Black Books Galore!
Guide to
Great African American
Children's Books

DONNA RAND

TONI TRENT PARKER

SHEILA FOSTER

John Wiley & Sons, Inc.
New York • Chichester • Weinheim • Brisbane • Singapore • Toronto

This book is printed on acid-free paper. ♾

Design and production by Navta Associates, Inc.

Permissions and credits begin on page 241.

This publication is designed to provide accurate and authoritative information in regard to the subject matter covered. It is sold with the understanding that the publisher is not engaged in render-
ing professional services. If professional advice or other expert assistance is required, the services
of a competent professional person should be sought.

Library of Congress Cataloging-in-Publication Data:
Rand, Donna.
    Black Books Galore! guide to great African American children's books /
Donna Rand, Toni Trent Parker, Sheila Foster.
        p.   cm.
    Includes bibliographical references and indexes.
    ISBN 0–471–19353–4 (acid-free paper)
    1. Afro-Americans—Juvenile literature—Bibliography.   2. Children's literature,
American—Afro-American authors—Bibliography.   I. Parker, Toni Trent.   II. Foster, Sheila.
III. Black Books Galore!   IV. Title.
Z1361.N39R33   1998
[E185]
016.973'0496073—dc21   98–10680

Printed in the United States of America
10 9 8 7 6 5 4 3 2 1

To the ABCs of my life,
Allison, Barry, and Christopher,
for their daily love, support, and inspiration!

D. R.

To Danny, and my three Super Readers!
Christine, Kathleen, and Jennifer.

T. T. P.

To my husband, George,
and Starr and Shawna,
the fruits of my labor.

S. F.

Contents

Foreword

by James P. Comer, M.D.

REARING CHILDREN in this complex age is a demanding job for all parents. Child rearing presents a special challenge to African Americans. Many conditions in our society transmit a negative message to our children about themselves and our group when successful functioning as children and adults requires a positive sense of group and self. Black parents, then, must counter the negative racial messages as they provide the appropriate knowledge and experiences needed for good overall development. This is particularly important in the years from birth to mid-adolescence.

Children's books can help when they are carefully chosen. That is why *Black Books Galore! Guide to Great African American Children's Books* is so important. The books listed and described have been carefully chosen by black parents for black parents, for children from birth through early teens. The many different types—story and picture books, concept books, board books, fiction and nonfiction, poetry and prose, biographies, fables, fairy tales, and more—will appeal to diverse interests and learning styles.

How Good Books Help Children Grow

Good books provide opportunities for parents to help children develop reading and language skills, a positive racial identity, and self-esteem, as well as the skills needed in many social situations. And when introduced to books early, children often develop a passion for reading and learning. When this is the case, young people can use books to help promote their own learning and development, with less and less pressure from parents and teachers.

Children are born with the potential to think, read, and express themselves at a high level. But it all must be developed if they are ever to do so adequately. They are born with the ability to relate to others, but also with an aggressive or survival energy that can be destructive and harmful unless it is channeled into the energy of learning, work, and play. Every interaction a child has with people, places, and things—mediated by caretakers—permits channeling of energy in a way that promotes desirable growth.

We see this taking place in the simple act of reading to a young child. We often read to our children at the end of a long, busy day. They have us all to themselves—home from work, no telephone, no other adults. They curl up in our laps, sometimes thumb in mouth, and it is a warm, cuddly bonding experience. Thus, reading is associated with a positive, safe emotional time.

Why Children Like Good Books

Children's stories often suggest to them that they are not going to be abandoned; that there is opportunity, protection, and safety in the world; and that reading is fun. Some books are about getting along with other people. Some are about honesty and fair play. Others suggest how children can meet their own needs without compromising the needs of other people. Some discuss feelings—sadness, anger, jealousy—and how children can manage them. Some promote perseverance and determination. In short, the content meets their needs.

Children want to hear these helpful and enjoyable stories—and see the pictures that help tell them—over and over again. They memorize the words and associate them with the pictures. Eventually, when we turn to a page they begin to "read" from memory. We get all excited and say, "Look, Mom, Nia [or Jamal] can read!" And when Grandma calls on the weekend we proudly report the great achievement of our little genius. The youngsters are pleased that we are pleased because they are programmed to please the adult caretaker. (Don't let their provocative and resistant behavior involved in their effort to establish some autonomy fool you.) Your pleasure and their pleasure in achievement motivate them to want to read and achieve even more.

Because they are reading or ready to read when they go to school, they receive good feedback about themselves from educators. They are thought of as bright and able and ready to learn. This makes a positive attachment between your child and educators much more likely. It also makes it much more likely that your child will be interested in school and helps educators to join parents in motivating reading and overall school learning. Achieving in school—reading in particular—deepens a child's self-esteem.

I hasten to point out, however, that neither school readiness nor good self-esteem or racial-group esteem rests primarily on a child's ability to read. Good child rearing lays the foundation for *all* these developments. Reading builds on and strengthens the foundation and helps to promote overall growth. Knowledge about development, then, can help you support it, as well as help you select or guide young people to useful reading materials.

What Children Need from Birth to Three

In the first three years children are little learning machines, bundles of energy seeking expression and trying to find out about themselves, including their racial and gender identity, and their immediate world—parents, families, friends, neighborhood, and so on. They are trying to bring their bodies, feelings, and behaviors in line with what is expected by the people who are important to them.

Good care—protection, love, guidance, and skill building—gives young children an inner core of good feelings about themselves. The child's performance in the neighborhood, with kin and friend, or in the family social network deepens the core of good feelings. This is the initial "stuff" of self-confidence and self-esteem.

What Children Need from Five to Eight

Between five and eight years of age, children should develop a passion for reading and learning, and they master the kind of behavior that is needed in school. They want to work—read, make things, do things. They also very much want to be like the adults around them—big people doing big-people things. This enables parents to encourage them to grow in positive ways. And good performance in school creates and deepens a sense of confidence and self-esteem. Also, racial and gender awareness grow, but a positive "take" must be promoted during this period; otherwise the negative message of the larger society can have a troublesome impact.

A positive sense of racial identity begins with answering the questions about race that children have in a calm and confident way, and by teaching them that racial antagonisms expressed by other people are the shortcomings of those people, not their own. It is important to help them learn how to handle these matters in ways that don't require them to spend a huge amount of energy on somebody else's problem, and to learn how to handle such antagonisms in a way that won't make matters worse.

What Children Need from Eight to Twelve and Up

Somewhere between eight and twelve years of age children begin to place themselves in the scheme of things. They begin to understand that they are part of a particular family and group with certain possibilities and limits and that they are different from certain other people and groups. Their behaviors, hopes, and aspirations begin to be shaped by their self-placement. Their confidence in school and ability to get along with others also influences these placements.

During this period children move strongly beyond membership only in a family to membership in groups in school. The relationships between parent and child need not be the kind of teenage rebellion that is often described. But the relationship must be changed in a way that enables young people to take more responsibility for their own lives. Parents must become less intrusive but remain as guides and supporters. This will allow young people to feel belonging both in the family and in the groups beyond the family.

Books about African culture and history and the American experience of blacks are helpful with the identity issue for young people who are having a good overall developmental experience. But books about African American history should show how the experiences of blacks and other groups were different. Information alone may not be helpful. For example, if books discuss African American inventors only in isolation, it's possible to conclude that by comparison, blacks invented very little. But if the great obstacles to achievement are understood, the achievement of African American inventors becomes remarkable. It is for this reason that I am particularly interested in biographies that show what blacks must overcome to achieve.

Many books will not make the necessary explanations, but books provide a general knowledge base and stimulate questions. The questions raised and the discussions that follow permit parents to help young people gain deep understanding. They also permit parents to have conversations with their children that are about something other than what the children are or are not doing that they should or shouldn't be doing. This creates an opportunity for close and more positive relationships.

It is worthwhile, then, for parents to give some thought to what is going on with young people developmentally, selecting and eventually suggesting books that will help them deal with all aspects of their growth. *Black Books Galore! Guide to Great African American Children's Books* can be most helpful in thinking about books for your child from birth to mid-adolescence. And don't stop there: keep reading and keep talking.

New Haven, Connecticut
June 1998

Acknowledgments

EIGHT YEARS AGO, we and several other mothers—Jennifer Barham, Linda Bari, Donna Gee, Lee Hill, Lee Mayfield, Jeanne Moutoussamy-Ashe, and Rhetta Vinson—shared a dream. As members of the not-for-profit Black Family Cultural Exchange, the predecessor of Black Books Galore!, we worked together to initiate, develop, and execute our first successful series of African American children's book festivals. Those festivals demonstrated the need for and paved the way for Black Books Galore! We would like to acknowledge the mothers of the Black Family Cultural Exchange, our friends, and to thank each of them, as individuals and as members of the visionary group, for the role they played, for their support in the early days, and for their continued good will.

We would also like to express our appreciation to Marie Dutton Brown, who encouraged us and has provided us with helpful insights into the publishing industry since the beginning of Black Books Galore!

We would like to acknowledge the help of Clara Villarosa of the Hue-Man Experience Bookstore, Denver, Colorado; Emma Rodgers of the Black Images Book Bazaar, Dallas, Texas; Ginny Moore Kruse of the Cooperative Children's Book Center, University of Wisconsin, Madison; and Josephine Anderson, Susan Baldwin, and Amy Lilien, librarians at the Ferguson Library, Stamford, Connecticut, in the preparation of this book.

We are particularly grateful to Carole Hall, our friend and editor-in-chief at John Wiley & Sons, Inc., for the faith and confidence that she demonstrated in encouraging us to write this book, and for her wise decision to team us with Christopher Jackson, our editor, to whom we are indebted for his mentorship and support during the development of this book. We would also like to extend our sincere appreciation to our managing editor, Marcia Samuels, for her guiding hand and commitment to this book.

We have also enjoyed the support of a host of talented authors and illustrators who have generously given their personal time to participate in our events. Our thanks to Tonya Bolden, Candy Dawson Boyd, James Michael Brodie, Ashley Bryan, Michael Bryant, Debbi Chocolate, Floyd Cooper, Pat

Cummings, Ron and Natalie Daise, Karen English, Toni Eubanks, Gwen Everett, Tom Feelings, George and Bernette Ford, Jan Spivey Gilchrist, Eloise Greenfield, Monica Greenfield, Gershom Griffith, Robert Guillaume, Cheryl Hanna, Vy Higgensen, Patricia Hinds, Darlene and Derek Hopson, Cheryl and Wade Hudson, Dolores Johnson, Sharon Bell Mathis, Robert Miller, Walter Dean Myers, Denise Lewis Patrick, Andrea and Brian Pinkney, Gloria and Jerry Pinkney, Connie Porter, James Ransome, Anna Rich, Brenda Roberts, Synthia Saint James, Cornelius Van Wright, Martha Vertreace, and Carole Boston Weatherford.

Introduction

SEVERAL YEARS AGO, we organized a small African American children's book festival in Sag Harbor, New York. A group of young boys, each about eleven years old, rode their bicycles by the event and stopped to see what was going on. One of the boys took a book, *Reflections of a Black Cowboy*, from one of our display tables and began to read it. After a while he looked up at Sheila, our founding partner, with an expression of surprise and disbelief. "There is no such thing as a black cowboy!" he said. "Oh, yes there is!" Sheila responded and handed him two other books about black cowboys, pioneers, and mountain men. He had no idea that black people had ever been a part of the adventurous American West. He had never seen a movie or television show—and certainly never a book—that featured blacks in this role. He was fascinated and delighted by this new revelation, and surprised himself by reading the entire book in the middle of that sunny summer afternoon!

Experiences like this are why we were compelled to write this book. We are three African American mothers—Sheila, Toni, and Donna—who own and operate Black Books Galore! In 1992, we began a mission to identify, publicize, and distribute quality African American children's books. What started as a project grew into a business and is now an ongoing quest and a consuming passion. This book is an outgrowth of that mission.

Our Story

Prior to the creation of Black Books Galore!, we, and seven other mothers, often commiserated with each other about how difficult it was to find a good selection of appropriate story books, picture books, books of poetry, history books, reference books—any books that were culturally validating for our children. We yearned for books that featured positive black characters who looked like our children and stories that reflected their world. It was the classic frustrating experience of a black parent when Sheila tried to find a collection of African American history and biography books for her daughter's school black history program. After an unfulfilling search through several bookstores, her disappointment and frustration inspired her to launch us into our mission.

We knew from the intensity of our own feelings and experiences that there were many other parents who felt the same way, so we developed an extensive book list that began to address the need. We also launched an exciting round of book fairs as a way of sharing the cache of books that we had discovered.

In the ensuing years we have developed a list of over 1,000 recommendable titles. The discovery process has been exhilarating. Our search for books has taken us from publisher to distributor, from catalog to web site, from library to bookstore, and from teacher to parent as we have sought out every available title. We now know that the development of our list will never end. There will always be another title that we have yet to discover and, of course, new and exciting works to look forward to.

We are now pleased to offer you this annotated list of 500 of our favorite books, with references to over 200 others, for and about African American children. We have selected books for children of all ages, from babies and toddlers to young teens, covering every category and genre from picture books and fairy tales to history books and novels. We believe that these books can help instill cultural pride, dignity, and self-esteem in our children.

This book is specifically for parents, guardians, relatives, family, friends, and educators who believe, as we do, that it is vitally important to introduce children to well-written, beautifully illustrated, and wonderfully self-affirming African American children's books.

There is no question that the black child's sense of identity and self-esteem are in a precarious state, living as we do in a country where African American culture, lifestyles, physical characteristics, and historical contributions are often devalued by the majority culture. Exposure to these books can reveal a whole new appreciation of self to the African American children in your life. We also believe that *all* children, regardless of race, should be exposed to these books so that they can learn to understand those who are different from themselves and foster greater acceptance and tolerance of others.

The first part of the Black Books Galore! mission was to identify the best books available for our kids. The second part of our charter was to exhibit and distribute these books, which we have done by supporting and running over a hundred African American children's book festivals and sales throughout the United States. During the past six years, we have had the opportunity to validate our premise that there is a tremendous desire and an overwhelming demand for these books. We have observed the reactions of thousands of children, parents, and educators to these books as we have taken our festivals to cities across the nation.

Our Book Festivals

Our book festivals are no ordinary events. We call them festivals instead of fairs because they are celebrations of African American children's books. Typically, we hold our festivals on a weekend day in a large venue that is well known and accessible to the community. Then we set up as many as thirty 8-foot-long, brightly covered tables with 300 to 500 titles of every description and literally thousands of books. Hundreds of parents, grandparents, teachers, and children come and go during the course of the day with strollers, diaper bags, and backpacks—after all, this is a family event! Admission is always free so that everybody can attend. The whole experience is designed to foster a love for books.

Our festivals have been held in a wide variety of venues, from local elementary schools to the Kennedy Center in Washington, D.C. Our appearance at the newly dedicated Arthur Ashe Tennis Stadium in Flushing, New York, in September 1997, was especially poignant because of Arthur's personal commitment to literacy. But regardless of the place, size, or scope of an event, our gratification has grown after each one because hundreds of families have come and clamored for our books. We have dozens of anecdotes that reinforce our charter and motivate us to move forward.

The Power of African American Children's Books

At an event in Chicago, a child took a book entitled *Jamal's Busy Day* off a table. His name was Jamal, and you can be sure that he had never seen a book featuring his own name, nor the ethnic names of his friends. There are actually dozens of books featuring Keishas, Tamikas, Tyrees, and other Afrocentric names. Children are more compelled to read when they recognize themselves in the stories and illustrations.

Donna's own little daughter, only two at the time and just learning to talk, was given a copy of *Bright Eyes, Brown Skin,* a picture book featuring four small children. She had never been heard to say her own name until she looked at this book, pointed to the little girl in the picture, smiled, and uttered, "Ahlson." Her name is Allison, and she had clearly identified with the little girl in the book, who looked remarkably like her. The book became one of her toddler favorites.

One last story: The 1996 version of *'Twas the Night B'fore Christmas* is a retelling of the traditional American Christmas poem. But in this version, Santa Claus and the family that he visits on Christmas Eve are black. We watched family after family discover this book at a festival in Charlotte, North Carolina. In every case, the parents were elated to find a book featuring a black Santa Claus, since they had been trying to convince their children for years that Santa is black! We sold scores of that title during that book festival alone because people identified with it.

The common thread between these three stories and others that we could tell is that these children and parents were validated and encouraged because there was finally recognition that stories about children of color were worthy of publication. We created this guide not only because we want to prove that these books exist, but also because we understand that it has been, and continues to be, challenging for parents and teachers to find them.

African American Children's Publishing

It has been extremely exciting to witness the recent proliferation of African American children's titles. However, we are keenly aware that even now the numbers of published works are still not representative of the need that exists. The Cooperative Children's Book Center of the University of Wisconsin, Madison, a library that monitors and studies newly published children's books, estimates that between 1993 and 1995, only 2 to 3 percent of children's publications "were about African and/or African American history, culture, and/or peoples," even though the African American population of the United States was about 12 percent. The number of African American publications rose very slightly in 1996 and 1997, but it is still insufficient.

But publishers, like other American businesses, are market driven. You can be sure that their motivation to publish is in direct response to demand and bottom-line sales results. It is critically important, therefore, that you, as parents and educators, understand that you play a significant role in the future of African American children's publishing. You can have an impact on publishers' decisions by exercising your economic clout—by requesting a larger selection of these books in your local bookstores and in your school and public libraries and by purchasing books for your children.

Why We Chose These Books

We are very excited about the selections that we have included in this guide. We have carefully crafted a meaningful collection of titles for each age group. The result is a broad cross-section of subjects and styles, created by a wonderfully diverse group of authors and illustrators to appeal to every child—from babies

4

to young adults. Our selections include a variety of picture and story books designed to entertain, teach, and enlighten small children, and a treasure trove of nonfiction books, chapter books, and novels intended to intrigue, motivate, and inspire more mature young readers. The selections include many books in each of the following special categories.

History, Heritage, and Biography Books. An impressive number of African American history, heritage, and biography selections are included in this guide to help children fill in the significant gaps in the African American story, and to gain a broader perspective of the roles and contributions of past generations of African American people who helped build our country.

Art, Poetry, and Music Books. Much of our African American culture is reflected in our art, music, and poetry. The cultural expressions that we have identified in this guide capture the best works of many of the most renowned and talented African Americans in the arts, from our past and present. Many of the works reflect the historical and emotional soul of African Americans.

Folktales, Fairy Tales, and Legends. We have included dozens of African American, African, and Caribbean folktales, fairy tales, and legends that reflect the values, fantasies, and belief systems of many centuries of black people. These books are important to ensure that we remain connected to our roots, and that our cultural legacy is passed on to the next generations.

African and Caribbean Books. We have ensured that there is an ample selection of books about African and Caribbean characters and subjects, since those cultures are naturally embraced in the African American experience.

Other books were selected because of their family-oriented themes. These books offer views of both traditional and nontraditional families and the interactions and relationships between parents, children, siblings, grandparents, aunts, cousins, and other family members. Still others contain messages about important values and virtues that children can incorporate into their daily lives.

We have also chosen books that are visually appealing. Children, even the older ones, are often attracted to a book because of the illustrations, even before they read it. And of course, it was important to us that the illustrations show positive images of black people.

A Parent's Point of View

We have read each book recommended in this guide from a parental point of view, and applied three guiding principles to our selections. First, we must feel that the stories are generally appropriate for the designated age group. You should make the final decisions about your child's reading and maturity level after reading the annotations. Secondly, we have been careful not to recommend books that stereotype black, female, or male characters, but instead develop them as individuals. Lastly, we have tested ourselves by asking if we would buy a given book for our children. If the answer is yes, then we have full confidence in recommending it to you.

There are two issues that we debated extensively prior to making certain selections. The first is the use of nonstandard English. There are several highly regarded works that employ Caribbean or black dialect. Proponents of these books argue that they have cultural and literary significance and that the language is acceptable if it is in the context of the story. Critics, however, denounce the nonstandard language as counterproductive to a child's language development. There is validity in both points of view, so we have clearly identified books that contain significant passages of nonstandard English for your consideration.

Similarly, there are books that use the N word extensively, which is obviously offensive, but may have a place within a given story. As an example, *Roll of Thunder, Hear My Cry* is a highly honored book that is told from the true-life perspective of the author's childhood, when that nomenclature was common. We have clearly identified books that use that term for your consideration.

We know that not every good or even excellent book is included in this selection. You may have a favorite title that is not included, or feel that the works of a respected author or illustrator are not adequately represented. We believe, however, that this broad selection is representative of the fine books that are available.

It is our hope that you will gain valuable insights into the myriad books that are available for the special children in your life and take every opportunity to introduce these books into their lives through their personal and school libraries.

How to Use This Guide

THE MAIN ENTRIES of this guide have been organized into four parts, which list books appropriate for the following reading levels:

- Babies and preschoolers
- Early readers (kindergarten to grade three)
- Middle readers (grades four to six)
- Young adults (grades seven to nine)

The titles in each part are arranged alphabetically. The entries are numbered sequentially, from 1 to 500, for easy cross-referencing. Throughout the book, numbers appearing in brackets, such as [257], refer to entry numbers, not page numbers.

Each numbered entry includes the title, subtitle, author, and illustrator; the publisher of the hardcover and softcover editions that are still in print; and the original publication date of the book. We have also made note of winners of the Coretta Scott King, Newbery, and Caldecott awards, and of books that have been recognized by the *Reading Rainbow* television program.

Our annotations offer brief descriptions of the books and include references to companion books, series titles, or sequels that may interest you. Books that contain nonstandard language are identified by one or more of the following phrases: "Nonstandard English," "Caribbean dialect," "Use of N word."

"The Creators" and Other Special Features

Pictures of book covers and text excerpts from many of the books are placed throughout to better impart the flavor of the books. In addition, twenty-four talented authors and illustrators are spotlighted in "The Creators" boxes to give you insight into their creative motivations. In the main entries, the names of these featured people are followed by a star (☆) and the page number on which their box appears. Here is a complete list of who to look for:

Appendix A lists several books that are of interest to parents and families. Appendix B describes the various book award programs and provides the full list of African American titles in each award program. Finally, there are four indexes to help you find what you want or to browse: an index of titles (both those of the entries and those of all other books mentioned within the entries), an index of authors, an index of illustrators, and an index of topics.

How to Get Your Hands on the Books in This Guide

The books in this guide should be available through your school or public library, or at bookstores. If they are not, you should be able to order them from your local bookseller. To find or order your selection, you should be prepared with a minimum of the title and the author's name.

Libraries may be able to accommodate your special request. If they do not have the book you want in their own system, they may be able to borrow it through an interlibrary loan arrangement. There are a number of African American specialty bookstores throughout the country whose staffs may be very knowledgeable about these and other children's books and who may be able to supply these titles for you easily. And of course you can always contact us, Black Books Galore!, at 65 High Ridge Road, #407, Stamford, CT 06905 (telephone: 203-359-6996; fax: 203-359-3226) to order any African American children's books. Please enclose a self-addressed, stamped business-size envelope if you would like a response to an inquiry.

Books for
Babies and Preschoolers

THERE IS AN IMPRESSIVE assortment of books available for even the youngest babies that can help establish an early appreciation of books and a love for reading. Within the collection of picture books are several wonderful board books specifically designed for babies and young toddlers. Board books have spill-proof, nontoxic, heavy cardboard pages that are easily turned by chubby little fingers. Fine examples are the companion titles *Good Morning Baby* [40] and *Good Night Baby*. Carry board books with you in the car, stroller, or diaper bag so they become familiar favorites for your little one.

Toddlers and preschoolers can also enjoy a wide selection of picture books known for their masterful illustrations, few words, and simple stories. Many of the books, such as those in the always popular Afro-Bets series [4], or the beautiful *Ashley Bryan's ABC of African American Poetry* [7], are designed to teach specific preschool concepts like the alphabet, numbers, shapes, or colors. Others, including *On the Day I Was Born* [85] and *Bright Eyes, Brown Skin* [16], help establish a positive self-image and a constructive view of the family and the world for a developing child.

Even though this young audience cannot read, they will reach the point where they know every word in their favorite books and will not allow you to deviate by even a single word. The toddlers learn and grow through repetition and will insist that you read the same books over and over and still over again. Then suddenly they will choose a new favorite that they will love with the same passion. Do not be surprised when, in a year or two, your child comes back to these early favorites when he or she is able to read them aloud to you!

Any time that a parent and child can become absorbed in an activity together, the time spent can truly be thought of as "quality time." Sharing a book is such an activity. The physical closeness of reading with your child as he or she sits on your lap or cuddles next to you for a bedtime story is both intimately rewarding and developmentally stimulating for the child. Reading, even if only for fifteen or twenty minutes a day, should be a part of every child's day.

Through reading, young children begin to develop language, vocabulary, and important prereading skills, while their imaginations, creativity, and curiosity are stretched. Many experts agree that storytime should be interactive, not strictly limited to reading the words on the pages. Using the story and illustrations, you can playfully ask your child to recall the last event or to anticipate the next, to describe the pictures, to count the objects, to point out certain letters or words, or to name the colors that he or she sees—all of which are developmentally enriching.

The important thing is to make books a natural and positive part of your young child's life. Keep introducing and reading new books as often as possible, and enjoy the experience of sharing the gift of books with your child.

A Is for Africa [1]

Written and photographed by Ifeoma Onyefulu

Hardcover and softcover: Penguin USA
Published 1993

Breathtaking color photographs of Nigerian villagers are the backdrop for this alphabet book with a difference. Each letter of the alphabet is represented by a unique African object. *F* is for the *feathers* pictured in the chief's hat. *I* is for *indigo*, used to dye the African fabrics; and *O* is for the *ornaments* that adorn the villagers' bodies. This book shares its format and illustration style with two companion books, *Emeka's Gift: An African Counting Story* [29], and *Chidi Only Likes Blue: An African Book of Colors.*

Aaron and Gayla's Alphabet Book [2]

Written by Eloise Greenfield ☆ 72
Illustrated by Jan Spivey Gilchrist ☆ 62

Hardcover and softcover: Black Butterfly, Writers & Readers
Published 1993

Playful preschoolers Aaron and Gayla learn their alphabet as they engage in everyday activities that showcase each letter. Interestingly, not all of the letters are associated with nouns. *D* is for I *dig* a hole, and *O* is for we *open* an *old* box. The companion book, *Aaron and Gayla's Counting Book,* does not stop at ten but takes the next step, featuring double-digit numbers up to twenty.

The Adventures of Sugar and Junior [3]

Written by Angela Shelf Medearis ☆ 150
Illustrated by Nancy Poydar

Hardcover: Holiday House
Published 1995

Preschoolers Sugar, an African American girl, and Junior, a Latino boy, are new neighbors who enjoy some wonderful experiences together. The book contains four short stories in which the two meet, bake cookies, go to a scary movie, and finally share an ice cream cone. Their warm friendship thrives in spite of their gender and ethnic differences.

Afro-Bets 123 Book [4]

Written by Cheryl Willis Hudson ☆ 102
Illustrated by Culverson Blair

Softcover: Just Us
Published 1987

This colorful primer helps teach and reinforce number recognition for preschoolers. In whimsical illustrations, the animated Afro-Bets kids bend and flex to form each number. Other titles in this effective series include *Afro-Bets ABC Book, Afro-Bets Book of Shapes,* and *Afro-Bets Book of Colors.* Preschoolers will read these books over and over again, while learning to recognize the figures and comprehend the concepts.

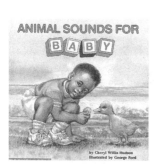

Animal Sounds for Baby [5]

Written by Cheryl Willis Hudson ☆ 102
Illustrated by George Ford

Board Book: Cartwheel, Scholastic
Published 1995

A toddler visits a petting zoo, where he makes fast friends with all of the farm animals and learns to imitate their unique sounds. Other titles in the What-a-Baby series include *Good Morning Baby* [40], *Good Night Baby,* and *Let's Count Baby.*

Ashanti to Zulu: African Traditions [6]

Written by Margaret Musgrove   Caldecott Medal
Illustrated by Leo and Diane Dillon

Hardcover and softcover: Penguin USA
Published 1976

African traditions from A to Z are explored in this alphabet book. Each letter represents an African object that is simply described to teach new facts about Africa, while the preschooler learns to recognize the sight and sound of each letter. The refined illustrations picture regal-looking African people.

Ashley Bryan's ABC of African American Poetry [7]

Written and illustrated by Ashley Bryan ☆ 16   Coretta Scott King Honor: Illustrator

Hardcover: Atheneum, Simon & Schuster
Published 1997

This book serves two purposes. Featuring poetic passages from twenty-five renowned African American poets and one African American spiritual, it introduces young readers to the breadth and diversity of African American poetry while at the same time teaching them their alphabet. The letters A to Z are not necessarily the first letter in each passage, nor is the word associated with each letter a noun. The illustrations are vibrant and the passages profound in this beautiful book.

At the Crossroads [8]

Written and illustrated by Rachel Isadora

Hardcover and softcover; William Morrow
Published 1991

The children of a South African township are excitedly anticipating the homecoming of their fathers, who have been away for months working in the mines. While they wait at the crossroads, the children sing and dance in this joyful story about family reunions.

The Baby [9]

Written by Monica Greenfield
Illustrated by Jan Spivey Gilchrist ☆ 62

Board Book: HarperFestival, HarperCollins
Published 1994

A baby's daily routine of eating, kicking, crying, sleeping, and then eating again—all under the watchful eye of his mother—is pictured in this story of Baby's day.

Baby Says [10]

Written and illustrated by John Steptoe

Hardcover and softcover: William Morrow
Published 1988

A baby, restricted to his playpen, tries everything he can to get his big brother's attention. Baby knows only two phrases, "Uh, oh," and "No, no," which his affectionate big brother uses to communicate with him. When the big brother is finally ready to help the little one out of the playpen, he says, "Okay, Baby, okay." Little ones will enjoy this book, especially if the baby talk is done with dramatic voice inflections.

Baby's Bedtime [11]

Written by Nikki Grimes
Illustrated by Sylvia Walker

Board Book: Golden, Western
Published 1995

A sleepy baby is bathed and prepared for bed by his loving parents. The illustrations of the baby and his doting daddy are especially heartwarming. Four companion titles, *Baby's Colors* [12], *No Diapers for Baby!* [81], *I Can Count* [49], and *Peekaboo, Baby* [89], are in this series produced in cooperation with *Essence* magazine to celebrate young African American children.

Baby's Colors [12]

Written by Naomi McMillan
Illustrated by Keaf Holliday

Board Book: Golden, Western
Published 1995

A little girl shares all of her favorite colorful things, including a bright red wagon, her new purple dress, and a fuzzy blue blanket. Each of the fourteen board-pages is brightly illustrated in different shades of the same color to reinforce the lesson. This book is part of the *Essence* Books for Children series, which also includes *Baby's Bedtime* [11], *No Diapers for Baby!* [81], *I Can Count* [49], and *Peekaboo, Baby* [89].

Bein' with You This Way [13]

Written by W. Nikola-Lisa
Illustrated by Michael Bryant

Hardcover and softcover: Lee & Low
Published 1994

A little girl runs through the park, noting the differences between people, but surmising that we are all the same. "Straight hair, curly hair—different but the same!" "Big nose, little nose. Light skin, dark skin—different but the same!" Even with our differences, she chants, "Isn't it delightful bein' with you this way?" This poem reflects a perfect sentiment for our children living in this multicultural society.

Ben Makes a Cake [14]

Written by Verna Allette Wilkins
Illustrated by Helen Clipson

Softcover: Tamarind, Red Sea
Published 1987

A bright-faced eight-year-old boy named Ben is a cake-making expert and aspiring chef. One Sunday morning, his mother asks him to make a cake for guests who are coming for tea. Ben considers the dozens of mouth-watering cakes and tarts that he could make and the ingredients that he will need. Ben will, of course, need a grown-up to help him with the oven, but other than that, he is on his own!

Billy's Boots: A First Lift-the-Flap Book [15]

Written by Debbie MacKinnon
Illustrated by Anthea Sieveking

Board Book: Dial, Penguin USA
Published 1996

Baby Billy is pictured on the front cover in his overalls and red boots. In eight delightful board pages, Billy searches for those boots. Young readers can actually flip open the diaper bag, closet, and chest of drawers in this interactive book to help Billy find his boots.

THE CREATORS

Ashley Bryan

ILLUSTRATOR

"With the birds trilling, my mother singing, and the general music-making that went on at home, it is only natural that I would one day do books of songs that had special meaning to me, the black American spirituals."

OUR FAVORITES

All Night, All Day: A Child's First Book of African-American Spirituals, 1991 [118]

Ashley Bryan's ABC of African American Poetry, 1997 [7]

Climbing Jacob's Ladder: Heroes of the Bible in African American Spirituals, 1991 [147]

Sing to the Sun, 1992 [276]

What a Wonderful World, 1995 [109]

Bright Eyes, Brown Skin [16]

Written by Cheryl Willis Hudson ☆ 102 *and Bernette G. Ford*
Illustrated by George Ford

Hardcover and softcover: Just Us
Published 1990

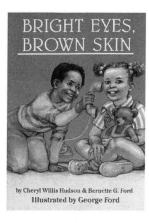

Four young children—Olivia, Jordan, Alexa, and Ethan—frolic through a day at school, confident in the beauty of their dark skin and eyes. The children's day is beautifully described in the rhyming text and illustrated in detailed watercolors that capture the sparkle in the children's eyes and the warmth of their skin tones.

Busy Baby [17]

Written by Naomi McMillan
Illustrated by Fred Willingham

Softcover: Golden, Western
Published 1995

Several adorable babies spend the day doing the things that babies do, while loving parents look on. This glossy-covered book is contoured on the right side to help small children grasp and turn the pages. Other titles in the Golden Super Shape Book series include *Look at You, Baby Face!* [68] and *See Me Grow Head to Toe.*

Caribbean Alphabet [18]

Written and illustrated by Frané Lessac

Hardcover: Tambourine, William Morrow
Published 1994

This would be just another ABC book, except *I* is for *iguana*, *S* is for *steel band*, and *R* is for *Rastafarian*, most unlike the typical *A*-is-for-*apple* versions! Bright, exotic full-color paintings depict a variety of fun island scenes in which there are four objects for each letter to reinforce letter recognition.

A Caribbean Counting Book [19]

Compiled by Charles Faustin
Illustrated by Roberta Arenson

Hardcover: Houghton Mifflin
Published 1996

Twelve counting rhymes, collected from nine islands of the Caribbean, are printed in bold type and illustrated with intensely colored tissue collages. The island of origin for each verse is indicated, and all are characterized by the rhythmic language patterns of the island people. *Caribbean dialect.*

The Chalk Doll [20]

Written by Charlotte Pomerantz
Illustrated by Frané Lessac

Softcover: Trophy, HarperCollins
Published 1989

A mother shares a few quiet moments with her daughter, Rose, reminiscing about the toys she played with as a child. Back in those days, Mother could not afford a real doll—a *chalk* doll—so she made a rag doll to play with. Rose thinks that the idea of a rag doll is delightful and decides to make one for herself, with her mother's help.

Cherries and Cherry Pits [21]

Written and illustrated by Vera B. Williams

Hardcover and softcover: William Morrow
Published 1986

Bidemmi makes up a series of stories from her vivid imagination and illustrates each story with her crayons. Each story that she tells has something to do with cherries and the discarded cherry pits, but she never quite finishes any one story until she begins telling one that involves herself. In her last cherry-obsessed story, she imagines herself eating cherries and planting the cherry pits until they grow into an entire grove of cherry trees, abundant enough to feed everyone from Nairobi to Brooklyn and from Toronto to St. Paul!

Coconut Mon [22]

Written by Linda Milstein
Illustrated by Cheryl Munro Taylor

Hardcover: Tambourine, William Morrow
Published 1995

The vividly drawn Coconut Mon peddles his coconuts, counting them down from ten to one as he sells his stock. He speaks with an exaggerated Caribbean accent, enticing his customers with cries of "Ssss-weet Coconuts, Goooood Coconuts," and "Crrr-isp Coconuts," to the delight of young readers. *Caribbean dialect.*

The Confetti Company Series [23]

Adapted by Naomi Fox
Illustrated by Neal Fox

Softcover and audiotape: Confetti Entertainment
Published 1993

Colorful books accompany audiotapes in this series of wonderfully adapted fairy tales. The characters featured in the books are members of the Confetti Drama Club and are pictured in the roles of favorite fairy tale characters. The richly textured voice of Robert Guillaume serves as the narrator on the audiotape, while young readers follow along in the book. Titles in the Confetti Company series include *A Christmas Carol, Cinderella, A Different Kind of Christmas, The Frog Prince, Hansel and Gretel, Little Red Riding Hood, Rumplestiltskin, The Shoemaker and the Elves,* and *Sleeping Beauty.*

Daddy and I [24]

Written by Eloise Greenfield ☆ 72
Illustrated by Jan Spivey Gilchrist ☆ 62

Board Book: Black Butterfly, Writers & Readers
Published 1991

Daddy and son are pictured doing household chores together in this heartwarming story. Their chores include everything from painting to doing the laundry, which sets a wonderful example of family responsibility for little boys! This book has three companion titles—*Big Friend, Little Friend; I Make Music;* and *My Doll Keisha*—by the same author and illustrator.

Dave and the Tooth Fairy [25]

Written by Verna Allette Wilkins
Illustrated by Paul Hunt

Softcover: Tamarind, Red Sea
Published 1993

Dave sneezes, losing a loose tooth in the process, but he cannot find it to give to the tooth fairy. Amusingly, he substitutes his grandfather's dentures, putting them under his pillow. When the tooth fairy comes, she is shocked and unable to afford the complete set of teeth that she finds. So, she returns to Tooth Fairy Land to get extra money. By the time she returns, Grandfather has found the missing tooth and put everything in its proper place, totally bewildering the conscientious tooth fairy.

Designed by God, So I Must Be Special
(African American Version) [26]

Written by Bonnie Sose
Illustrated by Bonnie and Holly Sose

Hardcover: Character Builders for Kids
Published 1991

" *He designed me with Special talents, gifts and abilities you see, which let me know that he has something Special in mind for me.*"

This oversized book is a tribute to the gifts that God has given to all children and a recognition that each child is unique and special. The primary-color illustrations are done in a childlike style that will appeal to small children.

Do Like Kyla [27]

Written by Angela Johnson ☆ 110
Illustrated by James E. Ransome ☆ 192

Hardcover and softcover: Orchard, Grolier
Published 1990

A little girl idolizes her big sister, Kyla, and mimics her through the day. Kyla is a loving big sister and an excellent role model for her younger sibling. This is a lovely book about sisterly love and the special relationship that can exist between sisters.

Eat Up, Gemma [28]

Written by Sarah Hayes
Illustrated by Jan Ormerod

Hardcover and softcover: William Morrow
Published 1988

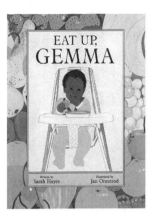

Try as they might, Mother, Father, and Grandma cannot get little Gemma to eat her food. One Sunday at church, a lady with a hat decorated with fruits catches Gemma's attention. When they get home, Gemma's big brother gets the inspired idea to decorate a plate with fruit to look like the lady's hat in order to get Gemma to eat! *Happy Xmas, Gemma* is a sequel about the active baby.

Emeka's Gift: An African Counting Story [29]

Written and photographed by Ifeoma Onyefulu

Hardcover: Cobblehill, Penguin USA
Published 1995

Captivating full-color photographs of the people of a village in southern Nigeria illustrate this counting story. *One* young Emeka is on his way to the next village to see his grandmother. Along the way he stops to find a gift for her. He considers *six* beautiful colored beads and *seven* musical instruments. Educational sidebars offer more detail about the interesting African curios. The companion titles, *A Is for Africa* [1] and *Chidi Only Likes Blue: An African Book of Colors,* present the alphabet and colors in the same photographic style.

Father and Son [30]

Written by Denize Lauture
Illustrated by Jonathan Green

Softcover: Paperstar, Putnam
Published 1993

A father and son share special moments in this book, illustrated with richly colored paintings of their activities on a Sea Island beach. A short poem describes their time together—spent horseback riding, boating, walking, and reading.

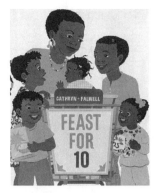

Feast for 10 [31]

Written and illustrated by Cathryn Falwell

Hardcover and softcover: Clarion, Houghton Mifflin
Published 1993

Count from one to ten and then count it again. A loving family counts down the ingredients it takes to make a delicious Thanksgiving feast, and then they count the ten preparation steps. This book is also available in a book/audio-tape set.

Fire Children: A West African Creation Tale [32]

Written by Eric Maddern
Illustrated by Frané Lessac

Hardcover: Dial Books for Young Readers, Penguin USA
Published 1993

Aso Yaa and Kwaku Ananse tumble to earth out of the mouth of the Sky God, Nyame, in this creative folktale about the origin of the world and the human race. The two are the first inhabitants of the earth, which Nyame has created. They secretly decide to make a family by shaping small clay models of themselves which, when baked, become children. Every time Nyame comes to visit he interrupts their secret project, so some children are baked longer than others, resulting in a rainbow of children, in hues from well-browned to honey-colored, and from yellow to white.

Flowers for Mommy [33]

Written and illustrated by Susan Anderson

Hardcover and softcover: Africa World
Published 1995

Aliya discovers nature's bounty in her own backyard. When she goes out to pick a basket of flowers for her beautiful mother, she is delighted by the rabbits, frogs, dragonflies, and butterflies that she sees. After enjoying the breeze and watching the clouds in the sky, Aliya delivers the loving gift to her mother.

Fruits: A Caribbean Counting Poem [34]

Written by Valerie Bloom
Illustrated by David Axtell

Hardcover: Henry Holt
Published 1997

Two sisters playing in the backyard sample a variety of exotic island fruits in this witty counting book. They count *one* guinep in a tree and eat it; *four* red apples, and eat them; and then *six* naseberries, which they also eat. By the time they get to ten, they have eaten fifty-five pieces of fruit and go to bed with tummy aches! The unusual fruits and Caribbean words are described in a glossary. **Caribbean dialect.**

Get Lost, Laura! [35]

Written and illustrated by Jennifer Northway

Hardcover: Western
Published 1995

Lucy and her cousin Alice are supposed to be taking care of Lucy's pesky baby sister, Laura. The big girls decide to play hide-and-seek, a ploy to get away from Laura. Later when they are unable to find Laura, they panic and begin to understand the meaning of the word "responsibility."

Getting Dressed [36]

Written by Dessie Moore
Illustrated by Chevelle Moore

Board Book: HarperFestival, HarperCollins
Published 1994

A little boy tells how he gets dressed in the morning with the help of his loving mother. Rich chalk colors are used to create the vibrant illustrations and the Afrocentric designs that border each page, making this simple book eye-catching to young readers. A companion book is *Let's Pretend.*

Debbi Chocolate

AUTHOR

"My purpose is always
the same: I write to entertain.
And more often than not,
I write to share my vision
of life's hope, its beauty,
and its promise."

OUR FAVORITES

Imani in the Belly, 1994 [200]

Kente Colors, 1996 [62]

My First Kwanzaa Book, 1992 [76]

NEATE: To the Rescue, 1992 [387]

On the Day I Was Born, 1995 [85]

Giant Hiccups [37]

Written by Jacqui Farley
Illustrated by Pamela Venus

Softcover: Tamarind, Red Sea
Published 1995

A lovely giant lives in the foothills near a small village. She never bothers any-one until she gets a ghastly case of the hiccups and disrupts the entire village. The townspeople come to offer her help, and they try a variety of the usual remedies: having her hold her breath, frightening her, and offering her water. They stumble upon the cure when they feed her a large portion of spicy food, but she still has plenty to share with her small friends.

The Gifts of Kwanzaa [38]

Written and illustrated by Synthia Saint James ☆ 200

Hardcover and softcover: Albert Whitman
Published 1994

Bold primary-color images of a loving family and their holiday celebration explain the story of Kwanzaa and its origin, the seven principles, and the cel-ebratory traditions associated with this African American holiday. A glos-sary offers proper pronunciations, English translations, and definitions of the new African words.

Golden Bear [39]

Written by Ruth Young
Illustrated by Rachel Isadora

Hardcover and softcover: Penguin USA
Published 1992

A cherubic toddler and his best friend, a golden teddy bear, are constant companions throughout the day. They do everything together, starting the day cuddling in a rocking chair and ending it by being tucked into bed side by side.

Good Morning Baby [40]

Written by Cheryl Willis Hudson ☆ 102
Illustrated by George Ford

Board Book: Cartwheel, Scholastic
Published 1992

This book explores the waking rituals of a chubby-faced baby. The happy baby awakes, dresses, and eats, preparing for her new day. The companion book, *Good Night Baby,* depicts bedtime rituals: a sleepy-eyed baby, exhausted from his day of play, bathes and enjoys a bedtime story before being put down for a good night's sleep. These books join *Animal Sounds for Baby* [5] and *Let's Count Baby* to complete the What-a-Baby series, which features African American babies doing the things babies like to do.

Grandfather and I [41]

Written by Helen E. Buckley
Illustrated by Jan Ormerod

Hardcover: Lothrop, Lee & Shepard, William Morrow
Published 1994

"But Grandfather and I never hurry. We walk along and walk along and stop . . . and look . . . just as long as we like."

A preschool boy finds that all the people he loves move too fast! His mom and dad are always in a hurry and his brother and sister are constantly in a rush. Grandfather, though, always seems to have time to walk with, talk with, and enjoy the company of the youngest member of the family. This is a touching story about the special bond that can exist between a child and grandfather. A companion title is *Grandmother and I* [43].

Grandmama's Joy [42]

Written by Eloise Greenfield ☆ 72
Illustrated by Carole Byard

Coretta Scott King Honor: Illustrator
Reading Rainbow Review Book

Hardcover: Philomel, Putnam
Published 1980

Rhondy knows that something is wrong with Grandmama, but she doesn't know what. She tries her usual tricks to make Grandmama smile, but cannot. Finally, Rhondy discovers that she and Grandmama must move from the home that they have shared for so long, because the rent is too high. Rhondy cajoles Grandmama into recollecting the bittersweet story of the death of Rhondy's parents and the day that Grandmama took her in to raise as her own, exclaiming that baby Rhondy was her joy.

Grandmother and I [43]

Written by Helen E. Buckley
Illustrated by Jan Ormerod

Hardcover: Lothrop, Lee & Shepard, William Morrow
Published 1994

Her mother's lap is nice for practical things like sitting in when she gets her shoe tied. Her father's lap is good when she wants to bounce or do tricks. Even her brother's and sister's laps are okay at times. But according to the young preschool girl in this story, nothing is as warm, wonderful, and supportive as her grandmother's lap. Endearing illustrations of the grandmother clearly show why she is so special. This book joins the companion book *Grandfather and I* [41] to make a wonderful set.

Half a Moon and One Whole Star [44]

Written by Crescent Dragonwagon
Illustrated by Jerry Pinkney ☆ 184

Coretta Scott King Award: Illustrator
Reading Rainbow **Review Book**

Hardcover: Macmillan
Softcover: Aladdin, Simon & Schuster
Published 1988

Young Susan lies in bed as the summer night settles in around her. The plants near her house close their petals and the animals snuggle down for their rest as the half moon and a whole star mark the beginning of nightfall. The gentle prose is illustrated in award-winning style.

Halloween Monster [45]

Written and illustrated by Catherine Stock

Hardcover and softcover: Simon & Schuster
Published 1990

Tommy participates in all the fun of the autumn season—playing in raked leaves, sipping cider, and carving Halloween pumpkins—in this easy-to-read book. As the time for Halloween trick-or-treating draws nearer, Tommy admits to his mother that he is afraid of the ghosts, goblins, and monsters and declares that he wants to stay home. Mom reassures Tommy, allowing him to enjoy this childhood pleasure.

Happy Birthday, Daddy [46]

Written by Teresa Reed
Illustrated by Stacey Schuett

Softcover: Aladdin, Simon & Schuster
Published 1996

James, Shaina, Binyah Binyah, and other characters from the Nickelodeon television series *Gullah Gullah Island* come together in this cartoon picture book to throw a surprise birthday party for Daddy. Now young fans of this television favorite can expand their pleasure to reading. Other titles in the Gullah Gullah Island series include *Armando's Great Big Surprise; Case of the Missing Cookie; Families, Phooey!; Guys and Dolls; It's a Breeze; Rain, Rain, Go Away;* and *Shaina's Garden.*

Honey, I Love [47]

Written by Eloise Greenfield ☆ 72
Illustrated by Jan Spivey Gilchrist ☆ 62

Board Book: HarperFestival, HarperCollins
Published 1995

A young child's positive outlook on life is rhythmically recounted in this poem about the people and things in her life that she loves, like the way her cousin talks and a ride in a car. This poem, originally published in 1978, has been republished and updated with contemporary illustrations of the optimistic child.

The Hunter Who Was King: And Other African Tales [48]

Adapted by Bernette Ford
Illustrated by George Ford

Hardcover: Hyperion
Published 1994

Three short African folktales are presented in this appealing pop-up book. Eight of the fourteen colorful pages spring into three-dimensional illustrations to bring the stories to life for young readers. The title story has a very elaborate scene of a great African feast, with all the colorful guests, in the palace of their queen.

I Can Count [49]

Written by Denise Lewis Patrick
Illustrated by Fred Willingham

Board Book: Golden, Western
Published 1996

An endearing little boy counts his belongings as he plays happily with them. He has *one* horse to ride, and *two* maracas to shake, but he seems happiest hugging his *five* puppies. Four companion titles from the *Essence* Books for Children series are *Baby's Bedtime* [11], *Baby's Colors* [12], *No Diapers for Baby!* [81], and *Peekaboo, Baby* [89].

I Don't Eat Toothpaste Anymore! [50]

Written by Karen King
Illustrated by Lynne Willey

Softcover: Tamarind, Red Sea
Published 1993

A toddler proudly boasts that she is a big girl, explaining that she can dress herself, can tidy up, no longer spills her dinner on the floor, and most importantly, no longer eats toothpaste! Bright, delightful illustrations make this a favorite for both toddlers and their parents.

I Like Me! [51]

Written by Deborah Connor Coker
Illustrated by Keaf Holliday

Hardcover: Golden, Western
Published 1995

A little girl, Nia Natasha Sierra Sims, revels in her uniqueness. Her mom tells her that she is the color of the leaves in the fall. Her dad tells her that her smile is as bright as the sunshine. She proudly proclaims that she likes herself in this positive, self-affirming preschool reader. This title and two companion books, *My Best Friend* [74] and *What I Want to Be* [110], make a set of positive self-image stories.

I Love My Family [52]

Written by Wade Hudson ☆ 102
Illustrated by Cal Massey

Softcover: Scholastic
Published 1993

In this positive, loving story about a family reunion, a young boy demonstrates pride in every member of the family from the oldest, Aunt Nell, who is almost one hundred years old, to the youngest, his baby cousin, Ahshon. The family eats, plays, and reminisces until it is time to part, knowing that there will be another reunion next year.

I Need a Lunch Box [53]

Written by Jeannette Caines
Illustrated by Pat Cummings ☆ 42

Softcover: Trophy, HarperCollins
Published 1988

A family prepares their first-grade daughter for the new school year by buying her needed school clothes and supplies, including a brand new lunch box. Her younger brother also wants a lunch box, so badly that he dreams of getting a whole collection of lunch boxes—a different color for every day of the week. The story is illustrated with vivid paintings that work with the text to help children learn the colors and match them to the written color names.

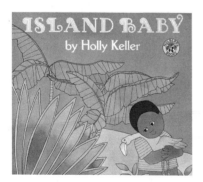

Island Baby [54]

Written and illustrated by Holly Keller

Hardcover and softcover: William Morrow
Published 1992

Simon spends his summer vacation helping Pop at his bird hospital. When Simon finds an injured baby flamingo, he takes it in and nurses it back to health, considering the bird to be his own pet. When the time comes to set the bird free, Simon is filled with mixed emotions.

It Takes a Village [55]

Written and illustrated by Jane Cowen-Fletcher

Hardcover: Scholastic
Published 1994

Young Yemi is supposed to take care of her baby brother while their mother sells mangoes at the market. Yemi loses sight of him and hurries around trying to find the missing child. She runs from stall to stall until she finally finds him, only to discover that he has been well cared for by their village neighbors, giving rise to the now-famous title adage.

Jaha and Jamil Went Down the Hill: An African Mother Goose [56]

Written by Virginia Kroll
Illustrated by Katherine Roundtree

Hardcover and softcover: Charlesbridge
Published 1995

> "Rock-a-bye baby in Mama's shawl,
> Snuggled up tightly, round as a ball.
> When Mama bends,
> You'll dip and you'll sway
> Like leaves in a soft breeze
> All through the day."

Forty-eight classic Mother Goose nursery rhymes have been rewritten with African-themed lyrics. Captivating color illustrations capture scenes of Africa from city to bush, from jungle to desert and of the multicultural people of the continent from Masai to Moslem and from farmer to fisherman. Even though the lyrics have been modified, the cadence of each verse remains the same and will be easily recognized by young Mother Goose fans.

Jamaica and Brianna [57]

Written by Juanita Havill
Illustrated by Anne Sibley O'Brien

Hardcover and softcover: Houghton Mifflin
Published 1993

Jamaica and Brianna have a misunderstanding that interferes with their friendship. Brianna makes fun of Jamaica's new boots, so Jamaica retorts with something equally unkind about Brianna's. Both girls feel hurt until they talk it out. Honesty and communication are key to successful relationships, as the two best friends discover. Jamaica's adventures are continued in three other books, *Jamaica's Find* [58], *Jamaica Tag-Along,* and *Jamaica's Blue Marker.*

Jamaica's Find [58]

Written by Juanita Havill
Illustrated by Anne Sibley O'Brien

Reading Rainbow Review Book

Hardcover and softcover: Houghton Mifflin
Published 1986

Jamaica turns in a hat that she found to the lost and found, but cannot, at first, bring herself to turn in the stuffed dog that she also found. When she finally does the right thing, she is gratified by the thanks of a new friend. All children will struggle with this dilemma the first time or two. Following Jamaica's lead may ease the conflict for young readers. Other Jamaica books are *Jamaica's Blue Marker, Jamaica and Brianna* [57], and *Jamaica Tag-Along.*

Jamal's Busy Day [59]

Written by Wade Hudson ☆ 102
Illustrated by George Ford

Hardcover and softcover: Just Us
Published 1991

Jamal understands the importance of his job as a student and his role as a family member, based on the positive role modeling of his parents. Every day, he prepares for his job of learning by washing up and brushing his teeth. He works hard at school, drawing pictures, doing math, and helping the teacher. Of course, the commute home is not easy, since the school bus is always so crowded! When he finally gets home, he does his homework, sets the table, and spends time with his family.

Jonathan and His Mommy [60]

Written by Irene Smalls-Hector
Illustrated by Michael Hays

Hardcover and softcover: Little, Brown
Published 1992

Jonathan and his mommy take a walk, a skip, a jump, a dance, and a run through the neighborhood, enjoying each other's company. This popular book exemplifies the love and affection shared between a mother and her child.

Joshua by the Sea [61]

Written by Angela Johnson ☆ 110
Illustrated by Rhonda Mitchell

Board Book: Orchard, Grolier
Published 1994

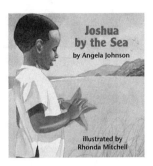

Little Joshua enjoys a special day on the beach along with his loving parents and attentive big sister. The illustrations show him enjoying the sun, sand, and sea. A gentle poem describes his special day. Other books about young Joshua are *Joshua's Night Whispers; Rain Feet;* and *Mama Birds, Busy Birds.*

Kente Colors [62]

Written by Debbi Chocolate ☆ 24
Illustrated by John Ward

Hardcover: Walker
Published 1996

Dazzling illustrations of African people are bordered with colorful West African kente cloth patterns in this unusual book of colors. Each color is named in the simple poetic text and matches the kente cloth that is shown being worn in a variety of traditional and nontraditional ways.

Kia Tanisha Drives Her Car [63]

Written by Eloise Greenfield ☆ 72
Illustrated by Jan Spivey Gilchrist ☆ 62

Board Book: HarperFestival, HarperCollins
Published 1997

Kia Tanisha is on the go! She jumps into her little play car and drives up the street, just like a grown-up, to briefly visit her friend before returning home. We first met this active little girl in *Kia Tanisha.*

THE CREATORS

Floyd Cooper

AUTHOR AND ILLUSTRATOR

"Illustrating children's books is a very exciting thing to do because it gives you the chance to have an impact on the way the world will be later. I believe that affection for other cultures leads to understanding, and I strive to create books that are a bridge between cultures."

OUR FAVORITES

Chita's Christmas Tree, 1989 [145]

Grandpa's Face, 1988 [185]

Happy Birthday, Dr. King!, 1994 [192]

Mandela: From the Life of the South African Statesman, 1996 [226]

Satchmo's Blues, 1996 [272]

Kim's Magic Tree [64]

Written by Verna Allette Wilkins
Illustrated by Lynne Willey

Softcover: Tamarind, Red Sea
Published 1990

In this imaginative story, Kim helps a Christmas tree escape from being discarded at the end of the season. In return for her kindness, the tree returns and offers Kim three wishes, which Kim and her friends quickly waste. The story is fun and the illustrations are delightful.

Knoxville, Tennessee [65]

Written by Nikki Giovanni
Illustrated by Larry Johnson

Hardcover: Scholastic
Published 1994

The simple pleasures of a summer in Knoxville, Tennessee—eating fresh corn, running barefoot, and going to church picnics—are the subjects of this early childhood poem. Bright watercolors accent this appealing and easily read book of few words.

A Kwanzaa Celebration: Pop-Up Book [66]

Written by Nancy Williams
Illustrated by Robert Sabuda

Hardcover: Little Simon, Simon & Schuster
Published 1995

Seven delightful pop-up images tell the story of Kwanzaa, teaching even the youngest children the meaning and spirit of the African American holiday. Small children love these stimulating three-dimensional books. There are so few pop-up books about African American children; this one is a must!

Let's Get the Rhythm of the Band [67]

Written by Cheryl Mattox
Illustrated by Varnette P. Honeywood

Softcover and audiotape: JTG of Nashville
Published 1994

This book explores a potpourri of African American musical styles, including African, folk, ragtime, and jazz. The history of each musical genre is described in a one-page summary, which is followed by two pages of sheet music representative of the style. The book is supplemented by an audiotape of the music. A companion set, *Shake It to the One You Love the Best*, explores music from the African, African American, Creole, and Caribbean traditions.

Look at You, Baby Face! [68]

Written by Madeline Carter
Illustrated by Keaf Holliday

Softcover: Golden, Western
Published 1995

Thirteen beautiful brown babies, in a variety of daily situations, clearly express their feelings by the looks on their faces. An early morning riser wakes up with a sleepy smile; a giggling, curly-headed baby grins during his bathtime play; a little one has just fallen down and cries; and a sad pouty-faced boy has just spilled his ice cream. This glossy-covered book is contoured on the right side to help small children grasp and turn the pages. Other titles in the Golden Super Shape Book series include *Busy Baby* [17], and *See Me Grow Head to Toe.*

A Lullaby for Daddy [69]

Written by Edward Biko Smith
Illustrated by Susan Anderson

Hardcover and softcover: Africa World
Published 1994

Inspired by loving parents, a little girl creates a lullaby for her daddy. The music and lyrics to her song are included. This is a sweet story about a child learning to give back, from the example of her parents.

Mary Had a Little Lamb [70]

Written by Sarah Josepha Hale
Photographs by Bruce McMillan

Hardcover and softcover: Scholastic
Published 1990

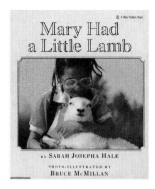

A classic rhyme is retold, with a new twist. In this version, Mary appears in colorful photographs and is an African American girl instead of the blue-eyed blond often associated with this verse.

Me and My Family Tree [71]

Written by Carole Boston Weatherford
Illustrated by Michelle Mills

Board Book: Black Butterfly, Writers & Readers
Published 1997

A little boy compares his facial features to those of his family in this rhyming verse. He has his brother's chin, his mother's hair, and his father's mouth, all illustrated in sensitive pictures of the child and those he loves. Other titles in this series of self-esteem topics include *Mighty Menfolk* [72], *My Favorite Toy, My Hair Is Beautiful . . . Because It's Mine!* [77], *My Skin Is Brown* [78], and *Grandma and Me.*

Mighty Menfolk [72]

Written by Carole Boston Weatherford
Illustrated by Michelle Mills

Board Book: Black Butterfly, Writers & Readers
Published 1997

A young boy recognizes strength and character in all of the men who surround him. In rhythmic verse, he identifies business neighbors, like the barber and store keeper; service workers, like the policemen and firemen, and family members, like his uncle, father, and grandfather, who influence his life and set fine examples for him. Other books in this series about positive self-images include *Grandma and Me, Me and My Family Tree* [71], *My Favorite Toy, My Hair Is Beautiful . . . Because It's Mine!* [77], and *My Skin Is Brown* [78].

Moja Means One: Swahili Counting Book [73]

Written by Muriel Feelings   Caldecott Honor
Illustrated by Tom Feelings ☆ 48

Softcover: Penguin USA
Published 1971

Children learn to count from one to ten in the Swahili language. The illustrations are dramatic charcoal drawings depicting various East African scenes. A highlighted word on each page indicates an African object to be counted and matched to each number. So, *mbili* (m.bee.lee), the Swahili word for "two," is depicted by two villagers. The companion book, *Jambo Means Hello: Swahili Alphabet Book,* is an equally well done book of letters; it too received the Caldecott Honor (1975), and it was a *Reading Rainbow* review book.

My Best Friend [74]

Written by P. Mignon Hinds
Illustrated by Cornelius Van Wright

Hardcover: Golden, Western
Published 1997

A young boy demonstrates a perfect understanding of the nature of relationships as he complains about all the things he does not like about his friend Omar: Omar broke his favorite model, and he always takes the window seat on the bus. On the other hand, he later recalls the list of special things that still make Omar his best friend: Omar shares his baseball cards and peanut butter cookies, and he tells funny jokes. This title, and its companion books, *I Like Me!* [51] and *What I Want to Be* [110], are positive self-image stories in the *Essence* Books for Children series.

My Best Friend [75]

Written and illustrated by Pat Hutchins

Hardcover: Greenwillow, William Morrow
Published 1993

Two little girls appreciate each other as best friends, even though their skills and abilities are different. One can climb higher in a tree; the other can eat spaghetti without making a mess. This delightful story of few words communicates a loving message of tolerance and acceptance.

My First Kwanzaa Book [76]

Written by Deborah M. Newton Chocolate ☆ 24
Illustrated by Cal Massey

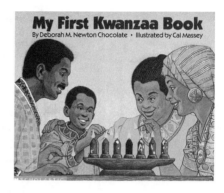

Hardcover: Scholastic
Published 1992

Descriptive illustrations of a thankful African American family and simple words introduce the youngest celebrators to the seven principles of Kwanzaa. A glossary describes the unfamiliar African words and other traditional symbols and words used during the Kwanzaa season in simple terms for young readers.

My Hair Is Beautiful . . . Because It's Mine! [77]

Written and illustrated by Paula deJoie

Board Book: Black Butterfly, Writers & Readers
Published 1997

Proud children brag about their curly, wavy, spiraly, braided, wiry, and wooly hair in this positive verse of self-love and appreciation. Other books in this series about positive self-image include *Grandma and Me, Me and My Family Tree* [71], *Mighty Menfolk* [72], *My Favorite Toy,* and *My Skin Is Brown* [78].

My Skin Is Brown [78]

Written and illustrated by Paula deJoie

Board Book: Black Butterfly, Writers & Readers
Published 1997

Beautiful children are proud of their toffee brown, cinnamon brown, honey-bee brown, and oak-tree brown skin in this positive book for toddlers. Other books in this self-affirming series include *Grandma and Me, Mighty Menfolk* [72], *Me and My Family Tree* [71], *My Favorite Toy,* and *My Hair Is Beautiful . . . Because It's Mine!* [77].

Nanta's Lion: Search and Find Adventure [79]

Written and illustrated by Suse MacDonald

Hardcover: William Morrow
Published 1995

Nanta, a young Masai girl, walks through the African plains looking for a
lion. As she walks, she sees many animals, but never a lion . . . or does she?
Each page is cut to show a piece of the puzzle, which is matched to the next
until, at last, the lion is revealed. This cute mystery book is a favorite of little
children, who will giggle every time they reach the conclusion, no matter how
many times they see it!

Nina Bonita [80]

Written by Ana Maria Machado
Illustrated by Rosana Faria

Hardcover: Kane Miller
Published 1996

In this affirming story about black skin, a white rabbit asks a little girl named
Nina for the secret to her beautiful black skin. Nina tells the rabbit several
incredible stories about her coloration, among them that she spilled black
ink on herself, drank large quantities of dark black coffee, and even that she
ate a bushel of blackberries to achieve her blackness! The rabbit tries each
method to turn himself black with no success. Finally, Nina's mother suggests that Nina is black simply because she looks like her black grandmother.

No Diapers for Baby! [81]

Written by Denise Lewis Patrick
Illustrated by Sylvia Walker

Board Book: Golden, Western
Published 1995

A lovable toddler is ready to be potty trained, so she trades in her diapers
for training pants in this inspirational book for two-year-olds. Even though
she has an occasional accident, her parents are loving and patient as she goes
through the process. This book is a companion to four others in the *Essence*
Books for Children series: *Baby's Bedtime* [11], *Baby's Colors* [12], *I Can Count*
[49], and *Peekaboo, Baby* [89].

Noah [82]

Written by Patricia L. Gauch
Illustrated by Jonathan Green

Hardcover: Philomel, Putnam
Published 1994

The well-known Bible story of Noah and the ark is told in this colorful picture book. The illustrations of the menagerie of animals are vibrant and eye-catching, but the intriguing feature is that Noah and his family are illustrated in the multiple colors of the black race.

Not Yet, Yvette [83]

Written by Helen Ketteman
Illustrated by Irene Trivae

Softcover: Albert Whitman
Published 1992

Yvette and Dad are busy preparing a surprise birthday party for Mom. Anxious, Yvette repeatedly asks Dad if things are ready. Dad answers over and over again, "Not yet, Yvette." Finally, Yvette's preparation and planning results in a successful birthday celebration. This is a charming story about the tremendous satisfaction that a child can receive by giving to and pleasing a parent.

Oh, No, Toto! [84]

Written by Katrin Hyman Tchana and Louise Tchana Pami
Illustrated by Colin Bootman

Hardcover: Scholastic
Published 1997

Little Toto is a handful for his grandmother, Big Mimi, who takes him to shop in her West African marketplace. Toto's appetite is greater than his reach. First he spills a tray of puffpuffs while reaching for the biggest one. Then he upsets an entire tray of hard-boiled eggs while diving for one. Finally, Toto takes a fall right into a tub of palm oil while trying to reach a banana! The exuberant two-year-old's mischief is complete when he rolls in the sand and becomes the muddiest child in the village.

"That banana looked so delicious! It made Toto very hungry. He climbed up next to the monkey and tried to grab the banana. 'Oh, no, Toto!' cried Pa Walter. But it was too late."

THE CREATORS

Pat Cummings
AUTHOR AND ILLUSTRATOR

"Hopefully, readers will find a bit of themselves, their world, and their stories reflected in my books. If they are strengthened, informed, embraced, or just tickled, then the book works."

OUR FAVORITES

Carousel, 1994 [142]

Clean Your Room, Harvey Moon!, 1991 [146]

I Need a Lunch Box, 1988 [53]

Jimmy Lee Did It, 1985 [208]

Willie's Not the Hugging Kind, 1989 [309]

On the Day I Was Born [85]

Written by Debbi Chocolate ☆ 24
Illustrated by Melodye Rosales

Hardcover: Scholastic
Published 1995

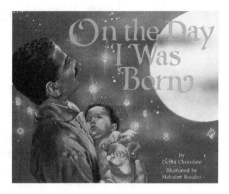

A baby boy is born to a family that celebrates a beautiful tradition. The new baby is held up to the full moon's light by his father and his dedicated relatives surround him to welcome him to the family. This book is so touching that every parent will want one as a keepsake for the new baby. The illustrations are so vivid and three-dimensional that they look like photographs.

One Fall Day [86]

Written by Molly Bang
Illustrated by Tom Kleindinst

Hardcover: Greenwillow, William Morrow
Published 1994

As a mother puts her little girl to bed, the child's doll and other favorite playthings are pictured in vivid three-dimensional dioramas, re-creating scenes from the young child's day.

One Hot Summer Day [87]

Written and photographed by Nina Crews

Hardcover: Greenwillow, William Morrow
Published 1995

A beautifully cornrowed preschooler enjoys the minor events of her urban life on a hot summer day. The little girl eats a Popsicle, plays on a slide, and tastes the rain from a sudden thunderstorm in a series of visually interesting photographic collages.

One Smiling Grandma: A Caribbean Counting Book [88]

Written by Ann Marie Linden
Illustrated by Lynne Russell

Hardcover and softcover: Penguin USA
Published 1992

Intense, colorful pictures of Caribbean island life illustrate a one-to-ten counting rhyme. The count begins with *one* smiling Grandma, then winds its way to *four* steel drums . . . *seven* conch shells . . . and comes full circle to that *one* smiling Grandma!

Peekaboo, Baby [89]

Written by Denise Lewis Patrick
Illustrated by Ray Simmons

Board Book: Golden, Western
Published 1995

A beautiful mommy and her playful baby play a toddler's favorite game—peekaboo. The child is illustrated with a bright, smiling face and so is Mom. This book is a companion book to four others in the *Essence* Books for Children series: *Baby's Bedtime* [11], *Baby's Colors* [12], *I Can Count* [49], and *No Diapers for Baby!* [81].

Pretty Brown Face [90]

Written by Andrea Davis Pinkney ☆ 172
Illustrated by Brian Pinkney ☆ 172

Board Book: Red Wagon, Harcourt Brace
Published 1997

A toddler sees his reflection in a mirror and studies his own image. He looks at the eyes, nose, lips, and hair on his pretty brown face while his proud father watches. A mirrored page at the end will allow little readers to admire their own beautiful faces. Other board books by the same husband-and-wife creators are *I Smell Honey; Shake, Shake, Shake;* and *Watch Me Dance.*

The Quilt [91]

Written and illustrated by Ann Jonas

Hardcover: Greenwillow, William Morrow
Softcover: Puffin, Penguin USA
Published 1984

A little girl studies the new patchwork quilt made by her mother and father using remnants from her younger years, including pieces of her pajamas, her first curtains, and the sheets from her crib. Wearing her footsie pajamas, she becomes so enthralled by the quilt that she imagines it as a map of a small town where her stuffed dog, Sally, has become lost. She searches each patch until she finds the dog.

Rain Talk [92]

Written by Mary Serfozo
Illustrated by Keiko Narahashi

Hardcover: Margaret K. McElderry Books, Simon & Schuster
Softcover: Aladdin, Simon & Schuster
Published 1990

The sounds of the rain—"Ploomp, Ploomp, Ploomp" and "Ping Ping Pingading" and "PlipPlipPlipPlipPlipPlip"—mesmerize a little girl as she watches it fall and waits for the rainbow that will follow the storm. Delightful illustrations of her rainy-day play fill the pages of this simple story.

See What I Can Do! [93]

Written by Denise Lewis Patrick
Illustrated by Thomas Hudson

Board Book: Golden, Western
Published 1996

A talented toddler shows off all her new skills, including eating with a spoon, doing puzzles, and throwing a ball. Her proud mommy is nearby to help celebrate her accomplishments.

Seven Candles for Kwanzaa [94]

Written by Andrea Davis Pinkney ☆ 172
Illustrated by Brian Pinkney ☆ 172

Hardcover: Dial Books for Young Readers, Penguin USA
Published 1993

The ancient African tradition of celebrating the harvest has been translated into Kwanzaa, a holiday now celebrated by many African Americans. The seven principles and celebratory customs are explored and beautifully illustrated in Pinkney's famous scratchboard style with colorful Afrocentric borders. A well-written one-page note to readers provides an excellent explanation of the holiday.

Shape Space [95]

Written and illustrated by Cathryn Falwell

Hardcover: Clarion, Houghton Mifflin
Published 1992

A young gymnast vaults through a whimsical poem, mixing and matching geometric shapes—squares, circles, rectangles, and semicircles—to create more complex objects. This book extends the young reader's knowledge of basic shapes to an understanding of their functional application.

She Come Bringing Me That Little Baby Girl [96]

Written by Eloise Greenfield ☆ 72
Illustrated by John Steptoe

Softcover: Trophy, HarperCollins
Published 1974

Kevin is prepared for a new baby brother, but to his surprise the new baby is a girl! To make matters worse, everybody's attention is turned to the baby, making Kevin feel left out. A conversation with his mother helps Kevin understand that he is still loved and that there is a special new role for him as a big brother. ***Nonstandard English.***

Snow on Snow on Snow [97]

Written by Cheryl Chapman
Illustrated by Synthia Saint James ☆ 200

Hardcover: Dial, Penguin USA
Published 1994

Bold, block-style paintings illustrate the story of a young boy's day playing in the snow. The brief, simple text includes repetitive word sequences to reinforce the action of this wintertime story.

The Snowy Day [98]

Written and illustrated by Ezra Jack Keats

Caldecott Medal
***Reading Rainbow* Review Book**

Hardcover and softcover: Penguin USA
Published 1962

Upon awakening, young Peter finds a yard full of fresh new snow. Outside, bundled in his snowsuit, he makes tracks and snow angels, sleds, and enjoys his wonderful winter playground. Other titles about the playful Peter include *Goggles, Letter to Amy, Pet Show, Peter's Chair,* and *Whistle for Willie.*

Something Special [99]

Written by Nicola Moon
Illustrated by Alex Ayliffe

Hardcover: Peachtree
Published 1997

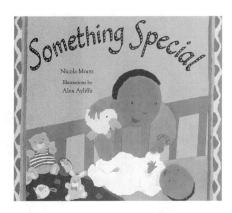

Charlie is frustrated and a little angry with his mother, who is too busy with the new baby to help him find something to take to school for show-and-tell. In fact, Mom puts him off for several days in a row because the baby always needs her attention. Charlie is desperate to find a unique item to take to school until he realizes the answer is right under his nose. Charlie takes his baby sister to show-and-tell and is met with enthusiasm for his one-of-a-kind presentation! Primary-color collages embellish this simple story.

THE CREATORS

Tom Feelings
AUTHOR AND ILLUSTRATOR

"The best illustrated books can stretch a child's mind and strengthen a child's spirit, preparing the child to face reality and reject the shallow and slick."

OUR FAVORITES

Daydreamers, 1981 [334]

The Middle Passage: White Ships, Black Cargo, 1995 [457]

Moja Means One: Swahili Counting Book, 1971 [73]

Soul Looks Back in Wonder, 1993 [403]

Tommy Traveler in the World of Black History, 1991 [289]

Sunday [100]

Written and illustrated by Synthia Saint James ☆ 200

Hardcover: Albert Whitman
Published 1996

Sunday's family activities are described, from sharing a pancake breakfast and going to church to eating dinner at Grandma's house. This book of few words establishes Sunday as a family day. Synthia Saint James illustrates her own text in her bold signature color-block style.

Sweet Baby Coming [101]

Written by Eloise Greenfield ☆ 72
Illustrated by Jan Spivey Gilchrist ☆ 62

Board Book: HarperFestival, HarperCollins
Published 1994

A young child looks forward to the birth of a new sibling with loving antici-pation in this rhyming verse. Although she is excited about the impending birth, she wonders what big sisters are supposed to do, whether the new baby will like her, and what the new baby will look like.

Tell Me a Story, Mama [102]

Written by Angela Johnson ☆ 110
Illustrated by David Soman

Hardcover and softcover: Orchard, Grolier
Published 1989

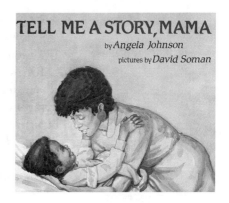

A little girl begs Mama to tell her a story at bedtime. "Which story?" Mama asks. The little girl then relates, in vivid detail, several of Mama's childhood stories that she has obviously heard many times before. As she recounts the often-told stories, Mama can scarcely get a word in edgewise. This poignant, multigener-ation family portrait is illustrated with tender watercolors.

Ten, Nine, Eight [103]

Written and illustrated by Molly Bang

Caldecott Honor

Hardcover and softcover: William Morrow
Published 1983

A little girl counts down from ten with her loving dad. They count the things in her bedroom, beginning with her *ten* toes and ending with *one* little girl tucked into bed. Little children love bedtime rituals and may love acting out this story with you as you put them to bed for the night.

This Is the Key to the Kingdom [104]

Written and illustrated by Diane Worfolk Allison

Reading Rainbow
Review Book

Hardcover: Little, Brown
Published 1992

A traditional verse is retold with softly muted watercolor scenes. A little girl finds the key to the kingdom, wherein lies the city, beyond which is a town. The poem takes her deeper and deeper into the intimate spaces of the kingdom, where she finds love and security before returning to her life in the city.

Traditional Fairy Tales Series [105]

Written and illustrated by Fred Crump

Softcover: Winston-Derek
Published 1988–1991

Traditional fairy tales are retold with an African American twist in this fun-to-read series of fifteen colorful books. The well-known characters are creatively drawn as African Americans, which will delight young readers. Titles in the series are *Afrontina and the Three Bears, Beauty and the Beast, The Ebony Duckling, Hakim and Grenita, Jamako and the Beanstalk, Little Red Riding Hood, Mgambo and the Tigers, Mother Goose, The Other Little Angel, A Rose for Zemira, Sleeping Beauty, Rumplestiltskin, Rapunzel,* and *Thumbelina.*

Tukama Tootles the Flute: A Tale from the Antilles [106]

Retold by Phillis Gershator
Illustrated by Synthia Saint James ☆ 200

Hardcover: Orchard, Grolier
Published 1994

Tukama is a naughty child who ignores his chores in this Caribbean version of *Jack and the Beanstalk*. Despite his grandmother's constant admonitions, he runs off to a forbidden place. He is captured by a two-headed giant and his wife, who intend to fatten Tukama up to eat for supper. In a suspenseful climax, Tukama uses his wits and engages the giant's wife with his tootling flute until he is able to escape.

Uh-oh! It's Mama's Birthday! [107]

Written by Naturi Thomas
Illustrated by Keinyo White

Hardcover: Albert Whitman
Published 1997

Jason's heart is in the right place as he goes out with his only dollar to buy a birthday present for his mama. His first choice, a dress, is too expensive, so he uses seventy-five cents to buy her some jelly bears. In an amusing sequence, Jason slowly eats the jelly bears, one color at a time, rationalizing that Mama does not like the green ones . . . the red ones . . . the yellow ones . . . until they are all gone! Remorsefully, Jason buys Mama a balloon with his last quarter, but accidentally loses it. He returns home, disheartened, only to find out that all Mama really wants is a hug.

> "*I open the bag of jelly bears. They sure look yummy . . . Red jelly bears are my favorite . . . Soon all the reds are gone. But that's okay—we have plenty left . . . I'll eat the greens. . . . Mama doesn't like green jelly bears anyway.*"

Waiting for Christmas [108]

Written by Monica Greenfield
Illustrated by Jan Spivey Gilchrist ☆ 62

Hardcover: Scholastic
Published 1996

Two children, full of anticipation, await Christmas morning while participating in a number of seasonal activities. They slide down the snowy hill, warm themselves by the fireplace, drink hot cider, and help decorate the Christmas tree. Beautiful family-oriented illustrations accompany the short poem.

What a Wonderful World [109]

Written by George Davis Weiss and Bob Thiele
Illustrated by Ashley Bryan ☆ 16

Hardcover: Atheneum, Simon & Schuster
Published 1995

Weiss and Thiele wrote the lyrics to this song made popular by the late, great Louis Armstrong. The colorful book is illustrated with multicultural children surrounded by rainbows, banners, ribbons, and stars—enjoying their wonderful world. The lyrics are printed in large type so the novice reader can read or sing aloud.

What I Want to Be [110]

Written by P. Mignon Hinds
Illustrated by Cornelius Van Wright

Hardcover: Golden, Western
Published 1995

In an old trunk in the attic, a young girl finds relics that inspire her to dream of what she might become. An explorer's hat transforms her into a great explorer in the Egyptian desert. With swimming goggles and fins she imagines herself as an underwater scientist. Her grandmother explains that her possibilities in life are as unlimited as her imagination. This is the third book in the series of positive self-image stories that includes *I Like Me!* [51] and *My Best Friend* [74].

What Will Mommy Do When I'm at School? [111]

Written and illustrated by Dolores Johnson ☆ 118

Hardcover: Atheneum, Simon & Schuster
Published 1990

A sensitive little girl, starting school, is deeply worried about her mother. She thinks through all of the daily events and activities that the two have shared in the past several years, and wonders how her mother will cope without her. Their loving relationship shines through in the intimate watercolor illustrations.

What's What?: A Guessing Game [112]

Written by Mary Serfozo
Illustrated by Keiko Narahashi

Hardcover: Margaret K. McElderry Books, Simon & Schuster
Published 1996

"What's hard?" "What's soft?" "What's light?" "What's dark?" The answers to a series of opposite questions will lead your young sleuth to guess what single object embodies the characteristics of all of the clues. A playful presentation of this game book can make entertaining fun for one child or an entire group.

When I Am Old with You [113]

Written by Angela Johnson ☆ 110   **Coretta Scott King Honor: Author**
Illustrated by David Soman

Hardcover and softcover: Orchard, Grolier
Published 1990

A young boy demonstrates his love and commitment to his elderly grandfather when he lists all the quiet activities that he is willing to do with his grandfather, including sitting in the rocking chair, swatting flies, and playing cards under a shade tree. Affectionate pictures of the two companions accompany the child's warm sentiments.

" When I am old with you, Grandaddy, I will sit in a big rocking chair beside you and talk about everything."

Where Jamaica Go? [114]

Written and illustrated by Dale Gottlieb

Hardcover: Orchard, Grolier
Published 1996

A spirited young island girl walks downtown, visits the beach, and returns home in three short stories told to a reggae beat. Colorful, childlike compositions of Jamaica's escapades illustrate the fast-paced stories. **Caribbean dialect.**

Will There Be a Lap for Me? [115]

Written by Dorothy Corey
Illustrated by Nancy Poydar

Hardcover and softcover: Albert Whitman
Published 1992

Kyle's favorite place is his mommy's lap, but as a new baby grows inside her, his special place disappears more and more each week. Then the baby comes and is always in Mom's arms, again blocking Kyle's way to her lap. At last Mom makes special time for Kyle and returns him to the warmth and comfort of the lap he loves. Many small children have had or will have this experience and can be assured of Mommy's unwavering love, despite any new babies.

Books for
Early Readers

A RICH COLLECTION OF TITLES is available for early readers in kindergarten through the third grade, ages five to eight, whose personal reading skills are in the process of developing. The variety of titles we have found for this age group is impressive, with clearly more titles available than for any other age group. These books are generally characterized as storybooks because of their combination of story lines and enticing illustrations.

The stories in this category range from those with very simple words and story lines, like *Dawn and the Round To-It* [157], about a little girl and her family, to some with much more complex plots, such as *Puzzles* [261], about a little girl with sickle-cell anemia. The differences in reading level among children in this age group, from those just learning to read to those who can read independently, can be enormous. Fortunately, children of this age

are still young enough to enjoy being read to, even if only occasionally, and these books lend themselves to read-aloud story time with an individual child or an entire group.

We've listed numerous books that can introduce children in this age group to black history and heritage, like *Juneteenth Jamboree* [213] and *The Story of Ruby Bridges* [280], as well as stories about famous African Americans like Harriet Tubman in *Minty* [230], and Benjamin Banneker in *Dear Benjamin Banneker* [159]. These biographies are often fictionalized to keep them as entertaining as possible, but the stories lay an important foundation for an understanding of the heritage of our people and ethnic pride.

Equally important are the number of books that are about pride, dignity, and self-respect, like *Somebody's New Pajamas* [278] and *Nappy Hair* [237]. In these and other books like them, the characters are strong and proud of themselves and their families.

An impressive feature of these storybooks is the quality of the artwork; many of these titles have won high acclaim for their artistic value. Engaging, eye-appealing illustrations are presented in a myriad of colorful mediums to make these books irresistible to young readers.

Primary readers should be encouraged to read. Their vocabularies and comprehension skills will expand with practice, preparing them for the challenges ahead. There will be many other distractions by the time they reach this age—television, video games, and other activities—so parents should take conscientious steps to support reading. Consider getting your child his or her own library card and making frequent trips to the library together. You might establish a designated time each day for your child to read quietly while enjoying a nice snack. Keep the experience pleasing—keep them reading!

The Adventures of Sparrowboy [116]

Written and illustrated by Brian Pinkney ☆ 172

Hardcover: Simon & Schuster
Published 1997

In this fun-loving fantasy, Henry the paper boy runs into a small sparrow while on his paper route. In the collision, Henry is magically transformed into a flying superhero, like his favorite comic strip hero, Falconman. He can see everything from his airborne vantage point, so he is able to witness the town bully's mischief and put an end to it.

Africa Brothers and Sisters [117]

Written by Virginia Kroll
Illustrated by Vanessa French

Hardcover: Simon & Schuster
Published 1993

When Jesse asks his dad why he has no siblings, Dad argues that he has a whole continent of brothers and sisters in Africa. The two identify nineteen of the many tribes of Africa and their connection to Jesse's life. The Ashanti make colorful fabrics, which Jesse loves to wear. The Ibo grow some of the best yams in the world, one of Jesse's favorite foods. A map of the African continent shows the geographic region of each tribe. Young African Americans will be enlightened by this introduction to their broad heritage.

All Night, All Day: A Child's First Book of African-American Spirituals [118]

Written and illustrated by Ashley Bryan ☆ 16

Coretta Scott King Honor:
Illustrator

Hardcover: Atheneum, Simon & Schuster
Published 1991

Twenty outstanding African American spirituals have been chosen by the author from a field of over a thousand such works, many of which are now regarded as American classics. This book of songs includes "This Little Light of Mine," "When the Saints Go Marching In," and "He's Got the Whole World in His Hand." Piano accompaniment music and guitar chords are included for each colorfully illustrated selection.

> " *She remembered the first time her father took her to a basketball game at Madison Square Garden. She loved it all: The noise of the crowd, the bright lights on the court, and especially the slam-dunks the players made look so easy! She knew right then and there that one day, she would be a professional basketball player, too . . ."*

Allie's Basketball Dream [119]

Written by Barbara E. Barber
Illustrated by Darryl Ligasan

Hardcover: Lee & Low
Published 1996

Allie is very excited when her dad brings home a new basketball. She goes to the neighborhood park to practice, but is quickly disheartened by her hoops failures and the taunting of the boys on the court. Allie is tough and determined, so she keeps trying until she sinks an impressive shot, which reminds her that her dream of playing professional basketball will require ongoing dedication and practice. The unique illustrations were achieved by using both traditional fine-art techniques and computer technology.

Alvin Ailey [120]

Written by Andrea Davis Pinkney ☆ 172
Illustrated by Brian Pinkney ☆ 172

***Reading Rainbow* Review Book**

Hardcover and softcover: Hyperion
Published 1993

Choreographer Alvin Ailey blazed a path in modern dance by blending African American dance movements with traditional modern-dance techniques. This simply told biography tells of Ailey's inspiration to dance and how he established himself as a genius in the field. Ailey's contribution to the larger American dance culture can be a source of pride and encouragement for any African American child.

Amazing Grace [121]

Written by Mary Hoffman
Illustrated by Caroline Binch

***Reading Rainbow* Feature Book**

Hardcover: Dial, Penguin USA
Published 1991

Grace loves to playact and plans to audition for her school's theatrical production of *Peter Pan*. She is deflated, however, when classmates tell her that she cannot play the lead role because she is black and a girl. Grace's wise grandmother teaches her a valuable lesson about self-esteem, helping her to realize that she can be whatever she wants to be and that she cannot allow others to put limitations on her. The sequel to this classic title, *Boundless Grace,* is another excellent story about this delightful young girl.

Annie's Gifts [122]

Written by Angela Shelf Medearis ☆ 150
Illustrated by Anna Rich

Hardcover and softcover: Just Us
Published 1994

Young Annie admires the way her brother plays the trumpet and the way her sister sings and plays the piano. She tries desperately to find her own performing talent. Despite her enthusiasm, and much to her own disappointment, Annie displays no musical ability. In this encouraging story, Annie's loving parents help her recognize one of her own unique talents and teach her to take pride in the gifts she has been given.

Aunt Flossie's Hats (and Crab Cakes Later) [123]

Written by Elizabeth Fitzgerald Howard
Illustrated by James Ransome ☆ 192

Hardcover and softcover: Clarion, Houghton Mifflin
Published 1991

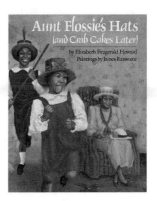

Sarah and Susan spend a fun afternoon with their Aunt Flossie, trying on her millinery. This launches their aunt on a round of stories about the day that she wore each hat. When they open the box with Aunt Flossie's favorite Sunday hat, they join in the storytelling, because they were all together the day that the hat blew into the lake. This book is also available in an audiotape/book set. A sequel, *What's in Aunt Mary's Room?*, continues the family's adventure.

Aunt Harriet's Underground Railroad in the Sky [124]

Written and illustrated by Faith Ringgold

Hardcover and softcover: Crown
Published 1993

The story of the Underground Railroad is told through the vision of a young girl named Cassie. In a dream, Cassie follows her brother, who has gone before her, retracing the route of their great-great-great grandparents' escape from slavery. Aunt Harriet (Harriet Tubman) speaks to Cassie along the way, personally directing her journey to safety and freedom in Canada. This story can help establish a young child's early understanding of this part of history. A brief biographical sketch of Harriet Tubman and a description of the Underground Railroad and its conductors are added bonuses. We first met young Cassie in the classic *Tar Beach* [287].

Baby Jesus, Like My Brother [125]

Written by Margery Wheeler Brown
Illustrated by George Ford

Hardcover and softcover: Just Us
Published 1995

" It's the night before Christmas, Tony. Christmas isn't just Santa Claus. It's Jesus' birthday and people come to church to pray."

As Tony and his big sister Keisha walk through town on Christmas Eve, young Tony sees many sights of the season, including a manger scene, carolers, Santa Claus displays, charity baskets, ornaments, and people exchanging gifts. Keisha uses each observation as an opportunity to explain the significance of Christmas as Jesus' birthday. Together, Tony and Keisha take in the warmth, generosity, and true spirit of the season. Young readers will be compelled to consider the deeper meaning of the Christmas season.

Barefoot: Escape on the Underground Railroad [126]

Written by Pamela Duncan Edwards
Illustrated by Henry Cole

Hardcover: HarperCollins
Published 1997

Forest animals bear witness to the flight of a Barefoot (an escaping slave) and the pursuing Heavy Boots (slave catchers). This poignant story is told and illustrated from the ground-level perspective of the animals, so all you see of the humans is their feet. The animals are compassionate toward the Barefoot and deliberately create obstacles to stall the Heavy Boots. Large print and the use of animal characters make the story accessible to young children, but the story will require some adult explanation.

Be Patient, Abdul [127]

Written and illustrated by Dolores Sandoval

Hardcover: Margaret K. McElderry Books, Simon & Schuster
Published 1996

Seven-year-old Abdul lives in Sierra Leone, where education cannot be taken for granted. School is not free, and children must work to help pay their own way. In this simply illustrated book, Abdul sells oranges, anxious to earn enough money to pay for school fees. Only after perseverance, hard work, patience, and the support of his parents is Abdul able to earn the money and return to school. Young readers should know that an education is a privilege that is not always available or free to all the children of the world.

The Best Bug to Be [128]

Written and illustrated by Dolores Johnson ☆ 118

Hardcover: Macmillan, Simon & Schuster
Published 1992

Kelly is very disappointed because she has been chosen to play the role of an insignificant bumblebee in the school play, a role that she feels is beneath her talent. Her parents' love and encouragement help Kelly decide to be the best bumblebee that she can. Her new commitment brings about fantastic results. You will love turning this inspirational story into an object lesson for your young readers.

Big Meeting [129]

Written by Dee Parmer Woodtor
Illustrated by Dolores Johnson ☆ 118

Hardcover: Atheneum, Simon & Schuster
Published 1996

Families from all over the region travel "down home" during the midsummer heat of August for the Big Meeting at the Little Bethel AME Church. The occasion reunites friends and family who come to celebrate the gospel, worshipping with song and plenty of preaching. After the meeting, the congregation plays, socializes, and eats together. Young readers who are church members may be able to relate to this story about an actual event in their own lives.

Big Wind Coming! [130]

Written by Karen English
Illustrated by Cedric Lucas

Hardcover: Albert Whitman
Published 1996

A farm family is making hasty preparations for the hurricane that is bearing down on them. As the wind and rain begin, a small girl realizes that she has left her favorite doll outside. The storm is ferocious and destructive, but some-how, except for a little mud, the doll is found safely after the storm. Windblown-looking illustrations add drama and realism to the story.

Jan Spivey Gilchrist

ILLUSTRATOR

"I wanted to become an artist when I was very young. As a matter of fact, I can specifically remember as far back as age four. I gave my mother a portrait I had drawn of her and she told me it captured her completely. I laughed about this years later, but it was the beginning of the strong support I would gain from my family and community for the years to come."

OUR FAVORITES

For the Love of the Game: Michael Jordan and Me, 1997 [177]

Indigo and Moonlight Gold, 1993 [203]

Lift Ev'ry Voice and Sing, 1995 [219]

Nathaniel Talking, 1989 [238]

Red Dog, Blue Fly: Football Poems, 1991 [397]

Bill Pickett: Rodeo-Ridin' Cowboy [131]

Written by Andrea D. Pinkney ☆ 172
Illustrated by Brian Pinkney ☆ 172

Hardcover: Gulliver, Harcourt Brace
Published 1996

The story of Bill Pickett, the first African American to be inducted into the National Cowboy Hall of Fame, is told in this biographical story book. Bill, the son of ex-slaves, became a heralded rodeo star, largely because of his dramatic bulldogging (steer wrestling) style. Bill incapacitated the steer in this man-vs.-beast sport by actually biting into the animal's lip! Scratchboard illustrations accentuate this true story about one of the few African Americans in this daring sport.

Bimmi Finds a Cat [132]

Written by Elisabeth J. Stewart
Illustrated by James E. Ransome ☆ 192

Hardcover: Clarion, Houghton Mifflin
Published 1996

Bimmi, a young Creole boy living on Galveston Island, is heartbroken when his beloved cat, Crabmeat, is found dead. The anguished boy finds another cat, but it obviously belongs to someone else. Bimmi is understandably torn between his desire for another pet to replace Crabmeat and finding the cat's rightful owner, which he ultimately does. His honesty is rewarded by the owner's considerate offer to share the cat. **Nonstandard English.**

The Black Snowman [133]

Written by Phil Mendez
Illustrated by Carole Byard

Hardcover and softcover: Scholastic
Published 1989

Young Jacob, anguished by poverty and disgusted with his blackness, is reinvigorated by a surreal encounter with a mystic black snowman made of sooty snow. The snowman's magical kente cloth scarf reveals to Jacob visions of the great heritage of the black race and helps instill a sense of pride and personal strength that he had never known.

" 'Who are these people?' Jacob asked.

'They are people like you,' the snowman replied. 'These are strong, brave Africans from whom you descend—black people who should make you proud of your great heritage.' "

Black, White, Just Right! [134]

Written by Marguerite W. Davol
Illustrated by Irene Trivae

Hardcover: Albert Whitman
Published 1993

In this lilting poem about a biracial child, a little girl delights in the fact that her mom is black and her dad is white, and that she is just right.

The Blue and the Gray [135]

Written by Eve Bunting
Illustrated by Ned Bittinger

Hardcover: Scholastic
Published 1996

Two young boys, one white and one black, are taught the significance of the location where their new interracial community is being built. Their friendship would have been unimaginable in 1862, when the same ground was the site of a bitter Civil War battle. In this rhyming text, the two boys begin to appreciate the fact that they can now be friends and neighbors, and decide that their homes will stand as monuments to their freedom.

Brown Angels: An Album of Pictures and Verse [136]

Written by Walter Dean Myers

Hardcover and softcover: HarperCollins
Published 1993

Walter Dean Myers gathered turn-of-the-century photographs of African American children from the attics, flea markets, and closets of generations of black families to create a new family album—an album of African American children. These touching black-and-white photographs illustrate eleven poignant poems. Each is bound to remind you of someone you once knew or someone in your own family. This exquisitely written book is popular with both adults and children.

Brown Honey in Broomwheat Tea [137]

Written by Joyce Carol Thomas
Illustrated by Floyd Cooper ☆ 34

Coretta Scott King Honor: Author
Coretta Scott King Honor: Illustrator

Hardcover and softcover: HarperCollins
Published 1993

Touching sepia-toned paintings illustrate each selection in this collection of twelve poems about the black child's beauty, uniqueness, and heritage. The simple verses describe and reinforce the value of our children. The companion title, *Gingerbread Days* [184], contains additional poems written and illustrated by the same award-winning team.

Buffalo Soldiers: The Story of Emanuel Stance [138]

Written by Robert Miller ☆ 156
Illustrated by Michael Bryant

Hardcover and softcover: Silver Burdett, Simon & Schuster
Published 1994

This high-action story is about Emanuel Stance, a member of the Ninth Calvary, one of the first all-black regiments in the United States Army. The Ninth Calvary, known as buffalo soldiers because their hair resembled that of the buffaloes, was chartered to protect pioneering settlers from the Indians. Stance distinguished himself as a leader and brave fighting soldier and, in 1870, was the first black to receive the Congressional Medal of Honor. Three other books in this series about pioneering African Americans are *The Story of Jean Baptiste Du Sable, The Story of Nat Love,* and *The Story of "Stagecoach" Mary Fields* [281].

Calvin's Christmas Wish [139]

Written by Calvin Miles
Illustrated by Dolores Johnson ☆ 118

Hardcover and softcover: Penguin USA
Published 1993

Calvin is unnerved when his friend, W.C., tells him that Santa Claus does not really exist. Calvin has been counting on Santa Claus to bring him a new bicycle for Christmas, but now does not know what to expect. Calvin's Christmas wish does comes true, confirming that Santa exists after all! Remarkably, Calvin Miles wrote this book at the age of thirty-nine, shortly after learning to read and write with the help of the Literacy Volunteers of America.

 Books for Early Readers

Can You Dance, Dalila? [140]

Written by Virginia Kroll
Illustrated by Nancy Carpenter

Hardcover: Simon & Schuster
Published 1996

Dalila's Gramma has exposed her to all kinds of dance styles, inspiring the young girl to try to perform each new dance she sees, including ballet, tap, jig, and even line dancing. Unfortunately, Dalila seems to have no aptitude for dancing. Then one day her Gramma takes her to see a West African dance troupe. Dalila is moved by their eurythmics and exuberantly joins in the *akpasa* (a group that dances to whatever feelings the music gives them), finally finding her niche! This is a story of a child's tenacity and the love and continuing support of her family to help her achieve her dreams.

Can't Sit Still [141]

Written by Karen E. Lotz
Illustrated by Colleen Browning

Hardcover: Dutton, Penguin USA
Published 1993

An energetic young girl guides us through the seasonal activities of her urban life. She frolics, dances, skips, and jumps through her neighborhood. Her contagious enthusiasm is captured in scintillating multimedia illustrations.

Carousel [142]

Written and illustrated by Pat Cummings ☆ 42

Hardcover: Bradbury, Simon & Schuster
Published 1994

Young Alex is unhappy because her father, away on a business trip, misses her birthday party. He has left a toy carousel as a birthday present, but her disappointment about his absence is still overwhelming. Alex is sent to bed, where she dreams that the carousel animals come to life and lead her on a magical adventure. Dazzling illustrations add to the story.

66

Celie and the Harvest Fiddler [143]

Written by Vanessa and Valerie Flournoy
Illustrated by James E. Ransome ☆ 192

Hardcover: Tambourine, William Morrow
Published 1995

Celie wants to win the prize for the best costume at the town's All Hallows' Eve parade. Her first entrance at the competition turns to humiliation when her costume falls apart in front of the crowd. Later, with the help of a mysterious magical fiddler, Celie re-enters the parade with an unsurpassable costume and interesting consequences. The story is illustrated with elegant paintings of the moonlit scenes. *Nonstandard English.*

Chinye: A West African Folk Tale [144]

Retold by Obi Onyefulu
Illustrated by Evie Safarewicz

Hardcover and softcover: Viking, Penguin USA
Published 1994

In this Cinderella-like story, Chinye is enslaved to her mean stepmother and selfish stepsister. When she is forced into the dark forest to fetch water for her inconsiderate family, she is guided and protected by loving spirits, and lavishly rewarded for her goodness and fine character. Jealous of Chinye's good fortune, the stepsister ventures out on the same mission but is met with entirely different results.

Chita's Christmas Tree [145]

Written by Elizabeth Fitzgerald Howard
Illustrated by Floyd Cooper ☆ 34

Hardcover and softcover: Simon & Schuster
Published 1989

Set in the horse-and-buggy days in Baltimore, this story portrays a loving family preparing for Christmas. The young daughter, Chita, enthusiastically participates in choosing a Christmas tree, baking cookies, and preparing a Christmas Eve family dinner. This is a timeless tale of a young child's joyful anticipation of Christmas morning. The sequel to this book is *Papa Tells Chita a Story.*

Clean Your Room, Harvey Moon! [146]

Written and illustrated by Pat Cummings ☆ 42

Hardcover and softcover: Simon & Schuster
Published 1991

Harvey's messy room is deplorable, as described in this frolicking, rhyming verse. Harvey must clean up his hodgepodge before he can watch any more television. This fun, colorfully illustrated poem will delight and entertain young readers.

Climbing Jacob's Ladder: Heroes of the Bible in African American Spirituals [147]

Selected by John Langstaff
Illustrations by Ashley Bryan ☆ 16

Hardcover: Margaret K. McElderry Books, Simon & Schuster
Published 1991

Nine Old Testament characters are praised in song in this colorful music book. The story of each black biblical hero is briefly presented and illustrated with bright paintings. Piano music and song lyrics are included for each character, among them the well-known "Rock-a My Soul" about Abraham, and the spirited "Didn't It Rain?" about Noah.

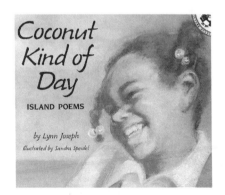

Coconut Kind of Day: Island Poems [148]

Written by Lynn Joseph
Illustrated by Sandra Speidel

Hardcover: Lothrop, Lee & Shepard, William Morrow
Published 1990

Thirteen poems are inspired by life on the Caribbean island of Trinidad. The title poem, "Coconut Kind of Day," makes you want to crack one open and drink the cool liquid inside!

Come Sunday [149]

Written by Nikki Grimes
Illustrated by Michael Bryant

Hardcover and softcover: William E. Eerdmans
Published 1996

LaTasha shares details about her Sunday at church through fourteen lyrical poems. LaTasha's verses include "Ladies' Hats," "Jubilation," and "Lady Preacher," all true reflections from a black church that young readers may recognize. Reverent worshippers are pictured in fluid watercolor paintings.

Coming Home: From the Life of Langston Hughes [150]

Written and illustrated by Floyd Cooper ☆ 34

Hardcover: Philomel, Putnam
Published 1994

The early life story of renowned African American poet Langston Hughes is shared in this well-written biography. Langston's early disappointments, travails, and other experiences helped to create the man whose poetic gifts grace African American literary history.

Cornrows [151]

Written by Camille Yarbrough
Illustrated by Carole Byard

Coretta Scott King Award: Illustrator

Hardcover and softcover: Putnam
Published 1979

As Grammaw braids Shirley Ann's hair, she explains the proud symbolism of cornrowed hair. "You can tell the clan or village by the style of the hair." "You would know the princess, queen, or bride by the number of the braid." This book is about our crowning glory—our hair, and can help instill dignity and cultural pride, as well as an understanding of the legacy of our braided hair.

The Creation [152]

Written by James Weldon Johnson
Illustrated by James E. Ransome ☆ 192

Coretta Scott King Award: Illustrator

Hardcover and softcover: Holiday House
Published 1994

Renaissance man James Weldon Johnson first wrote *The Creation* in 1919; it was later featured in *God's Trombones: Seven Negro Sermons in Verse* in 1927. The rhythmic verse of this poem tells the story of God's creation of the earth, and is enhanced by picturesque illustrations of the creation sequence. This book is excellent as a Sunday school text or bedtime reading.

Creativity [153]

Written by John Steptoe
Illustrated by E. B. Lewis

Hardcover: Clarion, Houghton Mifflin
Published 1997

In this story, Charlie learns about the ancestry he has in common with the new boy at school. Hector's skin color and features are like Charlie's, but his hair is straight and he speaks Spanish. Charlie befriends Hector and tries to help him adjust to the new school and neighborhood. Charlie even intends to help Hector with his English, which amuses Charlie's father because Charlie uses a very creative form of the language himself! Fluid watercolor illustrations enrich the story of the new friendship. **Nonstandard English.**

Dancing with the Indians [154]

Written by Angela Shelf Medearis ☆ 150
Illustrated by Samuel Byrd

***Reading Rainbow* Review Book**

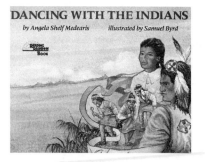

Hardcover and softcover: Holiday House
Published 1991

A turn-of-the-century African American family travels to visit the Seminole Indians, whose forefathers once befriended their grandfather and other runaway slaves. The family enjoys the annual get-together with the Seminoles, participating in traditional powwows, dances, and banquets. Young readers will gain insight into a little-known part of African American history through this poetic story.

Dark Day, Light Night [155]

Written by Jan Carr
Illustrated by James Ransome ☆ 192

Hardcover and softcover: Hyperion
Published 1996

Young Manda is having one of those difficult days when nothing seems right with the world. When she comes inside pouting, her Aunt Ruby helps her see things differently. Aunt Ruby shows Manda her crumpled old list of the things that make her happy, which she thinks about whenever she is feeling blue. She encourages Manda to make a list of her own. Manda slowly begins to itemize the positive things in her life until she realizes that there are many things to be happy about, especially her dear aunt.

Darkfright [156]

Written by Holly Young Huth
Illustrated by Jenny Stowe

Hardcover: Atheneum, Simon & Schuster
Published 1996

In this lyrical tale, Darkfright, a young island woman, is so afraid of the night that she goes to unusual lengths to lock it out of her house. She lights candles and lamps, pulls down window shades, and stays up all night, trying to keep darkness at bay. As a result, she is too tired during the day to enjoy the daylight she loves. It is only after a star falls from the night sky into her house and she nurses it back to health that she begins to release her fear. This humorous Caribbean tale will delight young readers. ***Caribbean dialect.***

Dawn and the Round To-It [157]

Written by Irene Smalls-Hector
Illustrated by Tyrone Geter

Hardcover: Simon & Schuster
Published 1994

Young Dawn wants her mother, father, and siblings to play with her, but they are always too busy, promising to play when they get around to it. Bored and lonely, Dawn comes up with a playful and creative answer to her own problem. Her actions inspire her family to invest quality time in their youngest member. This is a pleasing story about family dynamics and the resourcefulness and imagination of a young girl.

Eloise Greenfield

AUTHOR

"I write with the hope that my work will inspire, in children, a love for themselves, a love for language and literature, and a commitment to human values."

OUR FAVORITES

First Pink Light, 1976 [174]

Grandmama's Joy, 1980 [42]

Sister, 1974 [473]

Talk about a Family, 1978 [410]

William and the Good Old Days, 1993 [308]

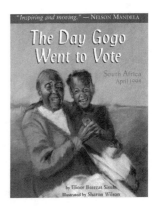

The Day Gogo Went to Vote: South Africa, April 1994 [158]

Written by Elinor Batezat Sisulu
Illustrated by Sharon Wilson

Hardcover: Little, Brown
Published 1996

One-hundred-year-old Gogo (*Grandmother* in the Xhosa and Zulu languages spoken in South Africa) explains to her young granddaughter that in spite of her age and the other challenges of getting to the polls, she, and all other black South Africans, must vote. It is their first opportunity to participate in the democratic process during their lifetime. The family and township rally around the historic occasion. Young readers can begin to understand the pride, privilege, and process associated with that event.

Dear Benjamin Banneker [159]

Written by Andrea Davis Pinkney ☆ 172
Illustrated by Brian Pinkney ☆ 172

Hardcover: Gulliver, Harcourt Brace
Published 1994

Benjamin Banneker, born free in 1731, was a brilliant self-taught mathematician and astronomer who became known as America's first black man of science. Banneker was the first black man ever to write and publish an almanac, an almost impossible feat in his time. Additionally, he became one of the first civil rights activists by corresponding with Thomas Jefferson, then the U.S. Secretary of State, to protest the enslavement of black people. This simple biographical storybook makes Banneker's story easily digestible for young readers.

Dinner at Aunt Connie's House [160]

Written and illustrated by Faith Ringgold

Hardcover and softcover: Hyperion
Published 1993

Exploring Aunt Connie's attic, Melodye and her cousin discover portraits of a dozen famous African American women, including Rosa Parks, Madame C. J. Walker, and Harriet Tubman. The portraits come to life and share their stories of achievement with the girls. The prestigious guests join the family for dinner and tell more about their contributions to history. This entertaining book is chock-full of information about these important women.

The Distant Talking Drum: Poems from Nigeria [161]

Written by Issac Olaleye
Illustrated by Frané Lessac

Hardcover: Wordsong, Boyds Mills
Published 1995

Poems from Nigeria describe a lifestyle different from our own, where tropical rains fall and weavers line the streets making cloth. The distant talking drums can be heard all day, calling out messages to the people in this brightly illustrated poem.

Down by the River: Afro-Caribbean Rhymes, Games, and Songs for Children [162]

Compiled by Grace Hallworth
Illustrated by Caroline Binch

Hardcover: Cartwheel, Scholastic
Published 1996

In this collection, the author recalls many of the rhymes, games, and songs that she grew up with in Trinidad. She learns later that these playful chants and games were actually inspired by the merriment of children all over the world. Bright, realistic illustrations reflect the energy and exuberance of the fun-loving children.

"I found an old book of fairy tales and read aloud. Miss Dessa snuggled under the patchwork coverlet, her eyelids drooping and her breathing soft. I carefully laid Miss Dessa's glasses on the dresser and Baby Sister tucked her in."

Down Home at Miss Dessa's [163]

Written by Bettye Stroud
Illustrated by Felicia Marshall

Hardcover: Lee & Low
Published 1996

Two young sisters meet and befriend an elderly neighborhood woman in this refreshing story about the special relationship between young and old. The two sisters visit Miss Dessa every day, offering her companionship as they work on a quilt, play dress-up, and swing from a tire tied to an old tree. At the end of one day, the sisters put Miss Dessa to bed with a bedtime story, endearing them to the old woman and to young readers.

Emerald Blue   [164]

Written by Anne Marie Linden
Illustrated by Katherine Doyle

Hardcover: Atheneum, Simon & Schuster
Published 1994

A little girl and her brother share their grandmother's Caribbean island home. They live a comfortable island life, which is vividly described in the text and illustrated in pastel renderings. Eventually, they sadly leave their paradise home and dear grandmother when their mother, who has been living in America, comes to take them home with her.

An Enchanted Hair Tale   [165]

Written by Alexis DeVeaux
Illustrated by Cheryl Hanna ☆ 88

Coretta Scott King Honor: Author
Reading Rainbow Review Book

Softcover: HarperTrophy, HarperCollins
Published 1987

A young boy, Sudan, has a head full of "wild, mysterious" hair. His dread-locks are so strange and so enchanted that children tease and grown-ups whisper, making Sudan ashamed of his misunderstood mane. Finally, Sudan meets a group of people with hair like his own. He learns to understand and enjoy what they have in common and to take pride in himself and his hair, setting an example of self-love for young readers. Fine black-and-white drawings illustrate the story.

Evan's Corner   [166]

Written by Elizabeth Starr Hill
Illustrated by Sandra Speidel

Hardcover and softcover: Penguin USA
Published 1967

Evan, who lives with his large family in a small urban apartment, laments to his mother that he has no place to call his own. Mother allows Evan to claim one corner in the apartment for himself. He enthusiastically decorates his nook, establishing his new territory, but still finds that something is missing. Finally, he realizes that privacy is important but so is sharing and being with his family.

Everett Anderson's Goodbye [167]

Written by Lucille Clifton
Illustrated by Ann Grifalconi

Coretta Scott King Award: Author
Reading Rainbow Review Book

Hardcover and softcover: Henry Holt
Published 1983

Young Everett experiences the five stages of grief following the death of his father. In this simple but profound poem, he comes to grips with the difficult reality of his father's death. This selection may be helpful to a young child who is coping with the death of a parent or loved one. Several books in the Everett series—*Everett Anderson's Christmas Coming, Everett Anderson's Nine Months Long, Everett Anderson's Friend, Everett Anderson's 1-2-3, Everett Anderson's Year, Some of the Days of Everett Anderson*—explore other emotional events in a child's life.

The Face at the Window [168]

Written by Regina Hanson
Illustrated by Linda Saport

Hardcover: Clarion, Houghton Mifflin
Published 1997

Dora is irrationally afraid of Miss Nella's powers after Miss Nella peers through the window just in time to catch Dora stealing mangoes from her tree. The neighborhood children ignorantly speculate that Miss Nella is spooky because they do not understand her peculiar behavior. When Dora's parents learn about the incident, they tell her the truth about Miss Nella, who is mentally ill. Dora visits Miss Nella to apologize for her mischief and learns a lesson about compassion and understanding. *Caribbean dialect.*

The Faithful Friend [169]

Written by Robert D. San Souci
Illustrated by Brian Pinkney ☆ 172

Caldecott Honor
Coretta Scott King Honor: Illustrator

Hardcover: Simon & Schuster
Published 1995

In this Caribbean folktale, Clement travels through Martinique accompanied by his best friend, Hippolyte, to seek the lovely Pauline's hand in marriage. Pauline's guardian, Monsieur Zabocat, who is reputed to be a wizard, is against the union and conjures up evil fates for the two. Each plot is discovered by Hippolyte, who sacrifices his own life to save his friends. Ultimately, good overcomes evil when Hippolyte's life is restored and the three friends are reunited.

Families: Poems Celebrating the African American Experience [170]

Selected by Dorothy S. Strickland and Michael R. Strickland
Illustrated by John Ward

Hardcover and softcover: Wordsong, Boyd Mills
Published 1994

The beauty and diversity of African American families are eloquently celebrated in this anthology. The dignified cover illustration of a handsome multi-generation family, as well as the other illustrations, convey the essence of this fine collection of twenty-three poems. Contributing poets include Arnold Adoff, Lucille Clifton, Nikki Giovanni, and Langston Hughes.

Finding the Green Stone [171]

Written by Alice Walker
Illustrated by Catherine Deeter

Hardcover: Harcourt Brace
Published 1991

Johnnie and his sister Katie each have a green gemstone that reflects its owner's good deeds by its degree of brightness. Johnnie loses his stone after behaving badly. He later realizes that the stone is not actually lost, but has become so dull and obscured by his poor behavior that it is difficult to see. When his behavior improves, his stone reflects the improvement. Use this story with young readers to point out that their behavior, good or bad, reflects directly on them.

Fire on the Mountain [172]

Written by Jane Kurtz
Illustrated by E. B. Lewis

Hardcover and softcover: Simon & Schuster
Published 1994

This is an energizing story about a young Ethiopian boy who accepts the challenge of his rich master to spend the entire night in the cold mountains with only a light cloak for warmth. If he succeeds, he will be rewarded. But if he fails, he and his sister will be banished. The boy successfully puts mind over matter, making it through the night by imagining that a fire, far off in the distance, is actually warming him. When he returns triumphantly, the master denounces him as a cheater for having taken comfort by the fire. In a humorous ending, the other servants, who resent the injustice, teach the master a practical lesson about fairness.

Fireflies for Nathan [173]

Written by Shulamith Levey Oppenheim
Illustrated by John Ward

Hardcover: Tambourine, William Morrow
Softcover: Puffin, Penguin USA
Published 1994

Six-year-old Nathan visits his grandparents in the country. They tell him boyhood stories about his father, who used to catch fireflies on summer evenings. Nathan convinces his grandparents to find the old firefly jar and to let him experience the magic. This is a pleasing story about the loving relationship between a child and his grandparents.

First Pink Light [174]

Written by Eloise Greenfield ☆ 72
Illustrated by Jan Spivey Gilchrist ☆ 62

Hardcover and softcover: Black Butterfly, Writers & Readers
Published 1976

Tyree misses his daddy, who has been away on business for a month. Tyree insists on waiting up for Daddy's arrival, who is not expected until dawn, just after the first pink light. Wisely, his mother gives up the bedtime battle, but wins the war by convincing Tyree to put on his pajamas and to curl up on the couch to wait. Tyree falls asleep, as expected, missing the first pink light and Daddy's actual arrival, but none of the joy of the reunion. Mother's wisdom and family love are prominent themes in this story.

Flossie and the Fox [175]

Written by Patricia McKissack ☆ 146
Illustrated by Rachel Isadora

Hardcover: Dial, Penguin USA
Published 1986

Flossie out-foxes a fox in this witty story. Flossie is asked to deliver eggs to a neighbor, but is warned about the wily fox. When the fox confronts her, she refuses to be intimidated because she has no proof of his identity. He tries to establish that he is a fox by showing her his soft fur, but she remarks that he may be just a rabbit. He shows her his pointy nose, but she believes that may mean he is a rat. Young readers will enjoy the developing story as Flossie drives the fox crazy. **Nonstandard English.**

Follow the Drinking Gourd [176]

Written and illustrated by Jeanette Winter   ***Reading Rainbow* Feature Book**

Hardcover and softcover: Knopf
Published 1988

A slave family flees its master, running for freedom on the Underground Railroad. They know the way because the directions are nested in the lyrics of a slave song. The song tells them to follow the drinking gourd, also known as the Big Dipper, which points to the north. Friends in safe houses along the way help the family through its harrowing journey. Young readers will gain insight into the ingenious communications strategies, survival methods, and subversive techniques used by travelers on the Underground Railroad. Lyrics and music to the song are included.

Virginia Hamilton

AUTHOR

"I will continue to explore
the known, the remembered,
and the imagined, the literary
triad of which every story is
made. After writing my first
book, it was my pleasure.
Writing still is. And that,
of course, is happiness."

OUR FAVORITES

Cousins, 1990 [331]

*Her Stories: African American Folktales, Fairy Tales,
and True Tales*, 1995 [359]

*Many Thousand Gone: African Americans from Slavery
to Freedom*, 1993 [378]

The People Could Fly: American Black Folktales, 1985 [393]

Sweet Whispers, Brother Rush, 1982 [483]

For the Love of the Game: Michael Jordan and Me [177]

Written by Eloise Greenfield ☆ 72
Illustrated by Jan Spivey Gilchrist ☆ 62

Hardcover: HarperCollins
Published 1997

Michael Jordan loves to play basketball and uses his God-given talent to excel at his game. In an analogy between themselves and Michael Jordan, two children realize that they can use their own special talents to excel in their lives. The children recognize that life may hold obstacles and challenges, but they understand that they can rise above them and soar toward their own goals, the way Michael Jordan soars to the basket. Young Jordan fans will enjoy the basketball scenes.

The Fortune-Tellers [178]

Written by Lloyd Alexander
Illustrated by Trina Schart Hyman

Hardcover and softcover: Penguin USA
Published 1992

A restless young carpenter seeks counsel from a fraudulent fortune-teller. The fortune-teller answers in ambiguous double-talk, leading the young man to believe in the incredible predictions about his future. In a turn of events, the fortune-teller's luck changes for the worse, while the young carpenter becomes a fortune-teller himself and manages to realize all of the fortunes that were foretold. Both story and illustrations are witty and entertaining.

The Freedom Riddle [179]

Adapted by Angela Shelf Medearis ☆ 150
Illustrated by John Ward

Hardcover: Lodestar, Penguin USA
Published 1995

It was a Christmas tradition on Master Brown's plantation that the first person to say "Christmas gift" to another on Christmas day would receive a gift. Jim, a slave, approaches his master and is first with the phrase, thus entitling himself to a present. Rather than the usual gift, Jim asks for his freedom if he is able to pose an unsolvable riddle. Master Brown agrees to the challenge. It takes Jim over a year to decide upon the riddle, but he finally presents one that stumps his master and earns him liberation.

Freedom's Fruit [180]

Written by William H. Hooks
Illustrated by James Ransome ☆ 192

Hardcover: Knopf, Random House
Published 1996

Mama Marina, a slave woman, is a conjurer who uses her magical ability and wits to buy her daughter Sheba and Sheba's beau out of slavery. This well-conceived story is one of many folktales associated with the Africans enslaved in the Low Country, along the coast of the Carolinas, who believed deeply in the magical abilities of conjurers. The illustrations are powerful, especially the cover art depicting the triumphant conjure woman.

Freedom's Gifts: A Juneteenth Story [181]

Written by Valerie Wilson Wesley
Illustrated by Sharon Wilson

Hardcover: Simon & Schuster
Published 1997

June 19, a holiday known as Juneteenth, marks the day in 1865 when slaves in Texas were told, two and a half years after the fact, that they had been emancipated. Aunt Marshall, an elderly ex-slave who was there when the original message came, uses the occasion of the annual Juneteenth celebration to tell her two young nieces about the significance of the day. After her compelling description of the event, both nieces better understand the gift of freedom.

Galimoto [182]

Written by Karen Lynn Williams
Illustrated by Catherine Stock

Reading Rainbow Feature Book

Hardcover and softcover: William Morrow
Published 1990

Kondi, a young African boy, spends a day gathering scrap wire so that he can make a *galimoto,* a push toy made from sticks and wires. Kondi must scavenge for the materials in order to complete his new toy. This story demonstrates the rewards of tenacity and sticking to your goals.

Gift of the Sun: A Tale from South Africa [183]

Written by Dianne Stewart
Illustrated by Jude Daly

Hardcover: Farrar Straus & Giroux
Published 1996

Thulani, a rural South African farmer, is bored by milking his cow, so he trades it for a goat. The goat eats up all of Thulani's seeds, so he trades it for a sheep. Shearing the sheep is too much work, so Thulani continues to make trades until he is left with only a bag of sunflower seeds. Inadvertently, the sunflower seeds bring a new form of prosperity to the farmer and his wife in this frolicsome story.

Gingerbread Days [184]

Poems by Joyce Carol Thomas
Illustrated by Floyd Cooper ☆ 34

Hardcover and softcover: HarperCollins
Published 1995

Twelve poems, one for each month of the year, celebrate themes of family love, individuality, and African American identity. Soft, entrancing illustrations accompany the verses. This second book of poetry is the perfect companion to *Brown Honey in Broomwheat Tea* [137], written and illustrated by the same renowned team.

Grandpa's Face [185]

Written by Eloise Greenfield ☆ 72
Illustrated by Floyd Cooper ☆ 34

Hardcover and softcover: Philomel, Putnam
Published 1988

Tamika has learned to recognize all of Grandfather's moods through his expressive face. She has seen joy, sorrow, and even fear pass over his brow but never anything close to anger. Then one day, Tamika sees him rehearsing for a play with an expression so terrifying that she does not know what to think. When her sensitive grandfather realizes that he has frightened her, he lovingly comforts her and assures her of his unconditional love.

Grandpa's Visit [186]

Written by Richardo Keens-Douglas
Illustrated by Frances Clancy

Hardcover and softcover: Annick, Firefly
Published 1996

High-tech Jeremy, who is hooked on computers, VCRs, and video games, and his career-oriented parents are a typical modern family. Grandpa makes a surprise visit and is alarmed by the impersonal family dynamics. When the electricity goes off one evening, Grandpa uses the occasion to engage the family in a playful evening with a rubber ball. The family reconnects and is reminded of the simple pleasure of sharing one another's company. This is a timely story that may remind both young readers and their families about their real priority: each other!

Great African Americans Series [187]

Written by Patricia C. and Fredrick McKissack ☆ 146
Illustrated by various artists

Hardcover: Enslow
Published 1991–1992

This biographical series profiles the lives of eighteen renowned African American men and women who have made significant contributions to our country and our world. Designed to be used by elementary school students either as a research source or for pleasurable leisure reading, the series has a large typeface and uses a generous number of sketches, photographs, and documents to embellish the stories. The series includes individual books about Marian Anderson, Louis Armstrong, Mary McLeod Bethune, Ralph J. Bunche, George Washington Carver, Frederick Douglass, Langston Hughes, Zora Neale Hurston, Martin Luther King Jr., Jesse Owens, Satchel Paige, Paul Robeson, Mary Church Terrell, Sojourner Truth, Madam C. J. Walker, Booker T. Washington, Ida B. Wells, and Carter G. Woodson.

Great Black Heroes Series [188]

Written by Wade Hudson ☆ 102
Illustrated by Ron Garnett

Softcover: Cartwheel, Scholastic
Published 1995

The first book in this series, *Five Notable Inventors,* tells the stories of five African American inventors and their creative genius and tenacity. Jan Ernst Matzeliger's shoe-lasting machine, Elijah McCoy's oil drip cup, Granville T. Wood's third rail, Madame C. J. Walker's hair growth preparations, and Garrett A. Morgan's gas mask were remarkable innovations contributed by these little-known inventors. Information about each inventor, the invention, and the patenting process is included. The second book in the series, *Five Brave Explorers,* explores the contributions of five noteworthy African American explorers: Jean DuSable, Matthew Henson, Mae Jemison, James Beckworth, and Esteban.

Gregory Cool [189]

Written and illustrated by Caroline Binch

Hardcover: Dial, Penguin USA
Published 1994

An all-American preadolescent, Gregory experiences culture shock when he visits his grandparents in Tobago for a four-week vacation. The weather, food, and daily life are just too different and too uncool for Gregory. As his vacation goes on he is suddenly struck by how much fun one can have doing "uncool" things. Gregory is just a kid at heart, who, like your own youngster, can afford a little more time in his childhood.

Grolier All-Pro Biography Series [190]

Written by Mark Stewart

Softcover: Children's Press, Grolier
Published 1996

Twelve African American professional and amateur athletes are profiled in this series of biographies. The life, challenges, and athletic accomplishments of each athlete are detailed and supported by color photographs, career time lines, and career statistics. This series includes individual books on Cedric Ceballos, Joe Dumars, Florence Griffith-Joyner, Randal McDaniel, Dikembe Mutombo, Hakeem Olajuwon, Jerry Rice, Barry Sanders, Emmitt Smith, Frank Thomas, Gwen Torrence, and Chris Zorich.

Happy Birthday, Martin Luther King [191]

Written by Jean Marzollo
Illustrated by Brian J. Pinkney ☆ 172

Hardcover: Scholastic
Published 1993

The life story of Martin Luther King Jr. is told in this elementary reader. The details of King's birth, education, life's work, and legacy are introduced to young children in storybook style to help them understand the importance of this monumental figure.

Happy Birthday, Dr. King! [192]

Written by Kathryn Jones
Illustrated by Floyd Cooper ☆ 34

Softcover: Simon & Schuster
Published 1994

After getting in trouble at school for fighting with another boy because he wanted to sit in the back seat of the bus, fourth-grader Jamal gets in trouble again at home when his Grandpa Joe learns about the scuffle. Grandpa Joe explains the story of Rosa Parks and the Montgomery bus boycott to help Jamal understand the history associated with sitting in the back of the bus. Jamal is so impressed with the story that he leads his class in a skit about the historic incident, which they stage in celebration of Martin Luther King Jr.'s birthday.

Hard to Be Six [193]

Written by Arnold Adoff
Illustrated by Cheryl Hanna ☆ 88

Hardcover: Lothrop, Lee & Shepard, William Morrow
Published 1990

A young boy is frustrated because being six years old does not live up to his expectations. There are still too many things that he cannot do that his ten-year-old sister can. His sensitive grandmother tunes in to his problem and successfully helps him understand how important it is to accept and enjoy the privileges, responsibilities, and opportunities of each age. You may enjoy sharing this story with your own children who are often too anxious to grow up!

Harriet and the Promised Land [194]

Written and illustrated by Jacob Lawrence

Hardcover and softcover: Simon & Schuster
Published 1993

Emotionally charged paintings and simple poetic text are offered in this artistic work about Harriet Tubman's life as a slave and later as a leader who led countless numbers of her people to freedom.

Hold Christmas in Your Heart: African American Songs, Poems and Stories for the Holidays [195]

Compiled by Cheryl Willis Hudson ☆ 102
Illustrated by various artists

Hardcover: Cartwheel, Scholastic
Published 1995

Sixteen holiday songs, poems, and stories are retold and colorfully illustrated in this seasonal anthology. This composite collection includes works by several well-known African American writers and illustrators, including Anna Rich, Lucille Clifton, Toyomi Igus, and Langston Hughes.

" *New Year's Wish*
Wish simply this:
To have the smarts
To save a part
Of Christmas
In your heart."
—*Cheryl Willis Hudson*

The House in the Sky: A Bahamian Folktale [196]

Written by Robert D. San Souci
Illustrated by Wil Clay

Hardcover: Dial, Penguin USA
Published 1996

This traditional Caribbean folktale tells the story of two lazy brothers who discover a magical abode in the sky that belongs to the spirit folk. While the spirit folk are away during the day, the brothers sneak into the house and steal all the food their hearts desire. One brother, though lazy, is still clever enough to eat and run. The other is both lazy and greedy, so he gets caught. Young readers will enjoy the drama and suspense and be thrilled by the unusual appearance of the spirit folk. **Caribbean dialect.**

THE CREATORS

Cheryl Hanna

ILLUSTRATOR

"Writing and illustrating books for children are privileges and pleasures which ultimately reconnect the artist with that most important part of one's inner character and history—childhood."

OUR FAVORITES

An Enchanted Hair Tale, 1987 [165]

Donovan's Word Jar, 1994 [336]

Hard to Be Six, 1990 [193]

Next Stop Freedom: The Story of a Slave Girl, 1991 [388]

The Story of "Stagecoach" Mary Fields, 1995 [281]

How Sweet the Sound: African American Songs for Children [197]

Compiled by Wade and Cheryl Hudson ☆ 102
Illustrated by Floyd Cooper ☆ 34

Hardcover and softcover: Scholastic
Published 1995

> " *Get on board, little children,
> Get on board, little children,
> Get on board, little children,
> For there's room for many a more.*"

This collection of twenty-three songs, including lyrics and music, features such classics as "Lift Every Voice and Sing," "Kum Ba Ya," and "Hambone." Each song is accompanied by commentary describing its origin, and soft, brown-hued illustrations. Children may be able to play or sing some of the selections, or at least be entertained by others, while absorbing important pieces of their musical heritage. A book/audiotape set is also available. A companion title is *Pass It On: African American Poetry for Children* [255].

Hue Boy [198]

Written by Rita Phillips Mitchell
Illustrated by Caroline Binch

Hardcover and softcover: Penguin USA
Published 1993

Hue is the smallest boy on his Caribbean island. His mother is concerned about his lack of growth, so she takes him to see the island's wise man, the doctor, and even Miss Frangipnia, who casts a spell over his head and gives him bathing herbs to make him grow. Still, Hue Boy does not grow. When he sees his Papa disembarking from a ship after several long months away at sea, he walks taller than he ever has with the pride of a loving son.

. . . If You Traveled on the Underground Railroad [199]

Written by Ellen Levine
Illustrated by Larry Johnson

Softcover: Scholastic
Published 1993

Everything a young reader wants to know about the Underground Railroad is detailed in this informative question-and-answer book. The format provides structure and is logically sequenced. Anecdotes about actual slaves who escaped on the Underground Railroad provide depth to the story. Another title in the series, . . . *If You Lived in the Time of Martin Luther King,* profiles the great leader's life in the same question-and-answer style.

Imani in the Belly [200]

Written by Deborah M. Newton Chocolate ☆ 24
Illustrated by Alex Boies

Hardcover and softcover: BridgeWater, Troll
Published 1994

A mother is distraught after a lion devours her children, who had wandered away from their West African village. Armed only with her faith, a portion of meat, a stick, and two stones, Imani seeks the lion to try to convince him to return her children. Instead, he swallows her, too! In his belly, Imani finds her children and other villagers who met the same fate. Imani uses her provisions to build a fire and cooks the meat to feed to the villagers, causing the lion's belly to blaze. His pain is so intense that he coughs out all of the victims. Bright, cut-paper illustrations support this Swahili folktale.

Imani's Gift at Kwanzaa [201]

Written by Denise Burden-Patmon
Illustrated by Floyd Cooper ☆ 34

Softcover: Simon & Schuster
Published 1993

A young girl, Imani, is part of a loving family that understands and celebrates the traditions of Kwanzaa. The family shares their Kwanzaa celebration with a new neighbor. The symbols and customs of Kwanzaa are introduced and demonstrated to young readers through Imani's kindness to her new friend.

In for Winter, Out for Spring [202]

Written by Arnold Adoff
Illustrated by Jerry Pinkney ☆ 184

Hardcover: Harcourt Brace
Published 1991

The beauty and specialness of the changing seasons remind Rebecca of the small events, activities, and traditions she has shared with her family during each season. These heartwarming poems depict a typical, loving family in a variety of seasonal activities.

Indigo and Moonlight Gold [203]

Written and illustrated by Jan Spivey Gilchrist ☆ 62

Hardcover: Black Butterfly, Writers & Readers
Published 1993

A young girl, Autrie, sits on the porch in the beautiful, dark night with the stars and moon shining on her. As her mother watches, Autrie compares the inevitable changes in the night sky to the changes she anticipates in her own life. In both cases she is unable to freeze the moment. This reflective story is exquisitely illustrated with deep, emotionally provoking paintings.

> " *Autrie knew she could not freeze the night or keep the neighborhood wrapped around her. She knew that Mamas don't sit and watch forever. That nights turn to days, starry nights to cloudy ones, and winds blow cold.*"

Irene Jennie and the Christmas Masquerade:
The Johnkankus [204]

Written by Irene Smalls
Illustrated by Melodye Rosales

Hardcover: Little, Brown
Published 1996

Johnkankus, a slave tradition celebrated at Christmas, brings momentary joy to Irene Jennie, a young slave girl. Irene's parents are absent for Christmas because they have been loaned to another plantation owner for the holidays. Irene Jennie takes some comfort in the exuberant masquerade parade performed by black dancers, singers, and acrobats, but remains deeply disappointed until she unexpectedly sees her parents performing at the end of the parade. The Johnkankus tradition, which originated in West Africa, is artfully described in this touching story.

Jasmine's Parlour Day [205]

Written by Lynn Joseph
Illustrated by Ann Grifalconi

Hardcover: Lothrop, Lee & Shepard, William Morrow
Published 1994

It is parlour day (market day) on the Caribbean island of Trinidad. Jasmine accompanies her mother to the marketplace to help set up their wares: fish and sugar cakes. But first, she visits with all of her other friends, who have also come to buy and sell at the parlour day. ***Caribbean dialect.***

Jenny [206]

Written by Beth P. Wilson
Illustrated by Dolores Johnson ☆ 118

Hardcover: Macmillan
Published 1990

The world according to young Jenny is captured in thirty-three short commentaries. Jenny tells young readers what she feels, thinks, and wants on a variety of subjects, including "Rain," "Teachers," "Summer Grass," "A Sister or Brother," "Grandpa's Snoring," and even "Bubble Bath." Young readers may or may not agree with all of Jenny's opinions, but they will certainly appreciate her positive outlook on life.

Jenny Reen and the Jack Muh Lantern [207]

Written by Irene Smalls
Illustrated by Keinyo White

Hardcover: Macmillan, Simon & Schuster
Published 1996

A young slave girl is warned about the scary Jack Muh Lantern, an African American folk character, who lurks in the woods waiting to entrap wanderers on All Hallows' Eve night. In this spine-tingling story, Jenny finds herself confronted by the monster, but in a moment of clarity is able to remember the anecdote that she has been told about how to ward it off.

Jimmy Lee Did It [208]

Written and illustrated by Pat Cummings ☆ 42

Hardcover: Lothrop, Lee & Shepard, William Morrow
Softcover: HarperTrophy, HarperCollins
Published 1985

This colorful primary reader follows the mysterious mischief of Jimmy Lee. Nobody is quite sure who Jimmy Lee is or what he looks like, but evidence of his misdeeds abounds. There are spills and tears, drawings on the wall, and other troublesome things that seem to happen only when Artie is around. Artie blames everything on the phantom, Jimmy Lee. Young readers will enjoy speculating about the culprit and solving the mystery of Jimmy Lee.

John Henry [209]

Written by Julius Lester
Illustrated by Jerry Pinkney ☆ 184

Caldecott Honor

Hardcover: Dial, Penguin USA
Published 1994

Nobody knows for sure whether John Henry was a real or a fictitious character, but it is said that he was the biggest and strongest man ever. According to the legend, John Henry competed successfully against a steam drill while breaking ground for the railroad through West Virginia. The intense illustrations of the laboring Henry convey the strength of his character. The story is written perfectly for an animated read-aloud about this larger-than-life character.

JoJo's Flying Side Kick [210]

Written and Illustrated by Brian Pinkney ☆ 172

Hardcover: Simon & Schuster
Published 1995

JoJo is preparing for her Tae Kwon Do yellow belt test. Her grandfather, mother, and friend all have sage advice for her about how to prepare. JoJo, however, finds the strength that she needs to succeed within herself, by drawing upon her feelings from a frightening personal experience. It is noteworthy that the athletic JoJo in this story is a girl!

Joshua's Masai Mask [211]

Written by Dakari Hru
Illustrated by Anna Rich

Hardcover and softcover: Lee & Low
Published 1993

Joshua is insecure about competing in the school talent show, where he plans to play the *kalimba,* an African instrument. He fears his performance will not be as spectacular as the dancing and rapping of some of his classmates. Joshua's uncle gives him a Masai mask to help him get into the spirit of the performance, but warns that the mask has magical powers. The mask magically transplants Joshua into the bodies of the classmates whom he envies. His brief experiences in other people's shoes prove to him, and will show young readers, that it is best to be oneself.

THE CREATORS

James Haskins

AUTHOR

"I was born in Demopolis, Alabama, and spent my childhood in a household with lots of children, a household where I felt a great need for privacy. One of the places I found privacy was in books. I could be anywhere at all, but if I was reading a book, I was by myself."

BLACK BOOKS GALORE!

OUR FAVORITES

Black Eagles: African Americans in Aviation, 1995 [427]

Get on Board: The Story of the Underground Railroad, 1993 [349]

Jumping the Broom [212]

Written by Courtni C. Wright
Illustrated by Gershom Griffith

Hardcover: Holiday House
Published 1994

The African American slave marriage ritual "jumping the broom" is described in this story. Lettie looks forward to the marriage of her sister and helps to sew the wedding quilt. The men build furniture for the new couple. The wedding feast is prepared, and a dress for the bride is made. Although the marriage celebration is a happy occasion, there are references to some of the harsh realities of slavery, such as threadbare clothes and the absence of a brother who was sold away to another plantation.

Juneteenth Jamboree [213]

Written by Carole Boston Weatherford
Illustrated by Yvonne Buchanan

Hardcover: Lee & Low
Published 1995

On June 19, 1865, Union soldiers arrived in Texas, two and a half years after the Emancipation Proclamation, and informed slaves that they had been freed. The day became known as Juneteenth and is still celebrated in many parts of the country. Modern-day Cassandra and her family participate in the festivities of this original African American celebration. The historical origins of the holiday are well developed and explained through the story.

"Some folks say the messenger took two years to reach these parts because his mule was slow. Others say slaveowners wanted to harvest one more cotton crop, so they kept the news from their slaves. Me? I don't know. . . . One thing is sure, though: Freedom was a long time coming, but it was mighty sweet."

Just Us Women [214]

Written by Jeannette Caines
Illustrated by Pat Cummings ☆ 42

Coretta Scott King Honor: Illustrator
***Reading Rainbow* Review Book**

Hardcover and softcover: HarperCollins
Published 1982

Aunt Martha and her niece are taking a trip in this simple story of female love and bonding. They plan to drive to North Carolina alone, with no boys or men on their carefree, fun-loving adventure.

Kelly in the Mirror [215]

Written by Martha Vertreace
Illustrated by Sandra Speidel

Hardcover: Albert Whitman
Published 1993

**"She looks like me!
. . . I mean, I look
like her! I look like
you, Mamma, when
you were a little girl!
I look just like you!"**

Kelly is upset because she thinks that she does not look like anyone else in her family. She goes to the attic and finds an old family album. When her mother joins her, the two look through the album together and realize that Kelly looks just like her mother did at the same age.

Kofi and His Magic [216]

Written by Maya Angelou
Photographed by Margaret Courtney-Clarke

Hardover: Clarkson Potter, Crown
Published 1996

A seven-year-old boy named Kofi tells the story of his West African village of Bonwire, which is known for the beautiful kente cloth that is woven there. Kofi magically transports young readers to other sites in his country, showing them the best and most beautiful parts of his land. Colorful photographs of the people and sights of Bonwire illustrate the story. Young readers who know about kente cloth will now understand more about its origin and the magic of its creation. A companion title, *My Painted House, My Friendly Chicken, and Me,* is another wonderful photographic essay about village life in Africa.

Kwanzaa Fun: Great Things to Make and Do [217]

Written by Linda Robertson
Illustrated by Julia Pearson

Softcover: Kingfisher
Published 1996

Seven days' worth of holiday crafts, activities, and recipes are included in this colorful Kwanzaa primer. The principles and symbols of the African American holiday are incorporated within the pages of activities. The book is beautifully illustrated with pictures of young celebrants.

The Leaving Morning [218]

Written by Angela Johnson ☆ 110
Illustrated by David Soman

Softcover: Orchard, Grolier
Published 1992

As a family packs its belongings in preparation for a move, the children sadly say good-bye to their friends and neighbors. Mom and Dad reassure the children that they will like their new home just as well. This simple story can help validate the feelings of young readers who are in a similar situation, and ease their anxiety about moving.

Lift Ev'ry Voice and Sing [219]

Written by James Weldon Johnson
Illustrated by Jan Spivey Gilchrist ☆ 62

Hardcover: Scholastic
Published 1995

James Weldon Johnson—novelist, poet, journalist, teacher, and the first leader of the NAACP—collaborated with his brother, J. R. Johnson, to write the song that became the African American national anthem. The song is illustrated with pictures of proud young children singing along. Every young African American should know this song and understand its place in our heritage.

> " *Lift ev'ry voice and sing,*
> *Till earth and heaven ring,*
> *Ring with the harmonies of Liberty.* "

Lion's Whiskers: An Ethiopian Folktale [220]

Written by Nancy Raines Day
Illustrated by Ann Grifalconi

Hardcover: Scholastic
Published 1995

An Ethiopian woman, Fanaye, marries a widower and becomes stepmother to a resentful boy. She loves the child, but he rejects her attempts to mother him. She consults a wise man, who sends her to get the ingredients for a potion that will make her stepson love her—three whiskers from the chin of a lion. The process of obtaining the lion's whiskers teaches Fanaye how to earn the boy's love. This story is uniquely illustrated with highly detailed collages.

> " *Fanaye stood her ground. Slowly she rubbed the lion's ear. Then she reached for his whiskers. Pluck! Pluck! Pluck! She had three hairs.* "

Little Lil and the Swing-Singing Sax [221]

Written by Libba Moore Gray
Illustrated by Lisa Cohen

Hardcover: Simon & Schuster
Published 1996

Little Lil is a selfless young girl who is prepared to sacrifice her ring, a prized possession, to help her mother, Mama Big Lil. In this warm story of family commitment, Lil's uncle pawns his saxophone to pay for Mama Big Lil's medicine when she becomes ill. Without the sax, the music that Mama loves is silenced. Lil decides that Mama needs the music as much as she does the medicine, so she decides to sell her ring. Her sensitivity and generous spirit are rewarded when she goes to trade in her ring for the saxophone.

Ma Dear's Apron [222]

Written by Patricia C. McKissack ☆ 146
Illustrated by Floyd Cooper ☆ 34

Hardcover: Atheneum, Simon & Schuster
Published 1997

This lovely story pays tribute to the black women of earlier generations who worked tirelessly as domestic workers but still had time to love and care for their own families. In this sweet story, David Earl learns to tell the day of the week by the color and style of his mother's apron. She has one for every day of the week, except Sunday, her day off—the day she spends with him.

Mac and Marie and the Train Toss Surprise [223]

Written by Elizabeth Fitzgerald Howard
Illustrated by Gail Gordon Carter

Hardcover: Four Winds, Simon & Schuster
Published 1993

Brother and sister Mac and Marie live in a house that overlooks a busy train track. Their Uncle Clem works for the railroad and advises them of his plan to throw them a surprise from his next train run. The children wait in anxious anticipation all day. Young readers will enjoy trying to guess the surprise with Mac and Marie, and will delight in the gift.

Magic Moonberry Jump Ropes [224]

Written by Dakari Hru
Illustrated by E. B. Lewis

Hardcover: Dial, Penguin USA
Published 1996

Erica and April love to jump rope but have trouble finding other playmates who enjoy the sport. When their uncle returns from Tanzania with a magical jump rope, their wishes come true. High-spirited jumping rhymes add to the fun of the story, and may become popular with the double-Dutch crowd in your neighborhood.

Make a Joyful Sound: Poems for Children by African-American Poets [225]

Edited by Deborah Slier
Illustrated by Cornelius Van Wright and Ying-Hwa Hu

Hardcover: Scholastic
Published 1991

Dozens of childhood poems and verses, written by twenty-seven African American poets, are presented here. The poems cover a wide range subjects and styles including the whimsical "Parade," by Karama Fufuka; the self-affirming "My People," by Langston Hughes; the biographical "Martin Luther King Jr.," by Useni Eugene Perkins; and the family-oriented "Love Don't Mean," by Eloise Greenfield. This lovely anthology belongs in every family's permanent collection.

Mandela: From the Life of the South African Statesman [226]

Written and illustrated by Floyd Cooper ☆ 34

Hardcover: Philomel, Putnam
Published 1996

In this simple but accurate account of the life of Nelson Mandela, a young reader will learn about Mandela's education and personal development from early childhood until the time that he became the president of South Africa. This book is a valuable guide to understanding who Mandela is and how he became such a great leader.

Masai and I [227]

Written by Virginia Kroll
Illustrated by Nancy Carpenter

Hardcover: Four Winds, Simon & Schuster
Published 1992

Linda becomes enthralled with the Masai people after studying about them in school. She contrasts the lifestyles and mores of the Masai with her own as an American. Lovely watercolor illustrations help to visually contrast the two worlds.

Max Found Two Sticks [228]

Written and illustrated by Brian Pinkney ☆ 172   ***Reading Rainbow* Review Book**

Hardcover and softcover: Simon & Schuster
Published 1994

Max finds two heavy sticks on the ground, which he employs to tap out rhythmic answers to questions in lieu of speaking. He "rah-tah-tah-tahs" and "thmps-di-di-thmps" all day long, communicating and imitating the beats of the city's sounds. The foot-tapping text matches the upbeat illustrations.

May'naise Sandwiches & Sunshine Tea [229]

Written by Sandra Belton
Illustrated by Gail Gordon Carter

Hardcover: Simon & Schuster
Published 1994

Big Mama reminisces with her young granddaughter over an old scrapbook. One picture reminds Big Mama of a special childhood experience, when she befriended another little girl whose family was much better off. Big Mama was embarrassed by the differences between their lifestyles. Her sensitive mother helped her understand that there was no shame in being poor and that with a little imagination and the right attitude, you could make an elegant party out of nothing more than may'naise sandwiches and sunshine tea. Valuable lessons about pride, dignity, and self-respect are incorporated into this touching story.

Minty: A Story of Young Harriet Tubman [230]

Written by Alan Schroeder   **Coretta Scott King Award: Illustrator**
Illustrated by Jerry Pinkney ☆ 184

Hardcover: Dial, Penguin USA
Published 1996

This fictionalized account of the life of young Harriet Tubman, also known as
Minty, tells of the struggles she endured during her quest for freedom and
her destiny as the leader of the Underground Railroad. This combination of
historical fact and fictionalized story is an effective and entertaining way to
transmit this important piece of history to young readers.

Mirandy and Brother Wind [231]

Written by Patricia C. McKissack ☆ 146   **Coretta Scott King Award: Illustrator**
Illustrated by Jerry Pinkney ☆ 184   **Caldecott Honor**

Hardcover: Alfred A. Knopf
Softcover: Dragonfly, Random House
Published 1988

The cakewalk was a popular remnant of the slave culture at the end of the
nineteenth century. At that time, festive dancers competed with their best step-
pin' to take home the prized cake. Mirandy, anxious to win, schemes to capture the wind as her dance partner. She is troubled, though, because her friend
Ezel also wants to be her partner. Mirandy creatively works out her problem
in this African American children's classic. **Nonstandard English.**

More Than Anything Else [232]

Written by Marie Bradby
Illustrated by Chris K. Soentpiet

Hardcover: Orchard, Grolier
Published 1996

Nine-year-old Booker T. Washington, who became the famous African
American leader and educator, works in the salt mines with his father and
brother. He has a burning desire to learn to read. In this fictionalized story,
Booker's ambition is ignited when his mother gives him his first book. She is
unable to read and so is he, but he is determined to learn. A local newspaper
man helps Booker decipher the black marks on the pages and shows him how
to write his name in the dirt. Booker's pure joy and optimism are evident in
his face in this richly illustrated book.

" *I draw the marks
on the dirt floor
and try to figure out
what sounds they
make, what story
their picture tells.* "

THE CREATORS

Cheryl Willis Hudson
AUTHOR

Wade Hudson
AUTHOR

"One can never take any image for granted. Images, whether in print, on film or television, or on stage, are constantly shaping the way we feel and what we think and believe. That is particularly crucial to the black community, which has been deliberately given negative images of its history and culture. I find it rewarding to help reshape and change those negative images to reflect the truth. I think the struggle to present the correct images— the truth—is the most important one facing us all."

—WADE HUDSON

OUR FAVORITES

Wade and Cheryl Willis Hudson: *How Sweet the Sound: African American Songs for Children,* 1995 [197]

Kids' Book of Wisdom: Quotes from the African American Tradition, 1996 [374]

Cheryl Willis Hudson and Bernette G. Ford: *Bright Eyes, Brown Skin,* 1990 [16]

Wade Hudson: *Pass It On: African American Poetry for Children,* 1993 [255]

Wade Hudson and Valerie Wilson Wesley: *Afro-Bets Book of Black Heroes from A to Z: An Introduction to Important Black Achievers,* 1988 [316]

Mufaro's Beautiful Daughters: An African Tale [233]

Written and illustrated by John Steptoe

Hardcover and softcover: William Morrow
Published 1987

Coretta Scott King Award: Illustrator
Caldecott Honor
Reading Rainbow Feature Book

Mufaro's two beautiful daughters are both beckoned to the city, where the king will select the worthiest young woman in the land to become his wife. Manyara, the selfish, spoiled sister, goes to great lengths to win the king's grace. Her egocentric nature makes her an unworthy choice for the king. The king prefers Nyasha, whose kindness and consideration earn his love and respect. This Cinderella-like folktale reinforces the rewards of virtue and good character.

My Dream of Martin Luther King [234]

Written and illustrated by Faith Ringgold

Hardcover: Crown
Published 1996

The author tells the story of Martin Luther King Jr. from the perspective of her own childhood dream. As her dream opens, she sees a world of people carrying bags full of prejudice, hate, ignorance, violence, and fear to exchange for bags of hope, freedom, peace, awareness, and love. Her dreams reflect real and imagined glimpses of the life of Martin Luther King Jr. to tell the story of his vision and civil rights leadership. By visualizing the story as the author tells it, young readers will be able to understand Dr. King's mission.

My Little Island [235]

Written and illustrated by Frané Lessac

Reading Rainbow Feature Book

Hardcover and softcover: HarperCollins
Published 1985

A young boy and his friend visit the Caribbean island of his birth. They meet new friends, eat delicious Caribbean food, take a drive, visit volcanoes, go to the market, and more. When the visit is over, they do not want to leave and agree to come back again soon.

My Name Is York [236]

Written by Elizabeth Van Steenwyk
Illustrated by Bill Farnsworth

Hardcover: Rising Moon, Northland
Published 1997

" *Still, I dream, and I carry my dream within me as we begin our quest to find a waterway to the western sea. I dream of finding freedom.*"

A little-known slave named York accompanied Captain Clark on the famous Lewis and Clark expedition in 1803. Although a slave, York stood side by side with Clark and experienced all of the adventure and thrill of their journey. The explorers encountered American Indians, white-water rapids, snowy passages, and brilliant views of the northern lights. Yet what York really sought was his own freedom. This is a quiet story about the quests of both the historic expedition party and one solitary man.

Nappy Hair [237]

Written by Carolivia Herron
Illustrated by Joe Cepeda

Hardcover: Alfred A. Knopf, Random House
Published 1997

Get past the provocative title and tune into the conversation at the family picnic, where everyone is talking about Brenda's nappy hair. You will quickly realize that they consider Brenda and her hair to be beautiful gifts from God. Written in call-and-response style, the family dialogue traces Brenda's nappy hair back through the ages to her African roots. "One nap of her hair is the only perfect circle in nature." Our little girls may come to appreciate their special place in creation and their beauty through this celebration of black hair.

Nathaniel Talking [238]

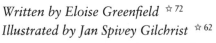

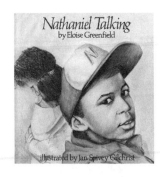

Written by Eloise Greenfield ☆ 72
Illustrated by Jan Spivey Gilchrist ☆ 62

Coretta Scott King Award: Illustrator
Coretta Scott King Honor: Author

Hardcover and softcover; Black Butterfly, Writers & Readers
Published 1989

Warm black-and-white pencil drawings illustrate eighteen poetic raps from an exuberant nine-year-old. Nathaniel reflects on a broad range of subjects from the perspective of his young life, including "Making Friends," "My Daddy," "Nine," and "Knowledge."

NBA by the Numbers [239]

Written by Bruce Brooks
Photographs by the National Basketball Association

Hardcover: Scholastic
Published 1997

Young sports fans will be thrilled by the dynamic photographs of notable NBA players in action that dominate this book about the popular game. Descriptions of certain elements of the game, and the corresponding photographs, are arranged to count from one, as in "One Alert Dribbler" (in this case Scottie Pippen) to fifty, as in "The Fifty All-Time Stars," picturing the NBA's top players picked in commemoration of the association's fiftieth anniversary.

Neeny Coming, Neeny Going [240]

Written by Karen English
Illustrated by Synthia Saint James ☆ 200

Coretta Scott King Honor: Illustrator

Hardcover: BridgeWater, Troll
Published 1996

Essie is excited about the impending visit of her favorite cousin, Neeny, who has moved away from Dasufskie Island (South Carolina). But now that she has lived on the mainland, Neeny no longer appreciates island life. Essie is disappointed by her cousin's new attitude, but gives Neeny a gift to bond them through shared memories. This book is illustrated in Saint James's signature block-color style. *Nonstandard English.*

The New King: A Madagascan Legend [241]

Adapted by Doreen Rappaport
Illustrated by E. B. Lewis

Hardcover: Dial, Penguin USA
Published 1995

A child, Prince Rakoto, suddenly becomes king when his beloved father dies in a hunting accident. His first act as king is to command that the royal doctors and magicians bring his father back to life, but they cannot. It takes the explanation of a wise woman to help Rakoto understand the circle of life and accept his father's death. This profound story with a tender message may be helpful in describing death to a young child.

Night on Neighborhood Street [242]

Written by Eloise Greenfield ☆ 72
Illustrated by Jan Spivey Gilchrist ☆ 62

Coretta Scott King Honor: Author
Coretta Scott King Honor: Illustrator
***Reading Rainbow* Review Book**

Hardcover and softcover: Penguin USA
Published 1991

Poetic glimpses of everyday life on an urban street are related in this lyrical book. Wispy pastel pictures convey family and neighborhood serenity.

Not a Copper Penny in Me House: Poems from the Caribbean [243]

Written by Monica Gunning
Illustrated by Frané Lessac

Hardcover: Wordsong, Boyd Mill
Published 1993

Scenes from daily life in Jamaica are poetically shared in this book. Among the fifteen short poems are: "Country Christmas," "Tropical Hurricanes," and "Jamaican Market Bus." The best features of the book are the vivid folk art paintings, which feature multihued children, tropical blue waters, and colorful island animals. *Caribbean dialect.*

Now Let Me Fly: The Story of a Slave Family [244]

Written and illustrated by Dolores Johnson ☆ 118

Hardcover and softcover: Simon & Schuster
Published 1993

Minna, an African girl, and a young boy, Amadi, are kidnapped from their village and then sold into slavery. The two survive the voyage to America with each other's love and support. Later they marry. Over time, Minna loses Amadi and their first son through the slave trade, and then two of their other four children to successful freedom runs. Family bonds remain intact and cannot be broken by the ravages of slavery. This profound story provides an excellent view not only of the brutality and inhumanity of slavery, but also of the spirit of our forefathers.

O Christmas Tree [245]

Written by Vashanti Rahaman
Illustrated by Frané Lessac

Hardcover: Boyds Mill
Published 1996

Anslem is anxious to go to the docks to be first in line when the shipment of real Christmas trees comes to his Caribbean island. Disappointingly, only dried-up, good-for-nothing trees arrive. Anslem tries to paint and decorate the raggedy pines but fails to achieve his dream of having a real tree for the holiday. On Christmas morning a thoughtful neighbor helps Anslem recognize the real Christmas foliage in his own front yard. Bright, festive folk art illustrations of the Caribbean holiday frame the story.

Off to School [246]

Written by Gwendolyn Battle-Lavert
Illustrated by Gershom Griffith

Hardcover: Holiday House
Published 1995

Wezielee is the daughter of a migrant sharecropper. The whole family works and the children go to school only after the farming seasons are over. Young Wezielee is so anxious to go to school that she cannot keep her mind on her chores. It is her week to cook for the family while they tend the fields. Her meals are disastrous, but her loving family is patient and understanding. It is inspirational to see how badly Wezielee wants to go to school and what she is willing to do to get there. ***Nonstandard English.***

> *"As Wezielee stirred the vegetables, she looked out the window. The schoolhouse glimmered in the sunlight. Maybe, if she hurried, she could walk up there once and say hello to the teacher. She'd still be back in time for dinner."*

Ogbo: Sharing Life in an African Village [247]

Written and photographed by Ifeoma Onyefulu

Hardcover: Gulliver, Harcourt Brace
Published 1996

Six-year-old Obioma tells the story of her *ogbo,* a group of children born within the same five-year period. The children of this *ogbo* grow up together in a small Nigerian village and share a special bond with one another. Each group is assigned a specific responsibility within the village. Obioma shares the stories of her family and friends and their respective *ogbos* in a fascinating photographic presentation.

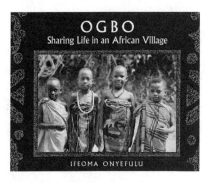

The Old, Old Man and the Very Little Boy [248]

Written by Kristine L. Franklin
Illustrated by Terea Shaffer

Hardcover: Atheneum, Simon & Schuster
Published 1992

As a young boy pays his daily respects to a village elder, he never imagines that he too will someday be old. The years pass, and the young boy becomes an old man receiving the same greetings from the village youth that he once gave to his elder. This is a tender book about the full cycle of life.

Only a Pigeon [249]

Written by Christopher Kurtz and Jane Kurtz
Illustrated by E. B. Lewis

Hardcover: Simon & Schuster
Published 1997

A young boy, Ondu-ahlem, lives and works in virtual poverty in Ethiopia. His only joy is his small coop of pigeons, which he tends with great care, sometimes sleeping next to the coop to protect the birds and their eggs. One day, he and his friends play an all-or-nothing game with their prized pigeons. On a signal, two boys throw their birds into the air. The boy whose pigeon returns home, leading the other pigeon to his side, wins and gets to keep both birds. Young readers will gain a sense of the life and values of this young boy in modern Ethiopia. A photograph at the back of the book shows the Ethiopian boy who inspired this story, surrounded by his pigeons.

The Orphan Boy [250]

Written by Tololwa M. Mollel
Illustrated by Paul Morin

Hardcover and softcover: Clarion, Houghton Mifflin
Published 1991

A star from the sky, named Kilekan, comes to earth embodied as a small boy to be a companion and son to an old man. Kilekan brings extraordinarily good luck to the old man by using celestial powers that he must keep secret. The old man becomes so curious that he breaks his trust with the boy in order to discover the secret, forcing Kilekan to return to his place in the sky. This gentle story, illustrated with intricate paintings, establishes how the Maasai people came to refer to the planet Venus as Kilekan, the orphan boy.

Our People [251]

Written by Angela Shelf Medearis ☆ 150
Illustrated by Michael Bryant

Hardcover: Atheneum, Simon & Schuster
Published 1994

An African American daddy tells his daughter about the great heritage and legacies of our people. He explains how our people built the great pyramids, invented the lightbulb, and accomplished much more. The young child is inspired by the stories and pleased to hear about our glorious past, but also looks forward to our brilliant future and her role in it. Use this excellent book to introduce children to black history and to frame their sense of racial identity.

Over the Green Hills [252]

Written and illustrated by Rachel Isadora

Hardcover: Greenwillow, William Morrow
Published 1992

Young Zolani and his mother journey across the South African countryside to visit Grandmother. Along the way, the two stop to shop, help a distressed neighbor, and rest by the roadside. Disappointingly, Grandmother is not at home when they arrive. The two wait patiently until they finally see Grand-mother coming down the road. Authentic landscapes of the South African countryside and scenes of rural village life support the simple story line.

Papa's Stories [253]

Written and illustrated by Dolores Johnson ☆ 118

Hardcover: Macmillan
Published 1994

A father and daughter bond during their special story-telling time in this heartwarming story. Papa regales Kari with creative stories told from her favorite books. As she grows, Kari begins to realize that Papa is not really reading the words in the books, and begins to understand that he cannot read at all. She is momentarily disappointed by the deception, but then recommits to their relationship and determines to help him learn to read. In a surprise twist, Papa demonstrates his own commitment to Kari.

THE CREATORS

Angela Johnson

AUTHOR

"I write children's books with the knowledge that I'm sharing a different world with young people. It is so very important for them to stretch beyond self-imposed or societal boundaries."

OUR FAVORITES

Do Like Kyla, 1990 [27]

The Rolling Store, 1997 [268]

Tell Me a Story, Mama, 1989 [102]

Toning the Sweep, 1993 [487]

When I Am Old with You, 1990 [113]

The Paperboy [254]

Written and illustrated by Dav Pilkey

Caldecott Honor

Hardcover: Orchard, Grolier
Published 1996

In the wee hours of the morning, while it is still dark outside and everyone is still asleep, a responsible young boy arises with his faithful dog to prepare for his paper route. In beautifully illustrated night scenes, he rides through his well-practiced route, delivering papers while the dog follows behind. He returns home just as everyone else is getting up, and goes back to bed to finish his night's sleep.

> "*All the world is asleep except for the paperboy and his dog. And this is the time when they are the happiest.*"

Pass It On: African American Poetry for Children [255]

Compiled by Wade Hudson ☆ 102
Illustrated by Floyd Cooper ☆ 34

Hardcover: Scholastic
Published 1993

The works of fourteen renowned African American poets from our past and present are featured in this important collection. A variety of subjects and styles are presented by poet laureates, like Langston Hughes and Gwendolyn Brooks. The poetry is illustrated with brown-hued paintings. The intent of this book is to pass our literary heritage from generation to generation, which makes it a natural addition to your child's permanent collection. The companion title, *How Sweet The Sound: African American Songs for Children* [197], does an equally fine job, presenting many songs from the African American experience.

The Patchwork Quilt [256]

Written by Valerie Flournoy
Illustrated by Jerry Pinkney ☆ 184

Coretta Scott King Award: Illustrator
Reading Rainbow Feature Book

Hardcover: Dial, Penguin USA
Published 1985

In this classic story, Tanya's grandmother begins working on a quilt, which captures Tanya's interest. Grandma explains how each square represents a piece of her life. She works on the project until she is overcome with an extended illness. The quilt was only half finished when Grandma became ill, so Tanya and her mother take over. Grandma recovers in time to help Tanya finish their mutual labor of love. *Tanya's Reunion* is an excellent sequel.

A Picture Book of Sojourner Truth [257]

Written by David A. Adler
Illustrated by Gershom Griffith

Hardcover and softcover: Holiday House
Published 1994

Freed slave Sojourner Truth was an early African American activist who stood up for her strong religious convictions and women's rights, and against the immorality of slavery. She acquired her name because she sojourned across the country speaking to great congregations of people. In this simply written biography, the life and works of this gifted African American woman are outlined for elementary readers. The Picture Book of... series includes other books on famous African Americans, including Frederick Douglass, Martin Luther King Jr., Jesse Owens, Rosa Parks, Jackie Robinson, and Harriet Tubman.

A Place Called Freedom [258]

Written by Scott Russell Sanders
Illustrated by Thomas B. Allen

Hardcover: Atheneum, Simon & Schuster
Published 1997

This is a triumphant story, inspired by the true story of the founding of Lyle Station, Indiana, about an emancipated black family that travels north from their Tennessee plantation to Indiana to build a new life. The industrious family works to buy land and then establishes their own farm. Papa travels back to the South periodically to lead other family members to the new home site. Soon other blacks come to the settlement until there are enough people to establish a town that they name Freedom.

Poppa's New Pants [259]

Written by Angela Shelf Medearis ☆ 150
Illustrated by John Ward

Hardcover: Holiday House
Published 1995

In a comedy of errors, Poppa's new pants, which were originally six inches too long, are cut off above the knee when each of the three women in the house, unbeknownst to one another, decides to surprise him by cutting and hemming the pants. The young son, an unknowing witness to the nighttime escapades, mistakes the three do-gooders for ghosts, adding a humorous subplot to the story.

Probity Jones and the Fear Not Angel [260]

Written by Walter J. Wangerin
Illustrated by Tim Ladwig

Hardcover: Augsburg Fortress
Published 1996

In this remarkably beautiful Christmas story, Probity Jones becomes ill on the night of the church Christmas pageant and is left at home alone when her family goes. Magically, an angel appears to Probity, wraps her in her arms, and sweeps her away to see the pageant from a heavenly point of view. Probity becomes the light that shines on the pageant.

Puzzles [261]

Written by Dava Walker
Illustrated by Cornelius Van Wright and Ying-Hwa Hu

Softcover: Lollipop, Carolina Wren
Published 1996

Nine-year-old Cassie has sickle-cell anemia and suffers the typical physical and emotional pains associated with the disease. Despite her medical challenges, Cassie is supported by loving and dedicated parents who maintain high expectations of her. Cassie's classmates do not understand her chronic condition until she produces a video for a science project that educates them about the illness and the effect on its victims. This is an important and enlightening story. A special introduction and a resource guide are included for adults interested in more information about the condition.

> "*I don't have sick cells. I have sickle cell disease, and it's not contagious.*"

Rachel Parker, Kindergarten Show-Off [262]

Written by Ann Martin
Illustrated by Nancy Poydar

Hardcover and softcover: Holiday House
Published 1992

Five-year-old kindergartener Olivia is delighted when a new classmate, Rachel Parker, moves in next door. As the two become acquainted, they begin to compete, upstaging each other at every turn, until their budding friendship falls apart. Their wise teacher puts the two in a situation where they must cooperate and begin to appreciate each other. Important lessons about jealousy, unproductive competition, and cooperation are clearly developed in this spirited book.

Rata-Pata-Scata-Fata: A Caribbean Story [263]

Written by Phillis Gershator
Illustrated by Holly Meade

Hardcover: Little, Brown
Published 1994

In this entertaining story, lazy Junjun does not feel like doing his chores. So, when Mommy asks him to go to the market for a fish, Junjun conjures up a magic word, "Rata-Pata-Scata-Fata," and a fish magically appears in his path. When Mommy tells Junjun to go for the goat, he repeats the magic phrase and instantly the goat is there. Every time Mommy asks for anything, Junjun relies on his magic spell. Although the results are actually brought about by a series of timely coincidences, Junjun believes in his magic!

The Real McCoy: The Life of an African American Inventor [264]

Written by Wendy Towle
Illustrated by Wil Clay

Softcover: Scholastic
Published 1993

Young readers will be inspired by knowing that Elijah McCoy, a free-born black man from Canada, was a premier engineer and inventor back in the mid-1800s. McCoy invented many things, for which he received little historical credit. Most noteworthy of his inventions was an oil drip cup that revolutionized the locomotive industry. Many others tried to develop better versions of the oil cup, but McCoy's original was always superior, which gave rise to the phrase "the real McCoy."

Red Dancing Shoes [265]

Written by Denise Lewis Patrick
Illustrated by James E. Ransome ☆ 192

Hardcover: Tambourine, William Morrow
Published 1993

An energetic little girl receives a shiny new pair of red shoes as a gift from her grandmother. She dances and twirls up the street to show off her new shoes, but has a sudden mishap that seemingly ruins the shoes. Dismayed, she allows her aunt to take them and attempt to clean them. A few minutes later, after a little wash and shine, the shoes are as good as new.

The Reverend Thomas's False Teeth [266]

Written by Gayle Gillerlain
Illustrated by Dena Schutzer

Hardcover and softcover: BridgeWater, Troll
Published 1995

Gracie's family is preparing to have Reverend Thomas over for dinner. Just before his arrival, the Reverend accidentally drops his false teeth into the Chesapeake Bay. Everyone frantically tries to retrieve the teeth, but to no avail. They all ignore Gracie's constant refrain that she knows how to find the lost chompers. Finally, she takes matters into her own hands and successfully uses a clever and truly funny tactic to get the Reverend's teeth back. Children will enjoy the whole ridiculous situation and the witty ending of this easy-to-read book.

Robert Lives with His Grandparents [267]

Written by Martha Whitmore Hickman
Illustrated by Tim Hinton

Hardcover: Albert Whitman
Published 1995

After his parents' divorce, and because of his mother's drug problem, Robert comes to live with his grandparents. He loves and appreciates his grandparents, but is embarrassed to admit that he does not live with his own parents. When his grandparents come to school for an open house, Robert is forced to admit his living arrangement. He is pleased and surprised to find out that he is not alone. Everyone is very positive about the situation, which is excellent reinforcement for children who live in nontraditional family situations.

The Rolling Store [268]

Written by Angela Johnson ☆ 110
Illustrated by Peter Catalanotto

Hardcover: Orchard, Grolier
Published 1997

An industrious little girl is inspired when her grandfather tells her a story about the rolling store, a mobile market that used to come to rural customers to sell them everything that they needed. She is so impressed with the idea that she and a friend load up a wagon to start their own business.

A Rookie Biography Series [269]

Written by Carol Greene
Illustrated by Steven Greene

Hardcover: Children's Press, Grolier
Published 1992

This elementary biography series introduces young readers to key historical personalities who excelled in a variety of fields. Each volume is chock-full of easy-to-read text, photographs, and other supporting illustrations. Six notable African Americans are featured in the series: Mary McLeod Bethune, George Washington Carver, Katherine Dunham, Martin Luther King Jr., Thurgood Marshall, and Jackie Robinson.

Rum-A-Tum-Tum [270]

Written by Angela Shelf Medearis ☆ 150
Illustrated by James E. Ransome ☆ 192

Hardcover: Holiday House
Published 1997

" *I sing and sway, I feel so fine,*
finger-snapping, toe-tapping in a line
I clap my hands and stomp my feet,
dancing along to the song of the street.
RUM-A-TUM-TUM, RUM-A-TUM-TUM,
RUM-A-TUM-TUM-TUM-TUM. "

The unique sights and sounds of turn-of-the-century New Orleans are captured in this rhyming text. Luscious illustrations of fruits, vegetables, and fish being sold by vendors on the cobblestone streets, and the vendors' street cries, will transport young readers to that place and time. There, they can join a young girl who is taking it all in, and then follow a high-stepping marching jazz band through the streets of the French Quarter. Only in New Orleans!

Running the Road to ABC [271]

Written by Denize Lauture
Illustrated by Reynold Ruffins

Coretta Scott King Honor: Illustrator

Hardcover: Simon & Schuster
Published 1996

Vividly illustrated children run across the landscape and past the people and places of Haiti on their way to school in this energetic poem. Each illustration is a complex mural of color and high action.

Dolores Johnson

AUTHOR AND ILLUSTRATOR

"I never thought that I would be a writer as a child, but I always felt I would do something with art. It's not that I thought I was an artist. All that I knew about artists was that they drew and painted all the time. Their paintings were hung in galleries and museums, and were sometimes sold for a great deal of money. As a child, it was difficult to imagine that as my future life. I simply loved to draw."

OUR FAVORITES

The Best Bug to Be, 1992 [128]

Now Let Me Fly: The Story of a Slave Family, 1993 [244]

Papa's Stories, 1994 [253]

What Kind of Baby-Sitter Is This?, 1991 [300]

What Will Mommy Do When I'm at School,? 1990 [III]

Satchmo's Blues [272]

Written by Alan Schroeder
Illustrated by Floyd Cooper ☆ 34

Hardcover: Doubleday
Published 1996

In this fictionalized biography, young Louis Armstrong, dreaming of becoming a musician, tries to save five dollars to buy the horn that he has seen in a pawnshop window. Just before he achieves his goal, Louis experiences a disappointing financial setback. In spite of that, he goes on to buy the trumpet and to become the most famous trumpeter of his time. The moral of the story is that goal-setting, hard work, determination, and the universal truth that nothing worth having comes easily are the keys to success.

Saturday at the New You [273]

Written by Barbara E. Barber
Illustrated by Anna Rich

Hardcover and softcover: Lee & Low
Published 1994

Shauna spends Saturdays in the family-owned New You Beauty Salon in this brightly illustrated story. She helps around the shop, folding towels and taking care of other small jobs, while enjoying the company of the regular customers. What Shauna really wants to be is a stylist, but she is limited to braiding her own doll's hair. When Tiffany, an ill-behaved young customer, sees the doll's hair, she settles down and orders the same style.

Sebgugugu the Glutton: A Bantu Tale from Rwanda, Africa [274]

Written by Verna Aardema
Illustrated by Nancy L. Clouse

Hardcover: Africa World
Published 1993

Sebgugugu is a very poor man who calls upon Imana, the Lord of R·
help provide for his family. Imana responds kindly on several occ·
viding a bounty of food for Sebgugugu and his family. Each time
tions Sebgugugu about what he must do to protect the endowm
always makes the foolish man risk what he has for what he t'
more. Strong cut-paper collages embellish this African folktale.

Shortcut [275]

Written and illustrated by Donald Crews

Hardcover: Greenwillow, William Morrow
Published 1992

Author Donald Crews recreates the story of the day that he and
his brothers and sisters decide to take a shortcut to Bigmama's
home, following the path of the train tracks. As it grows darker
and darker, they realize that an unscheduled freight train could
come by at any time. Then, finally, it happens! They hear a train
rumbling down the track and run for safety, narrowly avoiding
the danger. They continue their walk, vowing to keep their mischief a secret from Bigmama, their grandmother, and promise never to take
such a risk again. This book is the sequel to *Bigmama's,* in which Crews first
wrote about his summer vacations at his grandmother's house.

Sing to the Sun [276]

Poems and pictures by Ashley Bryan ☆ 16

Softcover: Trophy, HarperCollins
Published 1992

Illuminating mosaic illustrations brighten a collection of two dozen poetry
selections that celebrate the ups and downs of life. The poetic selections
include "Taste the Air," "Mama's Bouquet," "Storyteller," and "Pretty Is."

The Singing Man: Adapted from a
West African Folktale [277]

Adapted by Angela Shelf Medearis ☆ 150   **Coretta Scott King Honor: Illustrator**
Illustrated by Terea Shaffer

Hardcover and softcover: Holiday House
Published 1994

In the West African city of Lagos, a young man must declare his career plans
when he is initiated into manhood. When Banzar declares that he will become
a musician, he is banished from the village for choosing such an unproductive vocation. Over the years, Banzar becomes a very famous singer, intoning
songs about the history and heritage of his people. He returns home many
years later and is welcomed and honored for his accomplishment in this
sophisticated story.

Somebody's New Pajamas [278]

Written by Isaac Jackson
Illustrated by David Soman

Hardcover: Dial, Penguin USA
Published 1996

The lifestyle differences between Jerome and his friend Robert are obvious when Jerome spends the night with Robert. Robert has soft, comfortable pajamas, but Jerome does not, because his family has never been able to afford such luxuries. Jerome wants a pair of new pajamas, too, until he recognizes that the pajamas are not as important as the pride that he has in his family.

Storm in the Night [279]

Written by Mary Stolz   Coretta Scott King Honor: Illustrator
Illustrated by Pat Cummings ☆ 42

Hardcover and softcover: HarperCollins
Published 1988

When a grandfather and grandson are caught in a darkened house during a stormy night, an intimate evening of appreciation is shared between the two. There are several other books about Thomas and his grandfather: *Go Fish* [352], *Stealing Home* [405], and *Coco Grimes*.

The Story of Ruby Bridges [280]

Written by Robert Coles
Illustrated by George Ford

Hardcover: Scholastic
Published 1995

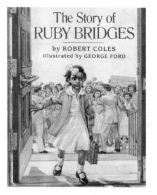

In 1960, six-year-old Ruby Bridges was the first black child to go to the all-white William Franz Elementary School in New Orleans, forcing school integration. This riveting fictionalized account of the true story describes the weeks of ridicule and protests that young Ruby endured. Ruby remained strong, demonstrating courage and character beyond her years, and made a difference for all children who would follow her.

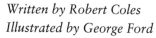

> "*E*very morning, Ruby had stopped a few blocks away from school to say a prayer for the people who hated her. This morning she forgot until she was already in the middle of the angry mob."

The Story of "Stagecoach" Mary Fields [281]

Written by Robert H. Miller ☆ 156
Illustrated by Cheryl Hanna ☆ 88

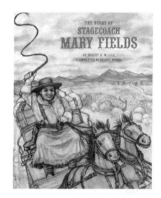

Hardcover and softcover: Silver Burdett, Simon & Schuster
Published 1995

"Stagecoach" Mary Fields was a true-life historical character who, after being emancipated from slavery, became the first black woman to carry the United States mail. This action-packed story tells of Mary's wild escapades and daring feats, which distinguish her as one of the larger-than-life legends of the early American West. Three companion titles about other African American characters of the Old West are *Buffalo Soldiers: The Story of Emanuel Stance* [138], *The Story of Jean Baptiste Du Sable,* and *The Story of Nat Love.*

Sukey and the Mermaid [282]

Written by Robert D. San Souci
Illustrated by Brian Pinkney ☆ 172

Coretta Scott King Honor: Illustrator

Hardcover and softcover: Simon & Schuster
Published 1992

Sukey lives with her mother and abusive stepfather. One day, while she is playing by the sea, Sukey meets a beautiful mermaid who befriends her and takes her to a kinder home below the surface. When Sukey returns to her own world, the mermaid continues to watch over Sukey's destiny and well-being, protecting her from the evil deeds of her stepfather.

The Sunday Outing [283]

Written by Gloria Jean Pinkney ☆ 184
Illustrated by Jerry Pinkney ☆ 184

Hardcover: Dial, Penguin USA
Published 1994

Ernestine wants to take the train to visit her aunt and uncle in this story about priorities. Her family is not able to afford the fare until Ernestine makes the mature and important choice to trade off the cost of new school clothes for the cost of the train ticket. Happily, she embarks on her adventure with the love and support of her family. This book is the sequel to *Back Home,* which first introduced us to Ernestine and her family.

Sweet Clara and the Freedom Quilt [284]

Written by Deborah Hopkinson
Illustrated by James Ransome ☆ 192

Reading Rainbow Review Book

Hardcover and softcover: Random House
Published 1993

Twelve-year-old Clara, a young slave, works in the big house sewing room. She hears stories about slave escapes to the North and begins to create a quilt that maps the way. She painstakingly sews the map to freedom, patch by patch, including every geographic detail that she can learn. When the quilt is completed, Clara, having memorized every detail of her work, makes her own escape, leaving the quilt behind for others to follow. This wonderfully dramatic story will captivate young readers. *Nonstandard English.*

The Talking Cloth [285]

Written and illustrated by Rhonda Mitchell

Hardcover: Orchard, Grolier
Published 1997

Amber visits her Aunt Phoebe, who is a consummate pack rat. She goes through her aunt's possessions until she comes upon an interesting piece of cloth. Young readers will learn about the *adinkra* cloth, which comes from the Ashanti tribe of Ghana, in this educational storybook. The cloth can tell stories about its owner by its color, design, and length. The cloth can also communicate feelings, messages, and social status. Brightly colored illustrations are crisply presented against a stark white background.

The Talking Eggs [286]

Written by Robert D. San Souci
Illustrated by Jerry Pinkney ☆ 184

Coretta Scott King Honor: Illustrator
Caldecott Honor
Reading Rainbow Review Book

Hardcover: Dial, Penguin USA
Published 1989

An imaginative folktale from the American South tells the story of a good-hearted young girl who is oppressed by her vain and selfish mother and sister. In this captivating Cinderella-like tale, Blanche flees into the woods to avoid her mother's wrath. There she meets an old woman, who guides her to a magical place. Blanche's goodness and respect for the old woman earn her a basket of eggs that are found to conceal gold, silver, jewels, and luxurious goods. Her jealous, lazy sister, Rose, goes to the woods to get her own fortune, but her flagrant disrespect and greed result in an entirely different reward.

Tar Beach [287]

Written and illustrated by Faith Ringgold

Coretta Scott King Award: Illustrator
Caldecott Honor
Reading Rainbow Feature Book

Hardcover and softcover: Crown
Published 1991

In her dreams, eight-year-old Cassie can fly over her Harlem neighborhood and lay claim to anything that she wants. She flies over the George Washington Bridge and owns it. She flies over the union building, where her father is working as a construction worker, to claim it for him. Ironically, he was not allowed to be a member of the union because he is African American. Cassie's selfless dreams of a better life for her family are inspirational. Another of Cassie's dreams of flight is told in *Aunt Harriet's Underground Railroad in the Sky* [124].

Teammates [288]

Written by Peter Golenbock
Illustrated by Paul Bacon

Hardcover and softcover: Gulliver, Harcourt Brace
Published 1990

This excellent, easy-to-read book tells the true story of the integration of major league baseball by Jackie Robinson. A young child can easily understand the integration strategy of Branch Rickey, the humiliation of Jackie Robinson, and the compassion of Pee Wee Reese, the white player who finally embraced Robinson on the field, both figuratively and literally. Photographs of the key characters are interspersed with illustrations that support the story.

Tommy Traveler in the World of Black History [289]

Written and illustrated by Tom Feelings ☆ 48

Hardcover and softcover: Black Butterfly, Writers & Readers
Published 1991

Tommy is unable to find books about black history in his public library, so he visits a doctor who has a private collection of books on the subject. As Tommy reads, he falls asleep and dreams that he is actually part of the historical stories of Phoebe Fraunces, Emmet Till, Aesop, Frederick Douglass, Crispus Attucks, and Joe Louis. The story is presented in a comic-book style that will attract and engage many young readers.

Tower to Heaven [290]

Retold by Ruby Dee
Illustrated by Jennifer Bent

Hardcover: Henry Holt
Published 1991

Yaa, an over-talkative village woman, constantly swings her walking stick as she talks, inadvertently striking Sky God. He warns her over and over again to be more careful, but her clumsiness continues. Finally, she strikes a final blow upon Sky God, so he retreats higher into the sky where she cannot reach him. Yaa and her people become desperate to find Sky God, so they try to build a tower up to the sky. They never quite reach their destination because of a shortcoming in their building process. The villagers' witty escapades will entertain young readers and challenge them to identify the error.

The Train to Lulu's [291]

Written by Elizabeth Fitzgerald Howard
Illustrated by Robert Casilla

Reading Rainbow Review Book

Softcover: Aladdin, Simon & Schuster
Published 1988

Babs and her big sister are traveling all alone on a train from Boston to Baltimore to visit their great-aunt Lulu for the summer. Mom has packed lunch and dinner, so they have plenty to eat. The two girls read, color, and play for the duration of the nine-hour trip, and take care of each other until they reach their destination, demonstrating uncommon maturity and responsibility.

Trouble [292]

Written by Jane Kurtz
Illustrated by Durga Bernhard

Hardcover: Gulliver, Harcourt Brace
Published 1997

A young Ethiopian boy always seems to find himself in the line of trouble, no matter what he does. Teklah's father makes him a game board, hoping to help occupy him while he tends the family's goats, so that he cannot get into trouble. Uncannily, however, Teklah gets involved in a series of troubled encounters that result in his losing the game board. In this witty story, things go full circle and Teklah manages to get a new game board at the end of the day.

'Twas the Night B'fore Christmas: An African-American Version [293]

Retold and illustrated by Melodye Rosales

Hardcover: Cartwheel, Scholastic
Published 1996

Clement Clark Moore's traditional holiday poem about Santa's visit to a family on Christmas Eve is told with a new twist. The characters now include members of a turn-of-the-century African American farm family and a black "Santy Claus." The illustrations come alive and reflect the joy and amazement of the story. ***Nonstandard English.***

Uncle Jed's Barber Shop [294]

Written by Margaret King Mitchell
Illustrated by James Ransome ☆ 192

Coretta Scott King Honor: Illustrator
***Reading Rainbow* Feature Book**

Hardcover: Simon & Schuster
Softcover: Houghton Mifflin
Published 1993

Sarah Jean's Uncle Jed was a traveling barber who always dreamed of owning his own barber shop and diligently saved to buy one. His dream was twice deferred, first when he temporarily sacrificed his savings to help pay for Sarah Jean's emergency surgery, and later when he lost his savings during the bank failures of the Great Depression. In this book, Uncle Jed's dream finally becomes a reality and Sarah Jean is there to help him celebrate and tell his story. Every picture conveys the special love and relationship between Uncle Jed, Sarah Jean, and other family members.

The Village of Round and Square Houses [295]

Written and illustrated by Ann Grifalconi

Caldecott Honor

Hardcover: Little, Brown
Published 1986

In the African village of Tos, the men live in square houses and the women and children live in round ones. A young girl is curious about this unique living arrangement. Gran'ma tells an entertaining story of how it came to be, and wisely surmises that they all live together peacefully because each one has a place to be apart and a time to be together.

The Wagon [296]

Written by Tony Johnston
Illustrated by James E. Ransome ☆ 192

Hardcover: Tambourine, William Morrow
Published 1996

A young slave boy has ambivalent feelings about the wagon that he and his father built for their master in this provocative storybook. The wagon is both a tangible emblem of his enslavement and the vehicle that can carry him to the freedom that he craves.

Wagon Train: A Family Goes West in 1865 [297]

Written by Courtni C. Wright
Illustrated by Gershom Griffith

Hardcover: Holiday House
Published 1995

Ginny and her family join other pioneering Americans heading west to California in a covered wagon over the Oregon Trail. Travel is slow and difficult. The pioneers face treacherous conditions, hunger, and personal pain during their journey to a new life in the West. This well-written story teaches something about the pioneering spirit and the fact that blacks were a part of the western expansion of the United States.

Wagon Wheels [298]

Written by Barbara Brenner
Illustrated by Don Bolognese

Reading Rainbow Review Book

Hardcover and softcover: HarperCollins
Published 1993

The incredible story of the Muldie boys and their father is told in this easy-to-read book of historical fiction. The boys—ages eleven, eight, and three—move with their father to Kansas and are then left alone for months while he goes on to find a better homestead. The boys live alone in a hole carved in the ground and care for one another under incredibly difficult circumstances, including a prairie fire that sweeps across their subterranean home. When their father sends word that he is settled, along with a rough map, the three young children travel alone for over 150 miles to reunite with him.

A Weed Is a Flower: The Life of George Washington Carver [299]

Written and illustrated by Aliki

Hardcover and softcover: Aladdin, Simon & Schuster
Published 1988

Born a poor, sickly slave, George Washington Carver was a special child who took every opportunity to learn and to attend school. He grew to be one of the most important agriculturists in American history. His work distinguished him among his peers and dramatically changed farming practices in this country. This version of Carver's life is presented at a primary level, so even the youngest readers can understand his achievements.

What Kind of Baby-Sitter Is This? [300]

Written and illustrated by Dolores Johnson   ☆ 118

Hardcover: Macmillan, Simon & Schuster
Published 1991

Kevin can tell with one look that he is in for one of those evenings when Mrs. Pritchard comes to baby-sit. But, to his surprise, Mrs. Pritchard tunes in to a baseball game and seems to know everything about the sport. Hmh! Maybe the evening will be okay! Like Kevin, young readers will learn that it is not wise to judge a book by its cover.

What Mary Jo Shared [301]

Written by Janice May Udry
Illustrated by Elizabeth Sayles

Hardcover: Albert Whitman
Softcover: Scholastic
Published 1966

Mary Jo is a shy schoolgirl who is too timid and insecure to share with her classmates at show-and-tell. She would really like to participate in the weekly event, but wants to think of something very unique and original to share with her class. She finally decides to present her father at show-and-tell, demonstrating creativity and pride that would warm any father's heart.

> " *But Mary Jo finally became determined to share something that no one else had shared. It got so she could hardly think of anything else.*"

> "*But what would life really be like without refrigerators and televisions? Without spaceships and rockets, VCRs and video games? Without indoor toilets? Noel couldn't imagine having to go to the bathroom alone in the cold and the dark.*"

When I Was Little [302]

Written by Toyomi Igus
Illustrated by Higgins Bond

Hardcover and softcover: Just Us
Published 1992

Young Noel and his grandfather spend a day fishing in this soulful book. The two engage in a very believable conversation about the differences between now and when Grandfather was a child. Grandfather explains to the incredulous Noel that there were no indoor toilets, televisions, VCRs, jet airplanes, or washing machines when he was a boy. The illustrations come to life in exquisite color, except the pictures of Grandfather's memories, which are presented in black and white for a striking visual effect.

Where Are You Going, Manyoni? [303]

Written and illustrated by Catherine Stock

Hardcover: William Morrow
Published 1993

Manyoni walks for two hours through the bush near the Limpopo River in Zimbabwe. She passes the malala palms, baboons, shady kloff, and red sand koppies (all of which are defined in the glossary), until she rendezvouses with her friend to finish the daily walk to school. The enthralling illustrations of the rural African landscape and wild animals are from Ms. Stock's personal memories of her visits to Zimbabwe.

White Socks Only [304]

Written by Evelyn Coleman
Illustrated by Tyrone Geter

Hardcover: Albert Whitman
Published 1996

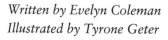

Grandma tells a story about the time when she was a child in the segregated South. One day she walked into town by herself. On her way home, she saw a water fountain with a "Whites Only" sign on it. Naively, she took off her black shoes and sipped from the fountain in her white socks. An angry white man confronted the child, but she was defended by an act of solidarity and defiance by other blacks. Children of today, possessing the same naiveté but none of the experiences of the past, may begin to understand the oppression felt by generations before them.

Who Built the Ark? [305]

Written and illustrated by Pam Paparone

Hardcover: Simon & Schuster
Published 1994

The story of Noah and the ark is told with rhythmic verse and colorful illustrations. Music is provided for gospel sing-along fun.

Wild, Wild Hair [306]

Written by Nikki Grimes
Illustrated by George Ford

Softcover: Cartwheel, Scholastic
Published 1997

Tisa has long, thick, wild hair that is very difficult to comb. She dreads her hair-combing sessions, so she hides from her mother whenever that time comes. In spite of her distaste for the hairdressing process, she is always proud of her beautiful long braids when Mother is finished.

Wild Wild Sunflower Child Anna [307]

Written by Nancy White Carlstrom
Illustrated by Jerry Pinkney ☆ 184

Hardcover and softcover: Aladdin, Simon & Schuster
Published 1987

Anna takes in nature's glory on a sunny summer day. She frolics in the meadow among the flowers, picks berries, splashes with the frogs, and watches the spiders spinning their webs. Finally, exhausted by the adventure, Anna falls asleep in the grassy meadow. This lyrical book enumerates many of the simple pleasures that await children outdoors.

William and the Good Old Days [308]

Written by Eloise Greenfield ☆ 72
Illustrated by Jan Spivey Gilchrist ☆ 62

Hardcover: HarperCollins
Published 1993

In this sensitive exploration of a child's innermost feelings, young William yearns for his grandmother's recovery after her extended illness. He reminisces about their wonderful times together and looks forward to the return of the good old days.

Willie's Not the Hugging Kind [309]

Written by Joyce Durham Barrett
Illustrated by Pat Cummings ☆ 42

Hardcover and softcover: HarperCollins
Published 1989

Young Willie gives up hugging his mom and dad, feeling that he is too old for such nonsense. But he soon starts to miss the warmth and security of those reassuring hugs. He finally realizes that he still needs the embrace of those he loves and those who love him. Leave this book around to help your remote young readers understand that demonstrative family affection has a place.

Wilma Unlimited: How Wilma Rudolph Became the World's Fastest Woman [310]

Written by Kathleen Krull
Illustrated by David Diaz

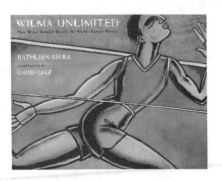

Hardcover: Harcourt Brace
Published 1996

The inspirational story of Wilma Rudolph is told in this simply written storybook. Wilma contracted polio as a child and spent many years in a leg brace. She was a determined young girl who worked tirelessly to rehabilitate her leg until, at the age of twelve, she was able to walk without assistance. Wilma became active in sports as a way of developing her weakened limb. She excelled in track, won a place on the United States Women's Olympic Team, and became the first American woman to win three gold medals.

Wood-Hoopoe Willie [311]

Written by Virginia Kroll
Illustrated by Katherine Roundtree

Hardcover and softcover: Charlesbridge
Published 1993

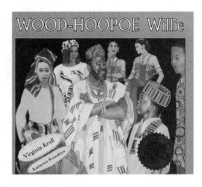

Willie, who loves music, is constantly tapping out rhythms—with chopsticks at the Chinese restaurant, with pencils at school, and on tabletops with forks and knives. Everywhere Willie goes, he finds something to get the beat going. Willie's grandfather muses that Willie has a wood-hoopoe, an African pecking bird, trapped within him and teaches Willie about African instrumentation. The family goes to a Kwanzaa festival, where Willie gets the unexpected opportunity to sit in for a missing drummer, releasing his wood-hoopoe talents. The vibrancy of the story is matched by the intensely colored, Afrocentric paintings.

Working Cotton [312]

Written by Sherley Anne Williams
Illustrated by Carole Byard

Coretta Scott King Honor: Illustrator
Caldecott Honor

Hardcover and softcover: Voyager, Harcourt Brace
Published 1992

A little girl tells about the daily toils of her migrant family, which picks cotton in the fields of California. The words are provocative and the illustrations extraordinary in this reflection of a difficult lifestyle. **Nonstandard English.**

> **"***I***'***m a big girl now.** Not big enough to have my own sack, just only to help pile cotton in the middle of the row for Mamma to put in hers."

Your Dad Was Just Like You [313]

Written and illustrated by Dolores Johnson ☆ 118

Hardcover: Macmillan, Simon & Schuster
Published 1993

Young Peter and his father are at odds with one another in this earnest story. Dad does not feel that Peter is serious enough about his schoolwork. To make matters worse, Peter has just carelessly broken an old cup on Dad's dresser. Peter cries to his grandfather, who then relates a compelling story about Dad when he was a boy, apparently very much like Peter at the same age. He also explains the significance of the old cup. The story helps Peter to better understand his father and motivates him to try to develop a more positive relationship with his dad.

You're My Nikki [314]

Written by Phyllis Rose Eisenberg
Illustrated by Jill Kastner

Hardcover and softcover: Penguin USA
Published 1992

Little Nikki is worried that her mother may forget about her because she is so busy with two other children and is going back to work. Nikki puts her mother to the test, asking her a series of tough questions to ensure that Mother will always be able to recognize her young daughter. Mother assures Nikki of her capacity to always know and love her.

Zora Hurston and the Chinaberry Tree [315]

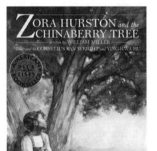

Written by William Miller
Illustrated by Cornelius Van Wright
  and Ying-Hwa Hu

Reading Rainbow Review Book

Hardcover and softcover: Lee & Low
Published 1994

The early life story of the renowned African American storyteller and author Zora Neale Hurston is inspirationally told in this book. As a young girl growing up at the end of the nineteenth century, Zora received conflicting messages about what girls could do. Her father urged her to wear dresses, read the Bible, and stay in her place. Her mother encouraged her curiosity and inspired her to see and do all that she could. Following her mother's death, Zora climbs a chinaberry tree where she can see a far-off city and contemplates the promise that she made to her mother to reach her fullest potential.

Books for
Middle Readers

THERE IS A DIVERSE SELECTION of sophisticated storybooks, chapter books, and nonfiction titles available to young readers in grades four to six, ages nine to eleven. Kids in this age group tend to be very specific about the genre and subject matter of the books they prefer. Some enjoy mysteries, others love to read serialized chapter books about a specific character, and still others will read everything that they can about sports, pioneers, or some other favorite interest.

Short chapter books and novels for secondary readers tend to have more complex plots. The subject matter is also more creative, ranging from the superstitious *Clara and the Hoodoo Man* [330], and the supernatural *Ghost Train* [350], to stories of preteen strife like *Once Upon a Time in Junior High* [391] and *Circle of Gold* [329].

There are also excellent books about black history and heritage, such as *Everyday People* [341], about the National Civil Rights Museum; and *Dear Mrs. Parks* [335], a book of letters written to Rosa Parks. Additionally, there are several biographical series that describe the accomplishments of famous African Americans, like the comprehensive Junior Black Americans of Achievement series [366].

Many parents and teachers will tell you that by the time children reach this age group they either love to read or they do not. For those who do, this list may help introduce new areas of interest. For those who do not, it is not too late to inspire them with books that appeal to their interests. The key is to introduce books that appeal to the child on a very personal level, and without too much pressure. By this time in their school careers, there is already plenty of required reading assigned, so a parent needs to offer supplemental reading solely for the child's pleasure.

The material in all of these books is appropriate for this age group, but the reading levels vary tremendously—from books for very skilled readers to books for those still developing reading and comprehension skills. Flipping through the pages of individual books will help you quickly assess the appropriateness for your child's reading level. Several of these titles are fully illustrated picture books even though the story lines are for this more mature age group, such as *Aïda* [318] and *Treemonisha* [416].

Afro-Bets Book of Black Heroes from A to Z: An Introduction to Important Black Achievers [316]

Written by Wade Hudson ☆ 102 *and Valerie Wilson Wesley*

Hardcover and softcover: Just Us
Published 1988

The accomplishments of forty-nine distinguished African Americans of the past and present are briefly told in this simply formatted reference guide. The heroes represent a great many fields of endeavor, demonstrating the breadth and depth of African American contributions to our society. A black-and-white photograph or illustration of every hero is prominently featured in each article. Among those included are Willie Mays, Ethel Waters, Zora Neale Hurston, and Booker T. Washington. Famous female personalities are featured in the companion book, *Afro-Bets Book of Black Heroes, Volume 2: Great Women in the Struggle,* by Toyomi Igus et al.

Afro-Bets First Book about Africa: An Introduction for Young Readers [317]

Written by Veronica Freeman Ellis
Illustrated by George Ford

Hardcover and softcover: Just Us
Published 1989

The lively Afro-Bets kids are guided through an African time line by a storyteller. They learn about Egyptian dynasties, Ashanti kingdoms, the slave trade, the independence movements of the 1960s, and other significant historical events of the African continent. Photographs, maps, and the illustrated Afro-Bets kids give visual interest to this beginning history guide.

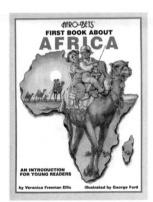

Aïda: A Picture Book for All Ages [318]

Written by Leontyne Price   **Coretta Scott King Award: Illustrator**
Illustrated by Leo and Diane Dillon

Hardcover: Gulliver, Harcourt Brace
Published 1990

Opera diva Leontyne Price tells the story of the opera in which she has performed the title role. Aïda is a princess who is torn between loyalty to her father, the king of Ethiopia, and her lover, the hero warrior of Ethiopia's enemy nation, Egypt. This mature story is one of deceit, jealousy, intrigue, and personal conflict. The vibrant marblelike illustrations are done extraordinarily well in an Egyptian motif, with the royals portrayed as beautiful black people.

All the Colors of the Race [319]

Written by Arnold Adoff
Illustrated by John Steptoe
Hardcover and softcover: William Morrow
Published 1982

Coretta Scott King Honor: Illustrator
Reading Rainbow Review Book

This provocative collection of poems explores the myriad colors that make up the "black" race. Many selections explore the thoughts and feelings of the biracial child. Others concentrate on the role that skin color plays in friendship, unity, family, and life in general. The collection is designed so that each selection can stand alone or can be read as a continuous narrative. The complex material may take some thoughtful interpretation on the part of young readers.

Amos Fortune: Free Man [320]

Written by Elizabeth Yates
Hardcover and softcover: Penguin USA
Published 1950

Newbery Medal

This is a true story about Amos Fortune, who was born At-mun, the son of an African king, and was heir apparent to the throne in his African village. But in 1710, his life was taken out of his hands when slave traders captured him and sold him into slavery. "Fortune"-ately, Amos was bought by a kind Quaker, who treated him well and taught him a productive trade, which is why he was named Fortune. Later, Amos was bought by another family, who also treated him well and allowed Amos to buy his own freedom when he was almost sixty years old. Amos's life as a freeman was marked by his kindness and honor. He bought others, including his wife, out of slavery and became a respected and productive citizen in New Hampshire.

Another Way to Dance [321]

"*That was the hardest thing . . . I'd look at myself in the mirror with all the other girls and I was always the first thing I saw. My own dark skin, my fuzzy hair, my long brown legs. I started feeling like I just stuck out so much.*"

Written by Martha Southgate
Hardcover: Delacorte, Bantam Doubleday Dell
Published 1996

Fourteen-year-old Vicki loves to dance classical ballet. She is thrilled to be accepted at the School of American Ballet in New York City for summer school. Once she gets there, however, she is subtly reminded that very few blacks are ever successful in professional ballet. During the summer, Vicki struggles with discrimination, which she has never experienced in her small New Jersey hometown. Even though her parents are in the midst of a painful separation, they provide love, support, and encouragement for their determined daughter.

Baby Grand, the Moon in July, & Me [322]

Written by Joyce Annette Barnes

Hardcover: Dial, Penguin USA
Published 1994

Ten-year-old Annie, her brother, and their parents are challenged by the conflicting needs of the two generations. The story is set in July 1969, at the time of the *Apollo 11* manned spaceflight to the moon. Annie's ambition is to be an astronaut when she grows up, so she is excited about the impending launch. Her older brother dreams of being a jazz musician and buys a piano, on credit, throwing the family into financial and emotional turmoil. Annie takes it upon herself to bring the fragmented family back together through a complex plan that is nicely developed in this well-written story.

Baseball Legends Series [323]

Written by various authors

Hardcover: Chelsea House
Published 1991–1995

The books in this series profile the personal lives and careers of baseball stars, including details about their key career games, statistics, and photographs. The series includes books about Satchel Paige, Hank Aaron, Willie Mays, Jackie Robinson, and Reggie Jackson. Basketball stars Charles Barkley, Kareem Abdul-Jabbar, Wilt Chamberlain, Julius Erving, Magic Johnson, Michael Jordan, Shaquille O'Neal, and Scottie Pippen, and football stars Jim Brown, Walter Payton, Deion Sanders, Emmitt Smith, and Lawrence Taylor are profiled in two companion series, Basketball Greats and Football Greats.

Black Stars in Orbit: NASA's African American Astronauts [324]

Written by Khephra Burns and William Miles

Hardcover and softcover: Gulliver, Harcourt Brace
Published 1995

This informative book details the challenges, contributions, and achievements of African Americans in the NASA space program, such as Edward J. Dwight, who was the first black admitted to the astronaut training program, in 1961; Colonel Vance Marchbanks, who became the first black chief flight surgeon in 1962; Colonel Guion S. Bluford Jr., who was the first African American in space, on the 1983 *Challenger* mission; and Dr. Mae Jemison, who in 1992 became the first African American woman in space.

The Block: Poems [325]

Poems by Langston Hughes
Collages by Romare Bearden

Hardcover: Viking, Penguin USA
Published 1995

Arresting collages by renowned African American artist Romare Bearden, which now hang in the Metropolitan Museum of Art, frame the evocative words of the equally prominent poet Langston Hughes. The two artists explore and pay tribute to life in Harlem in this composite work.

The Captive [326]

Written by Joyce Hansen

Coretta Scott King Honor: Author

Hardcover and softcover: Scholastic
Published 1994

> *" I was seized by a sudden jolt of terror. . . . I had been taken across the seas far away from all I knew and loved, to the land of the white foreigners who would try to make me a slave. I was kidnapped— a captive."*

Kofi, a West African prince, is betrayed by a fellow countryman and stolen away from his family, friends, and Sierra Leone homeland by slave traders in 1788. Young readers travel with him from the time of his terrifying bondage and voyage over the Atlantic in a slave ship to his landing in America, where he is sold into slavery. As Kofi struggles to survive in his treacherous new land, his West African family copes with the loss of their son. This riveting novel, told in wrenching detail from Kofi's perspective, will intrigue young readers, sensitizing them to the unfathomable tragedy of the victims—both the enslaved young man and the family left behind.

Chevrolet Saturdays [327]

Written by Candy Dawson Boyd

Hardcover: Simon & Schuster
Softcover: Puffin, Penguin USA
Published 1993

Joey Davis, a fourth-grade boy, faces a very difficult year of adjustment at home and at school in this realistic novel. Joey resents his mother's remarriage and his stepfather's persistent attempts to bond with him. Joey is also troubled by a difficult relationship with a teacher who tries to move him into a special education program, even though he has demonstrated an amazing aptitude for science. Joey's character is well developed as he struggles with his problems and receives unexpected support from his stepfather.

Christmas in the Big House, Christmas in the Quarters [328]

Written by Patricia C. and Fredrick L. McKissack ☆ 146

Illustrated by John Thompson   **Coretta Scott King Award: Author**

Hardcover: Scholastic
Published 1994

The lifestyle of the master's family in the plantation mansion and that of the slaves in their quarters during the Christmas season is contrasted in this elegant, artistic work. Set in pre-Civil War Virginia, two dramatically different stories of the holiday season are eloquently told. Authentic recipes, poems, and songs of the period are generously included to enrich the story line. **Nonstandard English.**

> "*After the big meal in the Quarters, gifts are presented. Santa visited the children earlier, but slave mothers usually give their children something personal, like an apron, basket, a strip quilt, or a hat. They attach a story or advice to it, so if they are separated by being sold, one from the other, the children will have a memory.*"

Circle of Gold [329]

Written by Candy Dawson Boyd   **Coretta Scott King Honor: Author**

Softcover: Apple, Scholastic
Published 1984

Young Mattie's family is devastated by the death of her father in this short, heartfelt novel. Ever since her husband's death, Mattie's mother has been dysfunctional as a mother. Mattie believes that a special act of love will stir her mother and restore the warmth to the family. Mattie gets a job and saves her money to buy a simple gold pin as a Mother's Day present. Challenged by the loss of her baby-sitting job and confrontations from friends, Mattie perseveres toward her important goal. Young readers will root for Mattie and her touching quest.

Clara and the Hoodoo Man [330]

Written by Elizabeth Partridge

Hardcover: Dutton, Penguin USA
Published 1996

Clara and her family live in the mountains of Tennessee at the end of the nineteenth century. The people are extremely superstitious and particularly afraid of Old Sugar, the hoodoo man, who they believe can "put a fix" on people. Clara and her little sister, Bessie, run into the hoodoo man while looking for herbs on the mountainside. Soon thereafter, Bessie comes down with a life-threatening case of mountain fever. Momma is convinced that the hoodoo man has cast a spell, but Clara believes that he is the only one who can actually save her sister with his healing herbs. She risks everything to find Old Sugar and to plead for his help in this dramatic novel, which is based on a true story.

> "*If a hoodoo man puts a bad fix on you, your ghost goes moaning and tramping around this earth forevermore, and you never get to heaven.*"

139

Cousins [331]

Written by Virginia Hamilton ☆ 80

Hardcover: Philomel, Putnam
Softcover: Apple, Scholastic
Published 1990

Eleven-year-old Cammy is a sensitive young girl thrown into emotional turmoil during a difficult period in her young life. Her beloved grandmother is confined to a nursing home. Her cousin Patty, who is thought to be perfect, is suffering from bulimia, a secret that Cammy must keep. And then Cammy faces the pain and guilt over Patty's untimely death when she witnesses her drowning at a school field trip. Cammy must cope with the aftermath of this terrible tragedy, which she does with the love and support of her father and grandmother.

Dare to Dream: Coretta Scott King and the Civil Rights Movement [332]

Written by Angela Shelf Medearis ☆ 150
Illustrated by Anna Rich

Hardcover: Lodestar, Penguin USA
Published 1994

Coretta Scott began preparing for her role in American history as a young girl. She learned very early about the importance of education and about everyone's right to be treated with respect and dignity. Educated as a teacher and trained as an opera singer, she met and married Martin Luther King Jr. Coretta became a critical part of the civil rights movement by supporting her husband's work, and later in her own right. This excellent biography establishes the historic context for Coretta's lifework and demonstrates her bravery and commitment.

Darnell Rock Reporting [333]

Written by Walter Dean Myers

Hardcover and softcover: Delacorte, Bantam Doubleday Dell
Published 1994

In this uplifting story, Miss Seldes, the school librarian, understands that Darnell needs a constructive connection to the school to keep him out of trouble. She suggests that he become involved in writing for the school newspaper, an idea that he hates. He decides to approach his newspaper assignment with as little effort as possible. So no one is more surprised than he when he becomes involved in an intriguing story that captures everyone's attention and casts him in an important role as the reporter. Darnell's sense of self is immediately elevated as he begins to recognize his strengths and the possibilities for his life.

Daydreamers [334]

Written by Eloise Greenfield ☆ 72
Illustrated by Tom Feelings ☆ 48

Coretta Scott King Honor: Illustrator
Reading Rainbow Review Book

Softcover: Puffin Pied Piper, Penguin USA
Published 1981

Two of the most dynamic artists in the field of children's books have teamed up to create this illustrated poem about our children, whose visions, experiences, fantasies, and daydreams lay the foundation for their adulthood. The pencil and pen-and-ink illustrations of the pensive children are extraordinarily well done.

Dear Mrs. Parks: A Dialogue with Today's Youth [335]

Written by Rosa Parks with Gregory J. Reed

Hardcover and softcover: Lee & Low
Published 1996

Rosa Parks changed the face of our nation with one simple act of courage in 1955. Since that time, she has been held in the highest esteem as a civil rights activist, inspirational leader, and role model for young people. In this frank question-and-answer book, Mrs. Parks openly answers the questions most asked of her by young people. The questions range from the very personal ("How old are you?" and "What is your favorite food?") to more complex subjects grouped in chapters entitled "Courage and Hope," "Knowledge and Education," "Living with God," "Pathways to Freedom," and "Making a Difference." Mrs. Parks responds from the heart, and conveys a sense of hope and a feeling for the possibilities.

Donovan's Word Jar [336]

Written by Monalisa DeGross
Illustrated by Cheryl Hanna ☆ 88

Hardcover: HarperCollins
Published 1994

Some kids collect trading cards, buttons, or bottle caps, but Donovan collects words. Whenever he sees a new or interesting word, he writes it on a slip of paper and puts it in his word jar. When his jar becomes too full, he must find a solution to that problem. This popular chapter book may motivate children to consider building their own vocabularies. There is also a wonderful underlying story line about a positive relationship between Donovan and his family.

Down in the Piney Woods [337]

Written by Ethel Footman Smothers

Hardcover and softcover: Random House
Published 1992

Annie Rye is ten years old and lives happily in the Piney Woods of Georgia with her parents, brother, and baby sister. Things get complicated when she finds out that her three half-sisters will also be coming to live with them. Then she realizes that there are still bigger problems in her life than the new additions to the family. Her family's security is threatened by aggressive racists who burn a cross in their yard. The blended family must come together quickly to withstand the threat. A sequel, *Moriah's Pond* [385], is another story about Annie Rye and her sisters. **Nonstandard English.**

Drew and the Bub Daddy Showdown [338]

Written and illustrated by Robb Armstrong

Softcover: Trophy, HarperCollins
Published 1996

Uncannily, when the cast is removed from eight-year-old Drew's arm, he can suddenly draw expertly. Drew creates and draws a comic book series about Super Agent Mason Stone from his vivid imagination. Drew's enterprising friends sell copies of the comics, elevating Drew to instant celebrity status at school. Drew and his friends use their new-found income to buy Bub Daddy, a two-foot-long, striped bubble gum. Drew's new endeavor draws fire from a tough teacher, the school bullies, and his parents. In an interesting effect, Drew's comic strip is imbedded in the story, making it a two-for-one hit! Other adventures about Drew and his friends are *Drew and the Filthy Rich Kids* and *Drew and the Homeboy Question.*

Ernestine & Amanda [339]

Written by Sandra Belton

Hardcover: Simon & Schuster
Published 1996

Preteens Ernestine and Amanda have a natural distaste for each other. They see each other at their piano lessons, and are brought together, too often, by two sisters, one of whom is a friend of Amanda and the other a friend of Ernestine. The rivalry is fueled by a piano competition that they both hope to win. The story is told in alternating chapters from Ernestine's and then Amanda's perspective, so sometimes the reader will get stories of the same event from two different points of view. In the end, the two girls come to terms with the fact that they do not dislike each other as much as they thought, which is not the same as saying that they are friends. The girls meet again in three sequels, *Ernestine & Amanda: Summer Camp, Ready or Not!*, *Ernestine & Amanda: Mysteries on Monroe Street,* and *Ernestine & Amanda: Members of the C.L.U.B.*

Escape to Freedom: A Play about Young Frederick Douglass [340]

Written by Ossie Davis

Coretta Scott King Award: Author

Softcover: Puffin, Penguin USA
Published 1978

The early life of Frederick Douglass is presented in this play, which is written for a cast of seven young actors. Readers can enjoy the script for their own pleasure and enrichment or perform it with friends. In either case, they will learn about Frederick's consuming quest to learn to read and the risks that he took to do so. His literacy led Frederick to a plan for his own escape and helped pave the way for his destiny as a powerful African American leader.

> "*Keep us ignorant, and we would always be his slaves! . . . Come hell or high water—even if it cost me my life— I was determined to read.*"

Everyday People: The National Civil Rights Museum Celebrates Everyday People [341]

Written by Alice Faye Duncan
Illustrated by Gerard J. Smith

Hardcover and softcover: Troll
Published 1995

This oversized book pictorially chronicles the events and people involved in the U.S. civil rights movement between 1954 and 1968. The National Civil Rights Museum, located in the Lorraine Motel in Memphis (where Reverend Martin Luther King Jr. was slain), now houses interactive exhibits, photos, and displays that tell the story of this impassioned period of our history. The book is the next best thing to a personal visit.

Followers of the North Star: Rhymes about African American Heroes, Heroines, and Historical Times [342]

Written by Susan Altman and Susan Lechner
Illustrated by Byron Wooden

Softcover: Children's
Published 1993

Twenty-six rhythmic poems about historical and contemporary African American people and events fill these remarkable pages about black history and heritage. The selections are about those who ran for freedom from the oppression of slavery, and many who continued to make a difference in more recent times, like Malcolm X, Medgar Evers, and Thurgood Marshall.

Forever Friends [343]

Written by Candy Dawson Boyd

Hardcover: Peter Smith
Softcover: Puffin, Penguin USA
Published 1986

Sixth-grader Toni Douglas faces the challenge of her young life as she studies in preparation for the entrance exam to the King Academy. There is tremendous pressure on her from her father to do well. In the midst of this and other typical preadolescent events, Toni's best friend is killed in a tragic car accident. Toni goes into an emotional tailspin, losing interest in everything, including the King Academy. In this heart-tugging novel, it takes the love, understanding, and patience of her friends and family to help Toni begin the difficult process of emerging from her grief to resume her promising life.

Frederick Douglass: The Last Days of Slavery [344]

Written by William Miller
Illustrated by Cedric Lucas

Hardcover and softcover: Lee & Low
Published 1995

Frederick Douglass was born a slave in 1817. Douglass, however, was always independent, unafraid to challenge others or to ask questions. An overseer targets Douglass, intent on breaking his spirit and free-thinking attitude. Douglass fights back, earning the respect of the overseer and demonstrating the pride and dignity for which he later becomes known. It is easy for young readers to appreciate this fictionalized biography.

Freedom Crossing [345]

Written by Margaret Goff Clark

Softcover: Apple, Scholastic
Published 1980

Laura Eastman, a young white girl, is forced to reevaluate her values when she discovers that her family is involved in sheltering fugitive slaves on the Underground Railroad. Since the death of her mother, Laura has been living in the South with relatives. Upon her return to her home in Lewiston, New York, she makes the startling discovery that her father and brother are involved in this illegal activity. In the suspenseful story, Laura must decide whether to help a young fugitive slave boy with his escape or to stand up for the law.

From a Child's Heart [346]

Written by Nikki Grimes
Illustrated by Brenda Joysmith

Hardcover and softcover: Just Us
Published 1993

Thirteen penetrating prayers and poems are written from a child's perspective about important aspects of their lives. "Good Morning Lord" is a prayer and acknowledgment to God; "Space" is a child's prayer for more room and a larger bed for her to share with her siblings. "Night Fight" is a heartbreaking prayer from a young boy to end his parents' frequent nighttime arguments. Other poems appeal for support, strength, and the opportunity to succeed in school and other childhood endeavors.

From Miss Ida's Porch [347]

Written by Sandra Belton
Illustrated by Floyd Cooper ☆ 34

Hardcover: Four Winds, Macmillan
Published 1993

Miss Ida's front porch is in the middle of Church Street and is the gathering place for the neighbors. On any given evening, adults and in-between kids— too young to hang out but too old to be put to bed—meet and share stories. On this night, memories of concerts by music icons Duke Ellington and Marian Anderson are the subject of the evening. This well-told story is related from the perspective of one of the in-between kids and makes for entertaining reading.

THE CREATORS

Fredrick McKissack

AUTHOR

Patricia C. McKissack

AUTHOR

"In the past there was a dearth of books for, by, and about African Americans. We have tried for twenty years to fill the void—and with some measure of success. But we can't rest on our laurels or claim a victory, because there is still too much work to be done. We hope our books encourage young children to read, but we also hope our efforts will inspire young children to write. The work must go on!"
—PATRICIA AND FREDRICK MCKISSACK

OUR FAVORITES

Patricia C. and Fredrick McKissack:
  Christmas in the Big House, Christmas in the Quarters, 1994 [328]

  Rebels Against Slavery: American Slave Revolts, 1996 [467]

Patricia C. McKissack:
  The Dark-Thirty: Southern Tales of the Supernatural, 1992 [434]

  Flossie and the Fox, 1986 [175]

  Ma Dear's Apron, 1997 [222]

From Slave to Civil War Hero: The Life and Times of Robert Smalls [348]

Written by Michael L. Cooper

Hardcover: Lodestar, Penguin USA
Published 1994

Robert Smalls courageously escaped slavery to join the Union Army in 1862. Smalls served as a Union soldier and later distinguished himself as an advocate for newly freed slaves and as an elected U.S. congressman. This interesting biography is supplemented with many black-and-white photographs, maps, and illustrations of Civil War scenes. The description of the war, the social and political climate, and other relevant details of the era help to establish a rich view of the time and Smalls's role in history.

Get on Board: The Story of the Underground Railroad [349]

Written by Jim Haskins ☆ 94

Softcover: Scholastic
Published 1993

The story of the Underground Railroad is chronicled in this informative book. Although slaves had been escaping since the inception of slavery, the term "Underground Railroad" was not coined until the mid-1800s. This thorough book is written for the young student interested in the history of the Railroad and its secrets. Information regarding the stations, station masters, conductors, train robbers, and other details are described and supplemented by historic photographs, black-and-white illustrations, and news clippings.

Ghost Train [350]

Written by Jess Mowry

Hardcover: Henry Holt
Published 1996

Thirteen-year-old Remi and his neighbor, Niya, are drawn into a murder mystery in this ghostly tale set in a tough Oakland, California, neighborhood. Remi, a recent Haitian immigrant, and the street-wise Niya witness a frightening murder and coverup by a trainman that takes place in a shipyard at an Oakland dock. The only problem is that the event happened fifty years before. Inexplicably, they become a part of the scene and confront the murderer in an attempt to lay the haunted case to rest forever. This suspense-filled, fast-paced story will draw young readers in, and hold them, until the surprise ending.

> " *Cold sweat sheened his body. He felt his heart hammering in his chest like the thud of those pounding pistons outside. Finally, he forced himself to push off the covers and crouch at the window.*"

Girl Wonder and the Terrific Twins [351]

Written by Malorie Blackman
Illustrated by Lis Toft

Hardcover: Dutton, Penguin USA
Published 1993

Maxine and her younger twin brothers, Anthony and Edward, are up to all kinds of misadventure in this collection of nine short stories about their shenanigans. Their creative and vivid imaginations guide them into trouble every time, even though they fantasize that they are superheroes. These delightful short chapters make ideal reading for middle readers or can be read aloud to younger children.

Go Fish [352]

Written by Mary Stolz
Illustrated by Pat Cummings ☆ 42

Hardcover and softcover: HarperCollins
Published 1991

Thomas spends a day with his grandfather, who amazes the boy with interesting bits and pieces of information about everything from fossils and dinosaurs to ancestral stories and folktales. In this warm story of male bonding, there is even time for a trip to the fishing pier and a game of Go Fish. Other books about Thomas and his grandfather are *Stealing Home* [405], *Storm in the Night* [279], and *Coco Grimes.*

A Good Soup Attracts Chairs: A First African Cookbook for American Kids [353]

Written by Fran Osseo-Asare

Hardcover: Pelican
Published 1993

Recipes for more than thirty-five West African dishes are presented in easy-to-follow recipes. A short introduction to each dish teaches children about the food, culture, and traditions of West Africa. Children will learn to cook foods of African cultures and get practice in reading for detail and following directions.

Great African Americans in Civil Rights [354]

Written by Pat Rediger

Hardcover and softcover: Crabtree
Published 1996

Martin Luther King Jr., Coretta Scott King, and Vernon E. Jordan Jr. are among the fourteen outstanding African American civil rights leaders profiled in this simply formatted reference book. A short essay on each leader's life, skills, and obstacles is supplemented by several photographs and informative, well-organized insets with information about their personalities, personal profiles, education, awards, special interests, and key accomplishments. Other books in the Great African Americans series are *Great African Americans in Business, Great African Americans in Entertainment, Great African Americans in Literature, Great African Americans in Music,* and *Great African Americans in Sports.*

The Great Migration: An American Story [355]

Written and illustrated by Jacob Lawrence

Hardcover and softcover: HarperCollins
Published 1993

A series of deeply toned paintings and a dynamic poem tell the story of the great migration of blacks from the South to the North in the early 1900s. Oppressed and poor, huge numbers of blacks moved north for the promise of a better life. The South was economically devastated by their departure, and life was not necessarily better for the migrants in their new promised land. This artistic work explains the major African American population shift and its political and economic consequences.

The Green Lion of Zion Street [356]

Written by Julia Fields
Illustrated by Jerry Pinkney ☆ 184

Hardcover: Margaret McElderry, Simon & Schuster
Published 1988

A stone statue of a lion is perched on the hill above Zion Street. In the full light of day, it is nothing more, but in the early morning fog, the lion seems to come to life in the imaginations of the children waiting for the school bus.
Nonstandard English.

THE CREATORS

Angela Shelf Medearis

AUTHOR

"Picture books are a child's first step into a lifetime of reading. I try to write in an exciting and humorous way so that the memory of reading my books will remain with a young reader forever."

OUR FAVORITES

Annie's Gifts, 1994 [122]

The Freedom Riddle, 1995 [179]

Poppa's New Pants, 1995 [259]

Rum-A-Tum-Tum, 1997 [270]

Treemonisha: From the Opera by Scott Joplin, 1995 [416]

Harlem [357]

Written by Walter Dean Myers
Illustrated by Christopher Myers

Coretta Scott King Honor: Illustrator
Caldecott Honor

Hardcover: Scholastic
Published 1997

The spirit of Harlem is described in this vibrant poem about the well-known urban area, a city within a city, that is a prism of African American culture. Finely detailed collages illustrate the lifestyle and people of Harlem.

Have A Happy . . . : A Novel about Kwanzaa [358]

Written by Mildred Pitts Walter
Illustrated by Carole Byard

Hardcover: Lothrop, Lee & Shepard, William Morrow
Softcover: Hearst
Published 1989

Ten-year-old Chris and his family usually celebrate Christmas, but he always feels a little let down because his birthday falls during the same time and gets lost in the hustle and bustle of the season. The family enjoys a different kind of holiday, however, when Chris's uncle introduces them to the African American celebration of Kwanzaa. Chris and his family experience a more meaningful season as they focus on each other and on their proud heritage.

Her Stories: African American Folktales, Fairy Tales, and True Tales [359]

Written by Virginia Hamilton ☆ 80
Illustrated by Leo and Diane Dillon

Coretta Scott King Award: Author
Coretta Scott King Honor: Illustrator

Hardcover: Scholastic
Published 1995

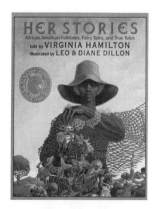

Nineteen stories are expertly told about black female folk and fairy characters. This enticing work is dedicated to mothers, grandmothers, and aunts, who have often been the bearers of such stories from generation to generation. Each story is exquisitely illustrated and is punctuated with a short commentary that adds insight into the nature and origin of the tale. Mature children, especially your daughters, will love this immediate classic. ***Nonstandard English.***

Honey, I Love: And Other Love Poems [360]

Written by Eloise Greenfield ☆72

Illustrated by Leo and Diane Dillon

Reading Rainbow Review Book

Hardcover and softcover: HarperTrophy, HarperCollins
Published 1978

Sixteen poems written from the perspective of children celebrate some of the everyday events and thoughts of their daily lives. Besides the ever-popular title poem, "Honey, I Love," other favorites like "Rope Rhyme" and "By Myself" are included. Black-and-white illustrations of beautifully coiffed black children embellish the prose.

The Hundred Penny Box [361]

Written by Sharon Bell Mathis

Illustrated by Leo and Diane Dillon

Newbery Honor

Hardcover and softcover: Penguin USA
Published 1975

Michael's great-great-aunt Dew, who is one hundred years old, lives with him and his family. Although her mind is not always sharp, she is clear about the importance of her box full of pennies—one minted in every year of her life. Michael is defiantly protective of his aunt and her old battered box against his mother, who wants to replace it with a smaller, neater box. This is an intimate story about sensitivity, compassion, love, and respect in a family.

I Am a Jesse White Tumbler [362]

Written and photographed by Diane Schmidt

Hardcover: Albert Whitman
Published 1990

This photographic essay about the Jesse White Tumbler team introduces young readers to the renowned group from the perspective of one of its young members. The tumbling program, based in the Chicago Cabrini-Green housing project, is designed to give young project residents a constructive, disciplined alternative to inner-city street life. The many photographs of the team in action supplement the positive story about the program and the personal development of its members.

Jazz: My Music, My People [363]

Written and illustrated by Morgan Monceaux

Hardcover: Alfred A. Knopf
Published 1994

Forty-one African American jazz artists are spotlighted in this book, including Jelly Roll Morton and Ethel Waters from "The Early Years," Duke Ellington and Billie Holiday from "The Swing Years," and Dizzy Gillespie and Miles Davis of "The Modern Jazz Era." Young music buffs will want this book as a key part of their reference collection and will enjoy reading about their favorite artists.

Julian's Glorious Summer [364]

Written by Ann Cameron
Illustrated by Dora Leder

Softcover: A Stepping Stone Book, Random House
Published 1987

Poor Julian! His best friend Gloria has a new bike and is riding all over the neighborhood, and Julian has not even learned to ride a bike yet. Embarrassed by his shortcoming, Julian does everything he can to avoid Gloria. Then a little fib he tells to cover himself grows to incredible heights in this delightful easy-to-read story. Other books in the series about young Julian include *Julian, Dream Doctor; Stories Julian Tells; More Stories Julian Tells;* and *Julian, Secret Agent.*

> " *I hate bicycles! . . . I hate the tubes, the tires, the wheels, the spokes, the pedals, the chain, the fenders, the handlebars, the reflectors, and the lights—and that's just the beginning.*"

Junebug [365]

Written by Alice Mead

Hardcover: Farrar Straus Giroux
Softcover: Yearling, Bantam Doubleday Dell
Published 1995

Things could not be worse for nine-year-old Junebug. His best friend Darnell just ran away to avoid a confrontation with a drug lord. His Aunt Jolita is mixed up with the wrong crowd and fighting with his mother. And the reading teacher who was helping his little sister has just quit out of fear of his rough New Haven, Connecticut, neighborhood. What's more, Junebug is about to turn ten years old, an age that he fears because that is when drugs, guns, and crime influences come into young boys' lives. Junebug is distracted from all of his problems by his dream of becoming a sailor. He writes his dreams on notes and stuffs them inside glass bottles that he launches into the sea. Junebug's story is one of hope and the possibilities for inner-city children to rise above their challenging environments.

Junior Black Americans of Achievement Series [366]

Written by various authors

Hardcover and softcover: Chelsea House
Published 1992–1997

Based on the popular Black Americans of Achievement series [425], this collection of twenty-seven hardcover and twenty softcover biographies profiles prominent African Americans in a wide variety of fields from both historical and contemporary times. Each book contains about eighty pages and up to eighteen black-and-white illustrations and photographs. The subjects include entertainers like Whitney Houston and Bill Cosby, civil rights leaders like Nelson Mandela and Booker T. Washington, and sports stars like Jesse Owens and Wilma Rudolph.

Just an Overnight Guest [367]

Written by Eleanora E. Tate

Hardcover: Just Us
Published 1980

Young Margie is undone when her mother invites four-year-old Ethel to stay with them overnight. Ethel, the biracial child of a poor, white single mother, is known as the wildest child in the neighborhood. Aside from being embarrassed at having the little girl in their home, Margie is jealous of the attention-stealing preschooler. One tortuous evening turns into weeks because Ethel's mother does not return as promised. It later turns out that Ethel is there to stay, and even worse, she is actually Margie's cousin! Young readers of this short chapter book will share Margie's embarrassment, disappointment, then finally compassion and understanding.

Just Like Martin [368]

Written by Ossie Davis

Hardcover: Simon & Schuster
Softcover: Puffin, Penguin USA
Published 1992

Young Stone is a member of his church's youth group and a devoted follower of the nonviolent philosophies of Dr. Martin Luther King Jr. When a racist's bomb explodes in his Sunday school classroom, killing two of his friends, Stone demonstrates his commitment by organizing his peers for a controversial nonviolent children's march. Stone must defy his father, who is much more militant, in this moving story set in the racially charged 1960s.

Just My Luck [369]

Written by Emily Moore

Softcover: Puffin, Penguin USA
Published 1982

Emily feels like a lonely misfit because her family is always too busy to spend time with her and her best friend has just moved away. Only her creepy neighbor, Jeffrey, has any interest in her. She falls in love with a puppy and decides to buy it to fill the void in her life. It costs two hundred dollars, a sum that she must raise quickly. When another neighborhood dog is lost and a reward is offered, Emily recruits Jeffrey to help her find the missing dog. Predictably, Emily and Jeffrey make an excellent team and develop a friendship based on this experience together.

Justin and the Best Biscuits in the World [370]

Written by Mildred Pitts Walter
Illustrated by Catherine Stock

Coretta Scott King Award: Author

Hardcover: Lothrop, Lee & Shepard
Softcover: Bullseye, Random House
Published 1986

Young Justin lives in a female-run house and is overwhelmed by the chores that are heaped on him by his mother and sisters. So he is excited when his grandfather invites him to his ranch out west. During the visit, Justin learns how to do men's work, but also learns that doing dishes, folding clothes, and making beds are not just for women. Furthermore, Grandpa teaches him to bake biscuits—the best in the world! The biscuits are entered in a baking contest and win first prize. The only thing missing from this entertaining story is the recipe for those biscuits.

> " *Justin felt a surge of love for his grandpa. He would always remember how to make a bed snug as a bug and fold clothes neatly. He grabbed Grandpa's hands. They walked downstairs, still holding hands, to get ready to ride the fence.*"

Kai: A Mission for Her Village [371]

Written by Dawn C. Gill Thomas
Illustrated by Vanessa Holley

Softcover: Aladdin, Simon & Schuster
Published 1996

A young Yoruba girl, Kai, living in the village of Ife in 1440, is called upon to make a daring journey with her sister. The village's yam crop has been destroyed by blight and they need food for the season. The two travel for four days to a neighboring village to borrow food. On their way they encounter snakes, washed-out paths, and lions. Each obstacle requires them to use their wits and to depend upon each other for support and security. In the end, the two are successful, and, just as importantly, closer than they have ever been. Kai's second book in the Girlhood Journeys series is *Kai: A Big Decision*.

THE CREATORS

Robert H. Miller

AUTHOR

"When the story of the American frontier is either told or read about, African American people are rarely mentioned. The opening of the West was a very pivotal time for America; it set the stage for the hero on horseback, the cowboy. I write about African American cowboys, pioneers, mountain men, and the Buffalo Soldiers, because we were just as much a part of building this great country as any other ethnic group that landed here."

OUR FAVORITES

Buffalo Soldiers: The Story of Emanuel Stance, 1994 [138]

A Pony for Jeremiah, 1996 [395]

The Story of "Stagecoach" Mary Fields, 1995 [281]

Reflections of a Black Cowboy: The Buffalo Soldiers, 1991 [468]

Keisha Leads the Way [372]

Written by Teresa Reed
Illustrated by Eric Velasquez and Rich Grote

Hardcover and softcover: Magic Attic
Published 1996

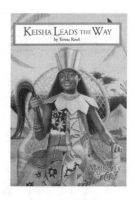

Keisha is a member of the Magic Attic Club. Its four members once found a key that unlocked a neighbor's attic, where costumes in an old trunk whisk them to new places and times. In this short adventure, Keisha is transported to ancient Central Africa, where she learns the importance each person's role in a family and community and the value of helping others. Keisha remembers these new lessons when she returns home to her family and her volunteer work at a local hospital. Other books in the Magic Attic Club series include *Keisha the Fairy Snow Queen, Keisha's Maze Mystery, Keisha to the Rescue,* and *Three Cheers for Keisha.*

Kid Caramel, Private Investigator: Case of the Missing Ankh [373]

Written by Dwayne J. Ferguson

Softcover: Just Us
Published 1996

Kid Caramel, fifth-grade sleuth, and his friend Earnie solve the mystery of a stolen crystal ankh that was taken from the city museum exhibit. Keen powers of observation, logic, and a creative plan to catch the thief help the two crack the case in this fun, fast-moving book. Young readers will enjoy solving the mystery with Kid and Earnie.

Kids' Book of Wisdom: Quotes from the African American Tradition [374]

Compiled by Cheryl and Wade Hudson ☆ 102
Illustrated by Anna Rich

Softcover: Just Us
Published 1996

Dozens of thought-provoking proverbs are passed on in this collection of sayings and adages that convey the wisdom of Africa through the ages. This collection of wise words is organized into sixteen sections. In the section on discipline you will read, "Do not try your luck once. Try it again and again." On the subject of patience, you will find, "The impatient man eats raw food." The last section offers adages about the seven principles of Kwanzaa.

Kids Explore America's African American Heritage [375]

Written by the Westridge Young Writers Workshop

Softcover: John Muir
Published 1993

Young students in grades three through eight actually "researched information, word processed, organized, wrote, proofread, and illustrated" this book as a part of the Westridge Young Writers Workshop in Denver, Colorado. Under the supervision of their teachers, the students compiled a comprehensive look at African American heritage, including impressive sections on famous firsts and heroes, stories, language and literature, and kids who made a difference. This book, written for kids by kids, includes photographs and illustrations, also done by the students.

Koya DeLaney and the Good Girl Blues [376]

Written by Eloise Greenfield ☆ 72

Softcover: Apple, Scholastic
Published 1992

For the first time in her life, Koya faces a situation that she cannot handle with her usual humor and delightful disposition. When her sister Loritha and her best friend Dawn have a major dispute, Koya's loyalties are torn between the two feuding girls. Then her cousin, a famous pop star, comes to town to perform a concert, which is rudely interrupted by the feisty audience. Koya's patience finally blows sky high as she confronts the rude spectators and later Loritha and Dawn. Young readers will see a perfect example of self-reliance when Koya finally asserts herself and does so without compromising her relationships.

The Lucky Stone [377]

Written by Lucille Clifton

Softcover: Yearling, Bantam Doubleday Dell
Published 1979

Tee sits with her beloved great-grandmother, who gives her a shiny black stone and tells her the one-hundred-year-old story of the enchanted good-luck piece. Grandma regales Tee with the good-luck stories of three people, including herself, who previously owned the stone. Tee is full of anticipation about the good fortune that the stone may hold for her. *Nonstandard English.*

Many Thousand Gone: African Americans from Slavery to Freedom [378]

Written by Virginia Hamilton ☆ 80
Illustrated by Leo and Diane Dillon

Hardcover and softcover: Knopf, Random House
Published 1993

Thirty-four brief, true stories about slavery are powerfully told. Each story relates a small piece of the historical truth about slavery. This book would make a fine classroom text or can be shared with your child to raise his or her awareness of what has gone before.

Mariah Loves Rock [379]

Written by Mildred Pitts Walter

Hardcover: Bradbury, Macmillan
Softcover: Troll
Published 1988

Mariah is a typical eleven-year-old who enjoys rock music. In fact, she and her friends, known as the Friendly Five, idolize rock star Sheik Bashara. When her dad announces that his daughter from a previous marriage is coming to live with them, Mariah is asked to make financial sacrifices, like foregoing a Sheik Bashara concert. Her resentment over the new sister's intrusion is apparent. Mariah works through the emotional tragedy and is able to see the concert after all, and even likes her new sister when they finally meet. A sequel, *Mariah Keeps Cool,* is also available.

Martin Luther King [380]

Written by Rosemary L. Bray
Illustrated by Malcah Zeldis

Hardcover and softcover: William Morrow
Published 1995

The life and works of Martin Luther King Jr. are captured in forty-seven over-sized pages of text and bright folk art in this exceptional book. The text begins by covering Martin's early life, when his childhood experiences began to shape his sensibilities. The major events of Martin's life are touched upon, including the day he became aware of and embraced Gandhi's philosophy of nonviolent protest, and his marriage to Coretta Scott. Every significant civil rights event during Martin's adult life is detailed, framing a young reader's understanding of the era and of King's leadership role.

> "Martin read about Gandhi for years. The more he read and heard, the more he wondered: Could black people in America do what Gandhi and his followers had done in India? Though he didn't know it at the time, Martin would one day have a chance to find out."

Me, Mop, and the Moondance Kid [381]

Written by Walter Dean Myers

Illustrated by Rodney Pate

Softcover: Yearling, Bantam Doubleday Dell
Published 1988

T. J. and Moondance are brothers who have been recently adopted from the Dominican Academy, an orphanage. Their best friend, Mop, is still without a family and the orphanage is about to close. The three kids play on a baseball team together, so they plan for Mop to attract the coach's attention and to entice him and his wife to adopt her. T. J., on the other hand, is reluctant to participate because he does not want his newly adoptive father to see how poorly he plays. The story unfolds through T. J.'s engaging first-person style. Several black-and-white illustrations add a fun touch to the short novel. This book is followed by the sequel, *Mop, Moondance, and the Nagasaki Knights.*

Meet Addy: An American Girl [382]

Written by Connie Porter

Illustrated by Melodye Rosales

Hardcover and softcover: Pleasant
Published 1993

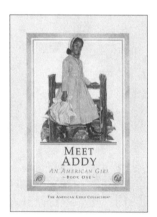

Addy, a young slave girl, dreams of escaping to freedom with her family. Just before their daring escape, the family is torn apart when her father and brother are sold away. Addy and her mother bravely make the escape alone, leaving behind a younger sister. The two settle in Philadelphia in 1864 and begin a new life. This book follows Addy and her mother as they adjust to their new life and continually plan the escape and reunion of the rest of their family members. Historical references and photos of actual events and personalities of the time are accurately incorporated into the story. Other books in the American Girl series about Addy are: *Addy Learns A Lesson: A School Story, Addy's Surprise: A Christmas Story, Happy Birthday Addy: A Springtime Story, Addy Saves the Day: A Summer Story,* and *Changes for Addy: A Winter Story.* **Nonstandard English.**

Meet Danitra Brown [383]

Written by Nikki Grimes
Illustrated by Floyd Cooper ☆ 34

Coretta Scott King Honor: Illustrator

Hardcover and softcover: William Morrow
Published 1994

Danitra Brown and her best friend, Zuri Jackson, are the subjects of thirteen high-spirited poems. Each poem reflects their personalities and friendship. Soft sepia illustrations capture the delight of these two girls. Many young girls will be able to relate to the best-friend theme celebrated in this book.

The Middle of Somewhere: A Story of South Africa [384]

Written by Sheila Gordon

Hardcover: Orchard, Grolier
Published 1990

Young Rebecca, who lives in a black township in South Africa, is afraid of being forced out of her home. The government wants to relocate her family and neighbors to a less developed area in order to accommodate expansion for white suburbanites. The villagers protest the attempts to move them, and Rebecca's father is arrested after a community-wide demonstration. The evils of apartheid come through strongly in this novel of a family's determination to stay together in their village.

> " *He told how he'd taken you to visit Mama in town. How Mama's madam has a girl the same age as you, who lives without fear because no one is telling her family that they have to move, no one is threatening to bulldoze their house. Yet every night you're afraid . . . because the bulldozers might come. . . a father has no choice but to protect his children—even against the government, if it is planning to harm them.*"

Moriah's Pond [385]

Written by Ethel Footman Smothers

Hardcover: Knopf, Random House
Published 1995

This story is based on the adventures of real-life sisters—Annie Rye, Maybaby, and Brat—who, while visiting their grandmother in rural Georgia, share a forbidden swim in Moriah's Pond. They agree to keep their mischief a secret, until Brat becomes critically ill from the contaminated pond water and begins to lose her vision. The sisters are forced to confess. The happy antics and soul-searching pain of the sisters is convincingly conveyed through the rich rural dialect of the storytelling sister, Annie Rye. We were first introduced to Annie Rye and her sisters in *Down in the Piney Woods* [337]. **Nonstandard English.**

Mouse Rap [386]

Written by Walter Dean Myers

Softcover: HarperTrophy, HarperCollins
Published 1990

"*You can call me Mouse, 'cause that's my tag*
I'm into it all, everything's my bag
You know I can run, you know I can hoop
I can do it alone, or in a group
My ace is Styx, he'll always do
Add Bev and Sheri, and you got my crew
My tag is Mouse, and it'll never fail
And just like a mouse I got me a tale."

Every chapter of this spirited story begins with a rap from the self-confident fourteen-year-old, Mouse. His summer is full of adolescent challenges: His prodigal father returns after an eight-year absence and tries to become part of his life again; then a new girl starts coming on to him while Sheri, a friend from his crew, tries to get him to compete in a dance contest. Most intriguing, though, is the rumor that a stash of money from 1930s mobsters is hidden in an abandoned building in his Harlem neighborhood, which Mouse and the crew plan to find. Young readers will be absorbed by this hip, contemporary story.

NEATE: To the Rescue [387]

Written by Debbi Chocolate ☆ 24

Softcover: Just Us
Published 1992

Naimah Gordon and her friends become actively involved in local and school politics when her mother's city council seat is contested by a tough and tricky opponent. The contender has been creating some racially charged issues to make Ms. Gordon look bad, seriously jeopardizing her reelection chances. Naimah is running against her mother's opponent's son in a student council election. A lesson in integrity, activism, and civic responsibility is conveyed through this fast-paced story. Neate's adventures continue in *Elizabeth's Wish*.

Next Stop Freedom: The Story of a Slave Girl [388]

Written by Dorothy and Thomas Hoobler and Carey-Greenberg Associates
Illustrated by Cheryl Hanna ☆ 88

Softcover: Silver Burdett, Simon & Schuster
Published 1991

Young Emily, a slave, dreams of freedom as she learns to read and write. Emily has heard about the Moses who led slaves to freedom. One night, Moses does come to escort her and others to freedom on the Underground Railroad. After a long and suspenseful trip, with slave catchers on their heels, the group is hidden by a Quaker family and then sent on to freedom in Pennsylvania.

Oh, Brother [389]

Written by Johniece Marshall Wilson

Softcover: Apple, Scholastic
Published 1988

Sibling relationships are tough enough, but even worse when two brothers, as different as night and day, share a room. In this entertaining story, Alex is the organized, industrious younger brother who is constantly victimized by his less disciplined, sloppy, older brother, Andrew. Andrew frequently borrows Alex's bike and ultimately loses it, which makes it very difficult for Alex to work his paper route. Andrew's friends tease and try to intimidate young Alex. There is plenty of anger and frustration between the two, but they are family, and come through for one another when it really counts.

Oh, Freedom!: Kids Talk about the Civil Rights Movement with the People Who Made It Happen [390]

Written by Casey King and Linda Barrett Osborne
Illustrated by Joe Brooks

Hardcover: Knopf, Random House
Published 1997

Kids conduct thirty-one interviews with adult friends, family members, and civil rights activists to learn firsthand about the days of the 1960s civil rights movement. Informative chapters thoroughly explore the Jim Crow era, non-violence, black power, and segregation. Three essays, and an important foreword by Rosa Parks, provide background information on various aspects of the era to help add perspective to the interviews.

Once Upon a Time in Junior High [391]

Written by Lisa Norment

Softcover: Apple, Scholastic
Published 1994

Shelby, who is white, and Amber, who is black, have enjoyed a long friendship throughout elementary school and are excited about entering junior high school together. The pair's relationship is threatened when other girls in the new school try to come between the interracial friends. This is a relevant story about one of the many societal pressures that young adolescents face as they grow.

> "Usually, I hate Monday mornings. I get this icky feeling in my stomach starting Sunday night. My stomach feels like it's full of those imaginary butterflies. The icky feeling gets worse and worse, until I wake up on Monday morning. Then I'll realize why I'd been feeling this way. It's because I'm nervous about spending another week in junior high school."

The Palm of My Heart: Poetry by African American Children [392]

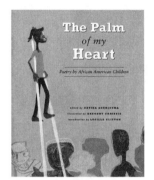

Edited by Davida Adedjouma
Illustrated by Gregory Christie

Coretta Scott King Honor: Illustrator

Hardcover: Lee & Low
Published 1996

Writer Lucille Clifton conducted a series of writing workshops for children of the Inner City Youth League and the African American Academy for Accelerated Learning. The works of twenty of these young poets are featured in this collection of poems that celebrate their blackness. Some of the poems, though extremely simple and brief, contain powerful concepts of racial pride and identity.

The People Could Fly: American Black Folktales [393]

Written by Virginia Hamilton ☆ 80
Illustrated by Leo and Diane Dillon

Coretta Scott King Award: Author
Coretta Scott King Honor: Illustrator

Hardcover and softcover: Knopf
Published 1985

Young children will enjoy this collection of twenty-four black folktales, told from the point of view of the slaves, that reflect parts of their African American heritage. Each tale is short enough to be suitable as a bedtime story, but they may require some explanation for younger readers since some of the concepts, phrases, and terms may be new. *Nonstandard English*.

A Place in the Sun [394]

Written by Jill Rubalcaba

Hardcover: Clarion, Houghton Mifflin
Published 1997

Young Senmut accidentally kills a dove while carving the figure of Sekhmet, the goddess of healing, which he was making to help his critically ill father. He is sentenced to a life of hard labor at a life-draining mining camp for killing the sacred bird. Still, he is determined to try to save his father, so he steals a small amount of gold from the mines to gild the carving. He and the carving are discovered and delivered to the Pharaoh, whose son is near death. The power of the carving heals the stricken son and earns Senmut the honor of being named as the royal sculptor. This story, set in the thirteenth century B.C., provides an interesting view into ancient Egyptian culture and beliefs.

A Pony for Jeremiah [395]

Written by Robert H. Miller ☆ 156
Illustrated by Nneka Bennett
Hardcover and softcover: Silver Burdett, Simon & Schuster
Published 1996

Jeremiah and his family escape slavery and begin a new life in the Nebraska territory. Jeremiah asks his father for a new pony, so the two go on a great adventure and capture a wild one, to the envy of a young Cheyenne boy, who later becomes a friend. The horse refuses to be broken and will not stay in captivity, a feeling that Jeremiah can relate to, so he allows the wild animal to go free. One day, to Jeremiah's surprise, the pony returns, on its own terms, and becomes a willing part of his life.

Profiles of Great Black Americans Series [396]

Edited by Richard Rennert
Hardcover: Chelsea House
Published 1993

Each of the ten volumes in this series contains biographical sketches about eight or nine important African Americans in a particular field of endeavor. The volumes are designed for quick and easy reference regarding each subject's childhood, education, and lifetime achievements, and includes several black-and-white illustrations for each subject. The series titles are: *Book of Firsts: Leaders of America,* which includes Shirley Chisholm and Douglas O. Wilder; *Book of Firsts: Sports Heroes,* which includes Althea Gibson and Bill Russell; *Civil Rights Leaders,* which includes James Weldon Johnson and Walter White; *Female Leaders,* which includes Marian Wright Edelman and Carol Moseley-Braun; *Female Writers,* which includes Alice Walker and Toni Morrison; *Jazz Stars,* which includes Count Basie and Billie Holiday; *Male Writers,* which includes Charles Chestnut and Ralph Ellison; *Performing Artists,* which includes Lena Horne and Sidney Poitier; *Pioneers of Discovery,* which includes Guion Bluford and Lewis Latimer; and *Shapers of America,* which includes Richard Allen and Mary McLeod Bethune.

Red Dog, Blue Fly: Football Poems [397]

Written by Sharon Bell Mathis
Illustrated by Jan Spivey Gilchrist ☆ 62

Softcover: Puffin, Penguin USA
Published 1991

Thirteen poems for young football lovers tell the story of the sport's season. Among the selections are "Touchdown," "Leg Broken," "Quarterback," and finally "Victory Banquet." If you have trouble getting your young jock to sit down and read (poetry or otherwise), perhaps this book will provide a breakthrough.

Seminole Diary: Remembrances of a Slave Family [398]

Written and illustrated by Dolores Johnson ☆ 118

Hardcover: Macmillan
Published 1994

A young girl and her mother look at an old diary passed down through their family from their ancestor, Libbie, a slave in 1834. The diary tells of Libbie's escape from slavery with her father and younger sister to Florida, where they lived with the Seminole Indians. The Seminoles fully accepted the blacks, and they shared a peaceful and productive life together. Eventually, however, the Seminoles were driven from their land by the U.S. government and escorted to an Oklahoma Indian reservation. Although a fictional account, the circumstances and story line are historically true and represent an important but little-known chapter of African American history.

Seth and Samona [399]

Written by Joanne Hyppolite
Illustrated by Colin Bootman

Hardcover and softcover: Bantam Doubleday Dell
Published 1995

This is an entertaining story about an unlikely friendship between a rambunctious fifth-grade African American girl and a very proper Haitian American boy. Somehow Seth becomes an accomplice to all of Samona's crazy antics, bonding the two in an impermeable friendship. Seth's commitment to Samona is tested when she decides to enter the Little Miss Dorchester pageant, where he knows she will be humiliated. Seth is torn between supporting her latest scheme and undoing her plan before the worst happens. Black-and-white illustrations of the two characters and their families are included throughout the easy-to-read chapters.

Sidewalk Story [400]

Written by Sharon Bell Mathis

Softcover: Puffin, Penguin USA
Published 1971

Lilly Etta Brown cannot stand idly by while her best friend, Tanya, and her large family are evicted from their apartment. She demonstrates her commitment and determination to help them in this story about true friendship. Inspired by another highly publicized eviction case, Lilly gets up the courage to call a local television reporter to interest him in the plight of her best friend, ensuring a positive outcome.

Smiffy Blue, Ace Crime Detective: The Case of the Missing Ruby and Other Stories [401]

Written by Walter Dean Myers
Illustrated by David J. A. Sims

Hardcover: Scholastic
Published 1996

Smiffy Blue, ace crime detective, and Jeremy Joe, his bumbling sidekick, solve a series of mysteries in this collection of four short stories. Each story is illustrated with pictures that have give-away clues that reveal the culprit even before Smiffy works through the silly case. Young readers will love the stories and Smiffy's sleuthing bloopers in this easy-to-read book.

Something to Count On [402]

Written by Emily Moore

Softcover: Puffin, Penguin USA
Published 1980

Young Lorraine faces emotional turmoil and behavioral problems at school after her parents' separation. The one thing that she needs is to be able to count on her father. But he does not call very often, and rarely comes when he says he will. Lorraine begins to believe that all of this is her fault. Eventually she begins to learn that she must distance herself from her unreliable father and accept the unconditional love and support of her mother.

> **"** *Since Daddy left, we hadn't talked about him. Ma never even told us why they broke up. But the last thing Daddy did say was, 'I'll be back for you. Wait and see.'*
>
> *It's been a month. I'm still waiting."*

Soul Looks Back in Wonder [403]

Compiled and illustrated by Tom Feelings ☆ 48

Coretta Scott King Award:
Illustrator

Hardcover: Dial
Published 1993

Renowned illustrator Tom Feelings has selected works by thirteen of the most distinguished African American poets, past and present—among them Maya Angelou, Lucille Clifton, Langston Hughes, and Marie Evans—to create a reflective book of poems dedicated to young sisters and brothers. The thirteen poems eloquently explore African heritage and the strength and beauty of black people. **Nonstandard English.**

Sports Reports Series [404]

Written by Ron Knapp

Hardcover: Enslow
Published 1994–1996

This biographical series features easy-to-read stories about some of America's greatest sports stars. Each title is complete with high-action photographs, statistics, and interesting factual sidebars about the subject. Nine African American athletes are featured in the series: Charles Barkley, Michael Jordan, Shaquille O'Neal, David Robinson, Barry Sanders, Deion Sanders, Emmitt Smith, Frank Thomas, and Thurman Thomas.

Stealing Home [405]

Written by Mary Stolz

Hardcover and softcover: HarperCollins
Published 1992

The peaceful lifestyle of Thomas and his grandfather is turned upside down when Aunt Linzy comes for an extended visit. Aunt Linzy, a cleaning fanatic, constantly bickers with Grandfather and is not interested in the sports that Grandfather and Thomas hold so dear. Grandfather tries to be patient and encourages Thomas to do the same, but it gets tougher with each passing day. The situation is amusing in this sports-oriented story, full of fast-paced baseball games, and will provide pleasant easy reading for preteens. Other books about Thomas and his grandfather include *Coco Grimes, Go Fish* [352], and *Storm in the Night* [279].

The Stories Huey Tells [406]

Written by Ann Cameron
Illustrated by Roberta Smith

Hardcover: Knopf, Random House
Published 1995

Huey is the younger brother of the well-known Julian of *Julian's Glorious Summer* [364] and other books. In this book, Huey relates five stories from his young experiences, all engagingly told from a kid's point of view. Our favorite was "The Rule." In Huey's family, everyone must try everything on their plate and must eat everything that they order in a restaurant. That is a double whammy for Huey when he orders trout (head and tail intact) and mushrooms for dinner. Young readers will empathize with Huey, and you will chuckle just imagining your own eight-year-old trying to contend with this dilemma! Read *More Stories Huey Tells* for more of Huey's antics.

Striped Ice Cream [407]

Written by Joan Lexau

Hardcover: HarperCollins
Softcover: Scholastic
Published 1968

Becky is the youngest of five children being raised by her hard-working mother. The family is extremely poor and has to make do with very little. Becky, always the recipient of hand-me-downs, understands that there is no money for new clothes, but hopes for at least a special dinner and striped (Neapolitan) ice cream for dessert. To Becky's surprise, her loving family fulfills all of her birthday wishes.

Susie King Taylor: Destined to Be Free [408]

Written by Denise Jordan
Illustrated by Higgins Bond

Softcover: Just Us
Published 1994

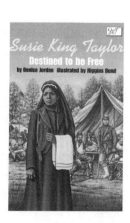

The little-known story of Susie King Taylor is told in this easy-to-read biography. Susie King Taylor, known as the educator of her people, founded a school where she taught black adults and children to read and write. Later she become the first black Civil War nurse, attached to a regiment of black Union soldiers. This remarkable woman, one of so many who have been lost in history, wrote an autobiography, an unusual accomplishment for a black woman of her times.

Sweet Words So Brave: The Story of African American Literature [409]

Written by Barbara K. Curry and James Michael Brodie
Illustrated by Jerry Butler

Hardcover: Zino
Published 1996

Forbidden to read and write, but determined to express themselves and tell their stories, many slaves defied the law and did learn, creating a literary legacy for all who followed. The history of African American literature, and the stories of many renowned African American writers, from Phillis Wheatley and Frederick Douglass to Alice Walker and Maya Angelou, are skillfully told. Full-page art, photographs, and documents illustrate this exceptional oversized history book.

Talk about a Family [410]

Written by Eloise Greenfield ☆ 72
Illustrated by James Calvin

Hardcover and softcover: HarperCollins
Published 1978

Ginny's life is about to change and she is unsure what to expect in this thoughtful book about complex family relationships. All she knows is that her mother and father are not getting along well. Her big brother returns home from his tour in the army and Ginny hopes that he can help mend whatever seems to be broken. But he cannot. When her parents announce their separation, Ginny's confusion, anger, and resentment give way to an understanding that they can still be a family, even if in a different configuration.

> " *Grandpa had been one of the best storytellers in Hog Hammock. He could tease and draw in his audience so skillfully that, by the end, everyone hung on his every word and movement. He was like a great actor in a one-man play.* "

The Terrible, Wonderful Tellin' at Hog Hammock [411]

Written by Kim Siegelson
Illustrated by Eric Velasquez

Hardcover: HarperCollins
Published 1996

Every year there was a storytelling contest in Hog Hammock, Gullah County. Young Jonas used to go to hear his grandpa, who was the best storyteller around, tell his tales. Now Grandpa is dead. So Grandma decides Jonas must carry on the family tradition. Young readers will relate to the nervous and insecure Jonas, and find out how he finds the strength to perform on his big night. **Nonstandard English.**

Themba [412]

Written by Margaret Sacks
Illustrated by Wil Clay

Softcover: Puffin, Penguin USA
Published 1985

After waiting for three long years, Themba is disappointed and worried when his father does not return as planned from the gold mines outside Johannesburg, where he has been working. Although young, and just a country boy, Themba knows that he must go into town to find his father. Several black-and-white illustrations embellish the short story of Themba's memorable and adventurous journey through modern-day South Africa.

Through Loona's Door: A Tammy and Owen Adventure with Carter G. Woodson [413]

Written by Tonya Bolden
Illustrated by Luther Knox

Hardcover: America's Family, Corporation for Cultural Literacy
Published 1997

Owen and Tammy, brother and sister, find their way into a bookstore while escaping a storm. The proprietor, Loona, engages them in lively discussion about African American history. They discuss Carter G. Woodson, the Father of Black History and driving force behind Black History Week (later expanded to a month). The two children become enthralled with his story and are soon whisked back in time to 1892, through a special door in the shop. They meet Woodson and learn more about the genesis of his extraordinary career and accomplishments. This enriching book is chock-full of impressive facts, and is an inspiration for kids to learn more about African American history.

> **"** . . . *and he knew that even though slavery was over, his people would never truly be free until they freed their minds of all the lies other people told about them. So he devoted his life—his whole being—to discovering and writing about the great works and glories of black folks."*

The Toothpaste Millionaire [414]

Written by Jean Merrill
Illustrated by Jan Palmer

Hardcover and softcover: Houghton Mifflin
Published 1972

Twelve-year-old Rufus Mayflower, amazed by the high cost of an everyday product, begins a profitable enterprise with a classmate to make and distribute a superior and more economical toothpaste. Important principles about business and free enterprise are embedded in this lighthearted story.

THE CREATORS

Andrea Davis Pinkney
AUTHOR

Brian Pinkney
AUTHOR AND ILLUSTRATOR

"For me, writing for children is like dancing—it lets my imagination whirl and encourages me to play with rhythm."

—ANDREA DAVIS PINKNEY

"I always knew I wanted to be an illustrator because my father is an illustrator, and I wanted to be just like him. I did everything he did. My desk was a miniature version of his desk. The paintbrushes and pencils I used were often the ones from his studio that were too old or too small for him to use. I had a paint set like his and a studio like his. Except my studio was a walk-in closet, which made it the perfect size for me."

—BRIAN PINKNEY

OUR FAVORITES

Andrea Davis Pinkney and
   Brian Pinkney: *Seven Candles for Kwanzaa*, 1993 [94]

Andrea Davis Pinkney: *Hold Fast to Dreams*, 1995 [447]

Brian Pinkney: *JoJo's Flying Side Kick*, 1995 [210]
   Max Found Two Sticks, 1994 [228]
   Sukey and the Mermaid, 1992 [282]

Toussaint L'Ouverture: The Fight for Haiti's Freedom [415]

Written by Walter Dean Myers
Illustrated by Jacob Lawrence

Hardcover: Simon & Schuster
Published 1996

Distinguished writer Walter Dean Myers adds meaningful narrative to the renowned series of forty-one provocative tempera paintings created by Jacob Lawrence. The paintings tell the story of Haiti's great liberator, Toussaint L'Ouverture, who fought for the island nation's independence from France in the early 1800s.

Treemonisha: From the Opera by Scott Joplin [416]

Written by Angela Shelf Medearis ☆ 150
Illustrated by Michael Bryant

Hardcover: Henry Holt
Published 1995

African American musical genius Scott Joplin created this ragtime opera in the early 1900s. The story of Treemonisha did not meet with critical success in its time, but it was awarded the Pulitzer Prize in 1976, and is now considered a cultural classic. In this nonmusical version, Treemonisha saves her fellow townspeople from the scheming cons of an evil conjure man, Zodzetrick. Although presented in story-book fashion, the story is a mature one that should be appreciated by older readers.

The Twins Strike Back [417]

Written by Valerie Flournoy
Illustrated by Melodye Rosales

Softcover: Just Us
Published 1980

Eight-year-old twins Natalie and Nicole are upset because no one seems to treat them as separate people. They are often referred to as "the twins" instead of by their own names. It is always assumed that they should have the same interests and strengths, but they do not! Even though they are best friends, they want people, including other family members, to accept them as individuals. The two devise a carefully planned ruse to trick their sister and friends, shocking them into acknowledging Nicole's and Natalie's individuality.

173

A Wave in Her Pocket: Stories from Trinidad [418]

Written by Lynn Joseph
Illustrated by Brian Pinkney ☆ 172

Hardcover and softcover: Clarion, Houghton Mifflin
Published 1991

Tantie (a term for Grandaunt in Trinidad) tells Amber and her cousins six colorful stories from the Afro-Trinidadian tradition. Several of the stories are about well-known folklore characters of the Caribbean island, such as the scary Soycouyant, which can "suck de blood" from its victims. Other stories are more sentimental, such as the title story about enduring love. A glossary defines some of the island colloquialisms for young readers. ***Caribbean dialect.***

The Year They Walked: Rosa Parks and the Montgomery Bus Boycott [419]

Written by Beatrice Siegel

Hardcover: Four Winds, Simon & Schuster
Published 1992

Rosa Parks's heroic act of nonviolent resistance, when she refused to give up her seat to a white rider on a bus, sparked the most widely watched civil rights demonstration in the history of the United States. A highly accessible, nonfiction account of the Montgomery bus boycott, this book describes in complete detail the call from black civic leaders to the African American community to unite for the boycott, and the strategies that the community used to hold their position for over a year, until they prevailed.

Ziggy and the Black Dinosaurs [420]

Written by Sharon M. Draper
Illustrated by James E. Ransome ☆ 192

Softcover: Just Us
Published 1994

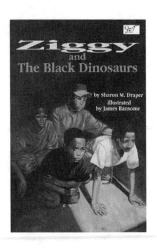

Preteen Ziggy and his three friends—Rico, Rashawn, and Jerome—thought that they were in for a boring summer in this delightfully boyish chapter book. The basketball hoop had been destroyed and the swimming pool had been closed, so there was nothing for the boys to do until they creatively formed their own club, known as the Black Dinosaurs. The four adventurous boys decide to bury their club's secret treasures, leading them to a box of buried bones. Now they have the mystery of their young lives to solve, and that is exactly what they do. The adventures of the Black Dinosaurs continue in *Lost in the Tunnel of Time* and *The Shadows of Caesar's Creek*.

Books for Young Adults

YOUNG TEENS TODAY are more sophisticated than in past decades. The books that we have identified for these young readers reflect that difference and build a bridge between childhood books and young adult novels. The topics, story lines and reading levels of these books are for young teens who are accomplished readers.

There is an excellent selection of historical novels that offer unique insights into specific aspects of slavery, including *Nightjohn* [461], about a young slave who wants to learn to read, and *Second Daughter* [471], about a young slave woman who sues her master for her freedom. Young students are not likely to hear stories like these in school, yet they are valuable for an understanding of what we have endured in this country. There is also a fair selection of nonfiction books on this era, like *North Star to Freedom* [463], about the Underground Railroad, and *The Amistad*

Slave Revolt and American Abolition [423], that contain detailed truths about the history and heritage of African Americans.

Some books contain mature subject matter, such as *Forged by Fire* [441] and *I Hadn't Meant to Tell You This* [448], both about child abuse and molestation. While these topics are tactfully handled, they are provocative issues that are discussed frankly in each book.

Teenage readers will also enjoy novels about young people like themselves who face more typical teen problems, such as peer pressure, self-esteem issues, racism, young love, and family struggles. Most of these books, like *Fall Secrets* [438] and *Poor Girl, Rich Girl* [466], will provide a short reading experience about situations that young teens can relate to.

Young teens and preteens should be encouraged to read for pleasure and relaxation, and as an alternative to television, video games, and the telephone. While they are being entertained by the stories, their comprehension and vocabulary skills will continue to grow and their view of the world will broaden.

African American Answer Book Series [421]

Written by R. S. Rennert

Softcover: Chelsea House
Published 1995

Six challenging books present an array of entertaining educational questions about African American history. Each book contains 325 questions in true-or-false and multiple-choice formats to help develop young readers' knowledge about the characters and events that have shaped their heritage. The series, based on the Black Americans of Achievements series [425], includes *African American Answer Book: Biography* and *African American Answer Book: History,* as well as titles on arts and entertainment, facts and trivia, science and discovery, and sports.

African-American Firsts: Famous, Little-Known and Unsung Triumphs of Blacks in America [422]

Written by Joan Potter and Constance Claytor

Illustrated by Alison Muñoz

Softcover: Pinto
Published 1994

Over 400 brief articles about breakthrough accomplishments of African Americans are contained in this reference book. Each noteworthy achievement is stated as an answer to a question such as: "Who was the first African American woman to serve on a president's cabinet?" and "Who was the first African American inventor to be granted a U.S. patent?" The range of firsts is in a variety of fields—business, entertainment, journalism, history, education, religion, and more. This informative guide is excellent for quick reference, research, or entertaining trivia games.

The Amistad Slave Revolt and American Abolition [423]

Written by Karen Zeinert

Hardcover and softcover: Linnet, Shoe String
Published 1997

Fifty-three slaves aboard the slave ship *Amistad* mutinied off the coast of Cuba, killing several Spanish officers, in 1839. The mutineers were captured off the coast of Long Island and brought to New Haven, Connecticut, to face trial. This book chronicles the controversial court battle over whether the slaves should be punished or set free. Abolitionists throughout the country used the case as a rallying point to highlight the injustice of slavery. Freed by the courts, the surviving *Amistad* slaves were returned to their home in Sierra Leone. Young readers will understand why historians see this event as one of many that would eventually lead to the Civil War and the abolition of slavery.

> " *Although the Africans could not understand the case against them, they understood enough of what went on to know that they were in serious trouble. Once again, they were overcome with despair.*"

177

Anthony Burns: The Defeat and Triumph of a Fugitive Slave [424]

Written by Virginia Hamilton ☆ 80

Softcover: Knopf, Random House
Published 1988

"*Overnight, without his ever knowing it, Anthony Burns became a symbol of freedom. But high up in the Court House he was a tired, miserable prisoner, alone save for his guard of petty criminals.*"

Anthony Burns was an escaped slave who was recaptured in Massachusetts shortly before the Civil War. He stood trial, with strong support of Northern abolitionists, to try to win his freedom, but was returned to his master in Virginia under the Fugitive Slave Act. His freedom was later purchased by his Northern supporters and he was given a scholarship to Oberlin College, where he studied for the ministry. The early death of this historical figure, at the age of twenty-eight, was, no doubt, a result of the stresses and hardships endured in his young life.

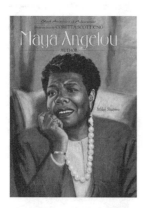
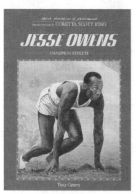

Black Americans of Achievement Series [425]

Written by various authors
Introduction by Coretta Scott King

Hardcover and softcover: Chelsea House
Published 1991–1997

This comprehensive collection of well-written biographies details the lives and times of notable African Americans from all walks of life (eighty-six in hardcover, sixty-three in softcover). The stories of these contemporary and historical personalities will help young readers understand the part that African American men and women have played and continue to play in the fabric of American life. Each title includes up to sixty black-and-white photographs and a complete reference section. The collection is ideal for a home or school library. The series includes biographies of civil rights leaders and builders of America such as Malcolm X, Nat Turner, and W. E. B. DuBois; writers such as Maya Angelou, Alex Haley, and Langston Hughes; twentieth-century leaders such as Barbara Jordan, Thurgood Marshall, and Colin Powell; entertainers and musicians such as Scott Joplin, Ella Fitzgerald, and Oprah Winfrey; scientists and explorers such as Ronald McNair, Charles Drew, and Matthew Henson; and sports stars such as Arthur Ashe, Muhammad Ali, and Michael Jordan.

Black Diamond: The Story of the Negro Baseball League [426]

Written by Patricia C. McKissack ☆146 *and Fredrick McKissack, Jr.*

Hardcover and softcover: Scholastic
Published 1994

Coretta Scott King Honor: Author

The extraordinary history of the black baseball players who were a part of the Negro Baseball League is told in this well-documented book. The players persevered through the Great Depression, racism, and other personal indignities in order to play the game that they loved. The comprehensive story is peppered with short anecdotes about individual players like Satchel Paige, Josh Gibson, and Buck Leonard. Photographs of teams, players, historical documents, and newspaper headlines add a special dimension to this historic story.

Black Eagles: African Americans in Aviation [427]

Written by Jim Haskins ☆94

Hardcover and softcover: Scholastic
Published 1995

This enriching book acclaims the achievements of generations of African American aviators who blazed a path in aeronautical history. Among those covered in this well-documented book are Eugene Bullard, who piloted planes for France during World War I; famous aviatrix Bessie Coleman, who barnstormed the country in air shows in the mid 1920s; and Mae C. Jemison, who in 1992 became the first African American woman in space. Black-and-white photographs embellish the text.

Black Profiles in Courage: A Legacy of African American Achievement [428]

Written by Kareem Abdul-Jabbar and Alan Steinberg

Hardcover: William Morrow
Published 1996

Former basketball great Kareem Abdul-Jabbar tells the stories of several of his own black heroes in this well-researched and well-written book. Abdul-Jabbar reveals the historic accomplishments of some renowned African Americans, such as Frederick Douglass and Rosa Parks, as well as several historically obscure blacks, such as Estevanico, an explorer whose expeditions and accomplishments were as significant as Marco Polo's or Balboa's, and Cinque, an African captive who, while in transit from Cuba, led a revolt on the slave ship *Amistad* in 1839.

The Bridges of Summer [429]

Written by Brenda Seabrooke

Hardcover and softcover: Penguin USA
Published 1992

Two very different African American cultures clash in this spirited novel about Zarah, a young black New York City teen who is forced to live with her grandmother on a rural island in South Carolina. Zarah finds the lack of running water, electricity, and other modern conveniences unbelievable. Furthermore, she does not understand her grandmother's old-fashioned ways, Gullah language, or strange spiritual beliefs. Zarah befriends a white girl who is more like herself, creating a local scandal in this story set on the fictitious Domingo Island, which is patterned after a real Carolina Gullah island. *Nonstandard English.*

The Broken Bridge [430]

Written by Phillip Pullman

Softcover: Bullseye, Random House
Published 1992

> *" Finding out something about yourself that other people have known and haven't told you makes you feel stupid, as if they were laughing at you for being so naive."*

Sixteen-year-old Ginny, a mixed-race child, lives with her white father in Wales. She was falsely told that her Haitian mother died when she was an infant. Life as a biracial, motherless child is difficult but became even more so when she learns that she has a white half brother, who is also sixteen years old. Ginny's father never mentioned his son, nor his first wife. More surprises are in store for Ginny as she plunges into her family's past. This is an intriguing novel with interesting subplots that will keep young readers turning the pages.

Charlie Pippin [431]

Written by Candy Dawson Boyd

Hardcover: Macmillan, Simon & Schuster
Softcover: Puffin, Penguin USA
Published 1987

Chartreuse "Charlie" Pippin undertakes an entrepreneurial scheme at school that gets her in trouble. Her bigger problem, however, is with her father, who overreacts to the situation. In fact, he is so angry that Charlie is confused by his rage. Charlie's mother explains that her father used to be a happier man until he went to fight in Vietnam, an experience that changed him forever. Charlie decides that the only way to understand her father's bitterness is to understand his wartime experience. She begins a restless pursuit of the truth in this compelling novel.

Children of Promise: African American Literature and Art for Young People [432]

Edited by Charles Sullivan

Hardcover: Harry N. Abrams, Times Mirror
Published 1991

Over one hundred African American poems, songs, and writings by notable writers Phillis Wheatley, Langston Hughes, Gwendolyn Brooks, and others, and over eighty illustrations and photographs fill this anthology, which traces the black experience in America from slavery through the twentieth century. One of the more poignant selections is the 1799 Petition to Stop the African Slave Trade, sent to the President and the legislature of the United States. It is presented along with a photograph of the petition's signature page, filled with signatures of seventy-four African American activists of that time.

Crocodile Burning [433]

Written by Michael Williams

Softcover: Puffin, Penguin USA
Published 1992

Seraki Mandindi, a South African teenager from Soweto, joins a theater group that is performing a poignant play about the horrors of apartheid in their country. The play becomes so successful that it is taken to a Broadway stage in New York City. Seraki and his group are thrilled with their New York experience but understand, all too clearly, how restricted they really are in South Africa. While they are in New York, they learn about the release of Nelson Mandela from his years of captivity and prepare to return to their own country with a renewed optimism about their futures.

The Dark-Thirty: Southern Tales of the Supernatural [434]

Written by Patricia C. McKissack ☆ 146
Illustrated by Brian Pinkney ☆ 172

Coretta Scott King Award: Author
Newbery Honor

Hardcover: Knopf, Random House
Published 1992

The ten spooky stories in this book are rooted in African American history or culture, and are sure to send shivers up the spine. Each chilling tale is written for independent reading or can be shared aloud after nightfall to thrill and enthrall young imaginations.

Definitely Cool [435]

Written by Brenda Wilkinson

Hardcover and softcover: Scholastic
Published 1993

Roxanne, a junior high school student, has to decide how important it is to be accepted by the cool crowd, even when their behavior and values do not match her own. She struggles to balance her acceptance in the new crowd with uncool virtues like maintaining a good relationship with her mother, earning good grades, and remaining true to past friendships. Roxanne makes a decision about who she will be when the cool group's activities escalate to cutting school and drinking. Young readers will understand Roxanne's dilemma in this book, which effectively captures the middle schooler's struggle with peer pressure.

The Diary of Latoya Hunter: My First Year in Junior High [436]

Written by Latoya Hunter

Softcover: Vintage, Random House
Published 1992

Inspired by an article that appeared in the *New York Times* about a graduating class of sixth graders in the Bronx, an editor contacted Latoya Hunter, an African American student in that class, and asked her to maintain a journal during her first year of junior high school. In this unusual and very personal book, Latoya's daily journal entries chronicle her experiences and emotions, like her struggle for independence, the pangs of first love, and her difficult relationship with her mother. Other entries, like those about a neighborhood shooting and a frightening sexual proposition, are more dramatic.

Ego Tripping and Other Poems for Young People [437]

Written by Nikki Giovanni
Illustrated by George Ford

Hardcover and softcover: Lawrence Hill, Chicago Review
Published 1993

This collection of thirty-two poems for teenagers is about their roots, struggles, and directions in life. This is one of only a few books that we found that is directed at adolescents and the questions and issues that surround this difficult stage in life.

Fall Secrets [438]

Written by Candy Dawson Boyd
Illustrated by Jim Carroll
Softcover: Puffin, Penguin USA
Published 1994

Jessie is very secure about her talent as she enters a new performing arts middle school, where she plans to develop her natural acting ability. Like most adolescents, however, she is insecure about many other things about herself. She struggles with academic rigors, social situations, and the relationships that she forms in her new school. Her deepest problem, however, is rooted in her basic insecurity about her dark brown skin and the frequent comparisons that are drawn between her and her golden-skinned sister. This novel is an engaging exploration of the effect that low self-esteem can have on a teen.

"And she loves you very much, and she did not ask to be born light-skinned like her father and me with hazel eyes and straight hair. I've told you time and time again that we are a rainbow people. African-Americans come in all shades of blacks and browns and creams—just like our family. When you celebrate your beauty, I'll rejoice."

Fast Sam, Cool Clyde, and Stuff [439]

Written by Walter Dean Myers

Coretta Scott King Honor: Author

Softcover: Puffin, Penguin USA
Published 1975

Twelve-year-old Francis, a.k.a. "Stuff," the new kid on a Harlem block, quickly becomes part of a circle of friends in this novel about the trials, tribulations, and experiences of average, urban preadolescents. His new friends, both boys and girls, support one another through everything, including peer pressures, school challenges, family situations, new loves, and losses. The preteen characters in this humorous story are well-developed through their realistic dialogue and reactions to the events in their young lives.

Fast Talk on a Slow Track [440]

Written by Rita Williams-Garcia
Hardcover: Lodestar, Penguin USA
Softcover: Bantam Doubleday Dell
Published 1991

Denzel Watson, a recent high school graduate, has every reason to believe that he is "all that." When he is accepted into a summer school program at Princeton University, Denzel expects to breeze through with his usual fast talk and charm. However, he does not do well because he is not prepared to do the hard work that it takes to compete with the other talented students. Discouraged, he does not return to school in the fall, choosing to be a door-to-door salesman instead. After months of soul-searching, Denzel grows up enough to accept the possibility of failure in order to take advantage of his educational opportunity.

"I got you read, brutha. We get one of you every year. Well-spoken chocolate chip cookies trying to skate through the program. Never make it beyond the second semester—which explains why there's a lot of well-spoken would-be's skating on what they coulda, shoulda been. Now, brutha, you still have a choice. You can either skate yourself on outta here with the rest of the would-be's or you can wake up, brutha. It's on you."

THE CREATORS

Gloria Jean Pinkney

AUTHOR

Jerry Pinkney

ILLUSTRATOR

"Books give me a great feeling of personal and artistic satisfaction. When I am working on a book, I wish the phone would never ring!"

—JERRY PINKNEY

OUR FAVORITES

Jerry Pinkney: *John Henry,* 1994 [209]

Minty: A Story of Young Harriet Tubman, 1996 [230]

The Patchwork Quilt, 1985 [256]

The Talking Eggs, 1989 [286]

Jerry and Gloria Pinkney: *The Sunday Outing,* 1994 [283]

Forged by Fire [441]

Written by Sharon M. Draper

Illustrated by John Clapp

Coretta Scott King Award: Author

Hardcover: Atheneum, Simon & Schuster
Published 1997

Young Gerald was neglected and sometimes abused by his drug-addicted mother. At the age of three, he was the victim of an apartment fire that he started while playing with a cigarette lighter. He was rescued from the fire by a neighbor, and then rescued from his tragic circumstances by his Aunt Queen, who became his guardian. Gerald thrives with the love of his aunt until she passes away on his ninth birthday. Gerald is forced to return to live with his mother, now married to an unsavory character, and his new little sister. He becomes fiercely protective of the little girl and is determined to save her from the sexual misconduct of his stepfather. Gerald grows into an inspirational young man who understands the responsibility of family and accepts the challenges of manhood at an early age.

Freedom Songs [442]

Written by Yvette Moore

Softcover: Puffin, Penguin USA
Published 1991

Fourteen-year-old Sheryl gets a dose of reality when she and her family drive from Brooklyn to North Carolina to visit their relatives. In the South, Sheryl is confronted for the first time with overt racism and Jim Crow laws. Her uncle is an activist with the Freedom Riders, who are setting up Freedom Schools and demonstrating against the racist practices of the South. Upon her return to New York, Sheryl is determined to help the freedom cause and organizes her friends and the community to raise money for the important cause.

The Friends [443]

Written by Rosa Guy

Hardcover: Henry Holt
Softcover: Bantam Starfire, Bantam Doubleday Dell
Published 1973

A friendship is born out of the neediness of two young girls. In this novel we meet fourteen-year-old Phyllisia, who is struggling for security after her family relocates from her Caribbean home to the tough streets of New York City. She is the object of teasing and ridicule by her new classmates and teachers. Edith, a delinquent and social misfit, extends herself in friendship to Phyllisia, somehow understanding their need for each other. ***Nonstandard English.***

The Girl on the Outside [444]

Written by Mildred Pitts Walter

Softcover: Scholastic
Published 1982

This novel is based on the true story of the integration of Little Rock High School in 1957. The high emotions of the era from the perspective of two fictionalized characters, Sophia, a white student, who resents the integration of her high school, and Eva, one of the nine black students who would be the first to enter the all-white Chatman High School, are effectively captured in this meaningful story.

Gold Diggers [445]

Written by Kwasi Koranteng
Illustrated by Pauline King

Softcover: Chelsea House
Published 1992

Kanjaga puts himself in peril when he accepts a job as an undercover agent, assigned to infiltrate and break up a ring of gold diggers who are stealing gold from the national mines of his small African country. Kanjaga enters the underworld, disguised as an escaped convict, in order to gain the acceptance of the criminals. Four of his police colleagues have died on this assignment, so he must use his wits and cunning, and be extremely careful not to expose himself in this suspenseful short novel.

Hang a Thousand Trees with Ribbons: The Story of Phillis Wheatley [446]

Written by Ann Rinaldi

Hardcover and softcover: Gulliver, Harcourt Brace
Published 1996

This book is a fictionalized account of the life of the famous poet Phillis Wheatley, who learned to read and write under the tutelage of her kind-hearted masters, the Wheatley family of Boston. Encouraged by the family, Phillis grew as a poet. Her young master, Nathaniel Wheatley, took her to England, where she was highly acclaimed for her work and became the first published African American poet. Upon her return to America, she demanded and won her freedom from the Wheatleys and then began a life-long struggle to find her place in American life.

Hold Fast to Dreams [447]

Written by Andrea Davis Pinkney ☆ 172

Hardcover: William Morrow
Softcover: Hyperion
Published 1995

Twelve-year-old Deirdre is uprooted from her familiar Baltimore home and all her friends when her father's promotion requires the family to move to suburban Connecticut. Deirdre is uncomfortable with the new school and the culture, which are predominantly white. This fast-moving novel explores Deirdre's relocation experiences, both good and bad, and could be helpful for adolescents facing a similar situation.

I Hadn't Meant to Tell You This [448]

Written by Jacqueline Woodson **Coretta Scott King Honor: Author**

Hardcover and softcover: Bantam Doubleday Dell
Published 1994

Twelve-year-old Marie is a popular black girl growing up in a middle-class community. When she develops an unlikely friendship with a poor white girl, a part of her childhood innocence is lost. Her new friend, Lena, shares a dark secret that forces Marie into the moral dilemma of her young life. She must decide whether she should keep the secret, or tell someone that Lena's father is molesting her. This is a dramatic story about a difficult subject. Be prepared to discuss it with your young reader, who may have questions about both the abuse and the responsibilities of friendship.

" I wanted to ask what he did and how. There were a million questions pressing against the back of my teeth. But Lena looked as though she had taken off. She looked hollow, vacant as sky, and I knew she had said all she was going to say about it."

If You Please, President Lincoln [449]

Written by Harriette Gillem Robinet

Hardcover: Atheneum, Simon & Schuster
Published 1995

In the midst of the Civil War, President Lincoln considered proposals to colonize liberated slaves on offshore islands. In this fictional story based on this notion, a young runaway slave becomes part of a poorly conceived and unauthorized plan to create such a colony on a small island. Four hundred ex-slaves are recaptured by an unscrupulous captain and transported to an island off of Haiti, where there are no provisions for their survival. When the few remaining victims are returned to America, they are falsely rumored to have lived like savages—cannibalizing, raping, and murdering one another for survival. This fascinating but emotionally tugging novel will evoke anger at the injustice and racism that the group experienced, but pride in their responsibility and resourcefulness.

Journey Home: Passage to Womanhood [450]

Written by Toni Eubanks

Softcover: People's
Published 1996

Fifteen-year-old Jessica goes to the library to research something about her African American heritage for her history class. She begins the exercise feeling humiliated because she feels that there is so little to tell about her African American forefathers, except that they were slaves. The librarian suggests that Jessica look at the journal of Tamara Woodson, a young African American girl who lived in Libertyville, a black western town, in the 1880s. In the journal, Jessica learns about African Americans in the American West, disproving her original notion that there was nothing new to tell about her black legacy. This stimulating novel, based on a real town and real characters, adds a rich new chapter to the African American story. A supplemental Teacher's Guide and a Student Guide are also available to support classroom use of this text.

Journey to Jo'burg [451]

Written by Beverly Naidoo
Illustrated by Eric Velasquez

Hardcover and softcover: HarperCollins
Published 1986

Thirteen-year-old Naledi and her younger brother journey from their small South African township to Johannesburg, hundreds of kilometers away, to get their Mma (mother). Mma is needed to care for their baby sister, who is dying of a severe fever. The children make the dangerous trip and find their Mma, with a little help from strangers, and are able to return with her. Along the way, they witness the atrocities of apartheid and racism that are more apparent in the large city. This quick-paced novel establishes a haunting view of the life of black South Africans, particularly before the demise of apartheid.

Just Family [452]

Written by Tonya Bolden

Hardcover: Cobblehill, Penguin USA
Published 1996

Ten-year-old Beryl's sense of security is threatened when she discovers a secret about her happy family. Beryl learns that her big sister, Randy, was born to her mother but a different father. This revelation turns Beryl's life upside down as she copes with the fact that she was never told and worries about what it all means. On a family reunion trip, Beryl learns the true meaning of family and accepts that her family is strong in spite of its past.

Kings, Gods, & Spirits from African Mythology [453]

Written by Jan Knappert
Illustrated by Francesca Pelizzoli
Hardcover and softcover: Peter Bedrick
Published 1996

Traditional myths and legends from all over the African continent are collected in this richly illustrated book. Most of the stories are no more than a page or two long, but tell ancient stories about Africa and its people, magical animals, spirits, saints, and more. Several two-page color illustrations and many black-and-white line drawings taken from the African tradition complement the thirty-five stories.

Last Summer with Maizon [454]

Written by Jacqueline Woodson
Softcover: Yearling, Bantam Doubleday Dell
Published 1992

Eleven-year-old Maizon and Margaret face a frightening threat to their friendship. During the summer, Maizon is offered a scholarship to a private boarding school, which will take her away from her familiar home and close relationship with Margaret. Their lives are further complicated by the death of Margaret's father and by Maizon's apprehension about being the only black girl in the boarding school. This well-written novel details how the girls deal with lagging self-esteem and conflicting emotions and how they support each other through each crisis. Other books about the title character are *Maizon at Blue Hill* and *Between Madison and Palmetto.*

Long Journey Home: Stories from Black History [455]

Written by Julius Lester
Hardcover: Dial, Penguin USA
Published 1972

This remarkable work of historical fiction, based on historical documents, tells the stories of six everyday black people—the kind of people whose lives create the body of black history. In the title selection, a man tells the story of fifty slaves who decided to go back home. They rose early in the morning and marched into the sea on their way back to Africa. Some said that they drowned. Others believed that the African gods rescued them and carried them back to their homeland. **Nonstandard English.**

> " *Well, one night they was talking and they decided they was going home. Decided that they wasn't going to slave no more. They was going home. So the next morning bright and early they got up. Long before the white folks was up they was up and they started walking. And they walked until they heard the roaring water. . . . They just marched on down to the beach, and without slowing down one bit, walked right on into the ocean.*"

Mama, I Want to Sing [456]

Written by Vy Higgensen with Tonya Bolden

Softcover: Point Books, Scholastic
Published 1992

Ever since she was eleven years old, all Doris could think about was singing. Even at a young age, she sang with her church's adult choir. As her extraordinary talent grows, so does her desire to become a professional singer. She gets her big break at the Apollo Theater in Harlem, winning an amateur talent competition. She becomes a big star, but her mother renounces her music as "worldly" and turns away from her daughter. Doris must find a way to keep her dream and reconcile with her headstrong mother in this contemporary story.

The Middle Passage: White Ships, Black Cargo [457]

Written and illustrated by Tom Feelings ☆ 48

Coretta Scott King Award: Illustrator

Hardcover: Dial, Penguin USA
Published 1995

The horrific story of the plight of Africans crossing the Atlantic on the Middle Passage is told through sixty-four exquisite black-and-white paintings. Each painting is highly detailed, with painful depictions of the dehumanizing treatment of the captives. A careful study of each illustration will reveal details of the voyage, including the cramped configuration of hundreds of slaves in the ship's hold, brutal whippings, and worse. Even though the subject matter is painful, young readers will recognize the strength of those who made the passage, as depicted in this masterful collection.

Mississippi Challenge [458]

Written by Mildred Pitts Walter

Coretta Scott King Honor: Author

Hardcover and softcover: Simon & Schuster
Published 1992

The civil rights era of the 1960s was a dynamic period and pivotal in the history of the United States. This book describes the civil rights movement as it existed in the state of Mississippi. The sobering text begins with a review of the historic background that led to the legal and social struggle for the basic rights of citizenship for blacks. The book, written from the perspective of black people who actually participated in the movement, unfolds with frightening details about the dramatic events of this explosive period.

Mississippi Chariot [459]

Written by Harriette Gillem Robinet

Hardcover and softcover: Simon & Schuster
Published 1994

In 1936, the lives of a sharecropper's family are forever changed when twelve-year-old Shortening Bread Jackson takes control of the family's problems. In this dramatic and suspenseful novel, Shortening Bread devises a plan to force the release of his father, who is serving time, unjustly, on a Mississippi chain gang. Shortening Bread's ploy is not only dangerous to his family, but to the entire black community. The courageous Shortening Bread saves his father, and then his family, from the wrath of their white oppressors with his own wit and strong sense of survival.

Motown and Didi: A Love Story [460]

Written by Walter Dean Myers   **Coretta Scott King Award: Author**

Softcover: Laurel Leaf, Bantam Doubleday Dell
Published 1984

This love story, set in the bowels of Harlem, involves Motown, a homeless seventeen-year-old dropout who sees himself as a street warrior, and Didi, a young woman trapped in the environment but full of hope and potential for her life outside the city. Motown saves Didi from an attempted assault, which ignites a powerful friendship and romance. In this mature novel, Motown and Didi face the realities of their world together. The riveting story captures, without glamour, the essence of the troubled ghetto.

> "Motown felt good. He walked down the street with Didi and people could see that they were in love. Strangers knew. If they had known his name, they could have said that he, Motown, had somebody to love. And who loved him."

Nightjohn [461]

Written by Gary Paulsen

Hardcover and softcover: Bantam Doubleday Dell
Published 1993

This is a true story about the strength and character of two slaves who defy their master and risk everything to read and write. Sarny, a young illiterate slave girl, encounters Nightjohn, an older slave who had once escaped but returned to bring the gift of reading to his people. Nightjohn teaches Sarny to read. The two pay a dear price for their defiance, but are bound by their commitment to each other and their hopes for their people. This compelling story of less than one hundred pages is blunt, brutal, and powerful, and will make a permanent impression on the minds of young readers. The 1997 sequel, *Sarny: A Life Remembered*, tells the story of Sarny's life after her emancipation. **Nonstandard English.**

> "You learn to read and they'll whip you till your skin hangs like torn rags. Or cut your thumbs off. Stay away from writing and reading."

THE CREATORS

James E. Ransome

ILLUSTRATOR

"What makes illustrating books so exciting is that because each book has a special voice, my approach toward each is different. Whether it be through my choice of palette, design, or perspective, there is always a desire to experiment and explore what makes each book unique."

Our Favorites

Celie and the Harvest Fiddler, 1995 [143]

Freedom's Fruit, 1996 [180]

Sweet Clara and the Freedom Quilt, 1993 [284]

Uncle Jed's Barber Shop, 1993 [294]

The Wagon, 1996 [296]

No Turning Back: A Novel of South Africa [462]

Written by Beverly Naidoo

Hardcover: HarperCollins
Published 1997

An abusive stepfather forces twelve-year-old Sipho from his township home into the streets of Johannesburg. There he joins a gang of other *malunde* [homeless] children, learning to survive the harsh realities of street life. Scrambling for every morsel of food, every nook or cranny to sleep in, and security from angry white antagonists, Sipho is given brief refuge by a white merchant and his family. This powerful novel, written in post-apartheid South Africa just prior to Mandela's election, offers vital insight into contemporary life for some black children in that country.

North Star to Freedom: The Story of the Underground Railroad [463]

Written by Gena K. Gorrell

Hardcover: Delacorte, Bantam Doubleday Dell
Published 1997

The story of the Underground Railroad is intelligently told in this comprehensive book. A historical perspective of slavery from its beginning through the Civil War establishes its economic, social, and political basis. The station-by-station expansion of the network is traced with stories and anecdotes about some little-known and well-known fugitives, slave catchers, abolitionists, and politicians. Numerous archival photographs, maps, and posters illustrate the book.

Phillip Hall Likes Me, I Reckon Maybe [464]

Written by Bette Greene
Illustrated by Charles Lilly

Newbery Honor

Softcover: Yearling, Bantam Doubleday Dell
Published 1974

The awkwardness of a young girl's first crush is humorously explored in this delightful novel. Beth Lambert likes Phillip Hall and, deep inside, knows that he likes her, too! To seal their unspoken affection, Beth finds herself allowing Phillip to outdo her in almost everything, including catching turkey thieves, winning calf-raising contests, and making mountaintop rescues. Sooner or later something has to give—and it does in this spunky tale. ***Nonstandard English.***

A Picture of Freedom: The Diary of Clotee, A Slave Girl, Belmont Plantation, Virginia 1859 [465]

Written by Patricia C. McKissack ☆ 146

Hardcover: Scholastic
Published 1997

Twelve-year-old Clotee, a slave girl who lives on a plantation in Virginia, learns to read and write surreptitiously while her young master is being tutored. Unable to reveal her secret for fear of reprisal, she keeps a diary—this book—about life on the plantation. When an abolitionist comes to tutor Master William, Clotee finds an ally in her desire for freedom. An interesting epilogue and notes at the end include historical photographs and insightful details about the period. ***Nonstandard English.***

Poor Girl, Rich Girl [466]

Written by Johniece Marshall Wilson

Hardcover and softcover: Scholastic
Published 1992

Miranda is in junior high school, where appearance is everything, which is why she hates wearing glasses. Miranda decides to get a job to earn enough money to buy contact lenses. In a humorous series of employment escapades, Miranda works as a camp counselor, baby-sitter, and dog walker, trying to find the perfect job to earn the money she needs. She learns about financial planning and personal responsibility. This contemporary adolescent story offers an entertaining reading experience for young teens.

Rebels Against Slavery: American Slave Revolts [467]

Written by Patricia C. McKissack ☆ 146   Coretta Scott King Honor: Author
    and Fredrick L. McKissack ☆ 146

Hardcover: Scholastic
Published 1996

Slave rebellions in all forms took place since the beginning of the institution of slavery. There was the violent rebellion led by Cinque on the slave ship *Amistad,* and a revolt led by Charles Deslondes, who led 500 slaves on a violent rampage on New Orleans in 1811, which is thought to be the largest slave uprising in this country. Slaves also protested passively with work slowdowns and other subtle actions that disrupted the day-to-day plantation routines. This book profiles many of the fascinating events and leaders of slave revolutions that took place in this country, giving them the credit that is so often attributed to white abolitionists.

Reflections of a Black Cowboy: The Buffalo Soldiers [468]

Written by Robert Miller ☆ 156
Illustrated by Richard Leonard
Hardcover and softcover: Silver Burdett, Simon & Schuster
Published 1991

The stories of the African American Buffalo Soldiers, who served in the Ninth and Tenth Cavalries in the nineteenth century, are colorfully told in this entertaining book narrated by Old Cowboy. The Buffalo Soldiers played an important role in opening up the western frontier, yet their stories are not well known. In this book of five short stories, several of these brave soldiers are acknowledged for their historic achievements and battles. The Reflections of a Black Cowboy series also includes a volume on pioneers, as well as one on cowboys and one on mountain men.

Roll of Thunder, Hear My Cry [469]

Written by Mildred D. Taylor
Hardcover and softcover: Penguin USA
Published 1976

Coretta Scott King Honor: Author
Newbery Medal

The Logan family's land is threatened by scheming white businessmen who seek to recover acreage lost to white families during the Civil War. Set in the rural South during the Depression, the story tells how the African American Logans must stand back-to-back to withstand the humiliation, racial assaults, and degradation that is heaped upon them. This is an intense novel, hallmarked by the dignity, strength, and self-support of the proud family. Other novels about the Logans are *The Road to Memphis, Let the Circle Be Unbroken, Song of the Trees* [479], and *The Well* [491]. **Nonstandard English. Use of N Word.**

Run for Your Life [470]

Written by Marilyn Levy
Hardcover: Houghton Mifflin
Softcover: Putnam
Published 1996

This novel is based on the true story of the Acorn Track Team, which was created by recreational director Darrell Hampton to offer an alternative to drugs and crime for the young girls of the Acorn Housing Project of Oakland, California. In addition to shaping a renowned sports team, Hampton becomes involved with the girls and their families to improve their grades. The novel features thirteen-year-old Kisha, who must balance her newfound commitment to her education and her sport with the obstacles of inner-city life. This powerful story will inspire young readers, enlarging their view of the possibilities.

"One day we were running at the Oakland track, which always made me feel special—I mean, who'd have thought old turkey feet could run four miles around a track?"

Second Daughter: The Story of a Slave Girl [471]

Written by Mildred Pitts Walter

Hardcover: Scholatic
Published 1996

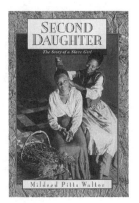

A provocative story set in the period of the American Revolution tells the story of two sisters who are the slaves of a colonial family in Massachusetts. The older sister, Bett, overhears many discussions about political strategy held in the home of her master. She learns that the Massachusetts Constitution and the Bill of Rights declare that all men are created equal and entitled to life and liberty, and that there is no difference in the document's language between those who are slaves and those who are not. Bett and another slave become two of the first slaves to brilliantly sue their masters for freedom, based on the legal language of the state's constitution.

Shimmy Shimmy Shimmy Like My Sister Kate: Looking at the Harlem Renaissance [472]

Written by Nikki Giovanni

Hardcover: Henry Holt
Published 1996

Selected works of twenty-three of the most renowned African American poets and writers of the twentieth century, including W. E. B. DuBois, Paul Laurence Dunbar, and Amiri Baraka, are collected in this distinguished anthology for mature young readers. Nikki Giovanni enriches the reading experience by exploring the writings and lending her own perspective in a commentary following each selection.

Sister [473]

Written by Eloise Greenfield ☆ 72

Hardcover and softcover: HarperCollins
Published 1974

Young Doretha, affectionately known as Sister by her family, was given an empty notebook by her father when she was nine years old. In the notebook, Doretha writes about the daily events in her life. Some of the events are painful, like the day her father died at a family picnic. Others are bittersweet, like the time that a dying neighbor gave her a treasured flute. Still others are joyous, like Doretha's discovery about her strong great-great-grandfather, who stood up for his dignity as a black man. As she reviews her memories four years later, she understands that each experience, good and bad, has helped make her who she is.

Skin Deep: And Other Teenage Reflections [474]

Poems by Angela Shelf Medearis ☆ 150
Illustrated by Michael Bryant

Hardcover: Macmillan, Simon & Schuster
Published 1995

Fifty contemporary poems reflect the innermost thoughts and feelings of teens on subjects ranging from the very serious "Babies," about an unwed teen mother of twins, to the emotion of "Forever," about a young love that was supposed to last forever, but lasted only for three months, and the witty "Report Card," about a student's excuse for bad grades. The poems, for both young men and young women, seem to be written especially for today's youth, but are actually timeless reflections of teen life.

Sky Man: 18 Pine Street [475]

Written by Stacie Johnson
Series Created by Walter Dean Myers

Softcover: Bantam, Bantam Doubleday Dell
Published 1993

Kids from Murphy High School gather after school to socialize at 18 Pine Street, the local pizza parlor. A new student, Sky Hodges, is a star basketball player who can lead the school's team to a championship. When his grades slip, threatening to keep him off the team, his friends rally to tutor him. Arrogantly, Sky refuses their help. The kids understand that only Sky can help himself. Other books in the 18 Pine Street series include *The Diary, Fashions by Tashia, Taking Sides,* and *The Test.*

Slam! [476]

Written by Walter Dean Myers   **Coretta Scott King Award: Author**

Hardcover: Scholastic
Published 1996

Seventeen-year-old Greg "Slam" Harris is an inner-city high school basketball star who dreams of an NBA career. But Slam has problems off court that he must face up to. His attitude, grades, and relationships are not nearly as well-tuned as his basketball game, and his coach is not willing to accept that from Greg. Greg has to grow up and learn to succeed in the game of life in order to realize his dreams. Fast-paced basketball action with detailed play-by-play descriptions will captivate young sports fans and draw them into this coming-of-age story.

> "*The second half started with me sitting on the bench. The coach looked over at me and I looked the other way. If he was expecting me to show humble he was wrong big time.*"

197

Sojourner Truth: Ain't I a Woman? [477]

Written by Patricia C. McKissack and Fredrick McKissack ☆ 146

Hardcover and softcover: Scholastic
Published 1992

Coretta Scott King Honor: Author

Isabella Van Wagener, who later became known as Sojourner Truth, lived under the harshness of slavery during her childhood. In her early years she worked in New York for several Dutch families, as her family was sold and resold to different masters. Sojourner was freed in 1828, after a law was passed liberating any slaves who were born before 1799. After her emancipation, Sojourner traveled the country as a consummate activist against slavery and for women's rights. Her strength earned her a reputation as a giant among abolitionists.

Somewhere in the Darkness [478]

Written by Walter Dean Myers

Hardcover and softcover: Scholastic
Published 1992

Coretta Scott King Honor: Author
Newbery Honor

Embittered by the loss of his mother and abandonment by his father fifteen years ago, Jimmy struggles with school and his adolescent life. Things are further complicated when a strange man walks into his life and declares himself to be Jimmy's father. Jimmy is forced to leave his surrogate mother to travel with his critically ill father. This poignant novel offers a roller-coaster of emotion for young readers, who will empathize with Jimmy.

Song of the Trees [479]

Written by Mildred D. Taylor
Illustrated by Jerry Pinkney ☆ 184

Hardcover: Dial, Penguin USA
Softcover: Bantam, Bantam Doubleday Dell
Published 1975

Coretta Scott King Honor: Author

The Logans are tested in this story about the strength of a southern African American family and its members' commitment to each other and to their land. Young Cassie learns about a plan to cheat Big Ma. In need of money, Big Ma has agreed to sell some of the giant old trees on her property, but an opportunistic lumberman plans to cut more than the agreed-upon amount. The family sends for Father, who is away working on a Louisiana railroad, to help defend their precious trees. Father's stands against the white lumberman are risky in the 1930s rural South, but his tactics work. Other books about the strong Logan family include *Roll of Thunder, Hear My Cry* [469], *The Well* [491], *The Road to Memphis,* and *Let the Circle Be Unbroken.* **Nonstandard English. Use of N Word.**

Sports Greats Series [480]

Written by various authors

Hardcover: Enslow
Published 1990–1996

This series explores the careers of ten great African American athletes. Career statistics and plenty of action photographs are included for each player. The series includes books about basketball greats David Robinson, Hakeem Olajuwon, Dennis Rodman, Reggie Miller, Dominique Wilkens, and Magic Johnson; football greats Bo Jackson and Herschel Walker; and baseball greats Bobby Bonilla and Darryl Strawberry.

Stolen Kisses [481]

Written by Michelle Mwansa
Softcover: Chelsea House
Published 1993

Young romantics will enjoy this lighthearted story about young love. A shy young schoolgirl named Patience meets and falls head over heels in love with a dashing young lawyer, Artwell. Patience is insecure about the new romance, fearing that Artwell may prefer her beautiful older sister. Their romance blooms in spite of Patience's fears. This story is one of several in the Chelsea House Heartbeats series of romantic novels for teens, which includes *The Gift of Life*, *The Jasmine Candle*, *The Place of Gentle Waters*, and *When the Drums Speak of Love*.

Straight Up!: A Teenager's Guide to Taking Charge of Your Life [482]

Written by Dr. Elizabeth Taylor-Gerdes, Ph.D.
Illustrations by Cortrell J. Harris, Sr.

Softcover: Lindsey
Published 1994

This positive guide, written expressly for teenagers, is an empowering tool that offers sage, no-nonsense advice and challenges young people to take responsibility and accountability for their futures. Seven straight-up chapters deal with getting into the game of life; a young black person's African American legacy; the role of the family in a teen's development; racism; overcoming obstacles; taking personal responsibility for one's life; and the guiding principles for a successful life. Parents should give this guide to their teens and encourage them to read it, reread it, and refer to it often for constant reinforcement.

THE CREATORS

Synthia Saint James

AUTHOR AND ILLUSTRATOR

"My hope is that my writing and illustrating children's books encourages children to find the joy in reading and learning, in addition to inspiring the many creative artists among them to become our future writers and illustrators."

OUR FAVORITES

The Gifts of Kwanzaa, 1994 [38]

Neeny Coming, Neeny Going, 1996 [240]

Snow on Snow on Snow, 1994 [97]

Sunday, 1996 [100]

Tukama Tootles the Flute: A Tale from the Antilles, 1994 [106]

Sweet Whispers, Brother Rush [483]

Written by Virginia Hamilton ☆ 80

Coretta Scott King Award: Author
Newbery Honor

Hardcover: Philomel, Putnam
Softcover: Avon
Published 1982

Fourteen-year-old Tree is responsible for the care of her home, and of an older, retarded brother, while their mother works. One day, a charming stranger, Brother Rush, comes into her life. It takes several weeks before Tree realizes that Brother Rush is actually the ghost of her uncle who has come to take her back in time to her earlier childhood. In the past, Tree discovers hidden secrets about her family that help her make better sense of her current life and to understand her mother's choices and motivations. This intense time-travel story will capture young readers' imaginations as they explore the deep emotions of this African American family.

This Strange New Feeling [484]

Written by Julius Lester

Coretta Scott King Honor: Author

Softcover: Scholastic
Published 1982

Three true stories are compiled in this book about the intense love relationships of young slave couples. Each captivating story is chock-full of the challenges that the young lovers confronted in the face of slavery to be together, to be free, and to enjoy the universal promise of love.

Those Who Love the Game: Glenn "Doc" Rivers on Life in the NBA and Elsewhere [485]

Written by Glenn Rivers and Bruce Brooks

Hardcover: Henry Holt
Softcover: Trophy, HarperCollins
Published 1993

As a youngster, Glenn "Doc" Rivers always knew he wanted to be a professional basketball player. Though his teacher chastised him for his dream, he pursued it and became a point guard for the Atlanta Hawks and the New York Knicks. This book chronicles his life in the NBA and is dedicated to the idea that one should never give up on one's dream. Rivers discusses his career, the players who influenced him, and racism within professional basketball. Eight pages of black-and-white photographs of Doc in action and with family and friends are included.

> "*The easiest time to quit is at the beginning. . . . Not just because of frustration. Most people don't quit because they aren't good—they quit because they are bored, bored by the endless repetition of practicing a skill or a move or a shot. It is incredibly tedious. You do it over, and over, and over. And then over some more.*"

To Be a Slave [486]

Written by Julius Lester
Illustrated by Tom Feelings ☆ 48

Newbery Honor

Hardcover: Dial, Penguin USA
Softcover: Scholastic
Published 1968

The heart-wrenching realities of slavery are revealed in this poignant collection of slave interviews. The author discovered a priceless collection of first-hand slave narratives that were used by abolitionists to sway public opinion against slavery in the pre-Civil War period. Other slave interviews conducted by the 1930 Federal Writers' Project revealed the innermost feelings of those who were slaves. In painful personal accounts, the indignity of the auction block, the harshness of plantation life, and other difficult aspects of slavery are told to young readers from the mouths of those who were slaves.

Toning the Sweep [487]

Written by Angela Johnson ☆ 110

Coretta Scott King Award: Author

Hardcover: Orchard, Grolier
Softcover: Scholastic
Published 1993

Terminal illness forces Grandma Ola to leave her California desert home to go live with her daughter, Diane, and teenage granddaughter, Emily, in Cleveland. Emily makes a videotape for Ola, featuring her friends and scenes from her beloved home, to help Ola face her loss. The discrete personalities, complex mother-daughter relationships, and internal struggles of the three generations of women in this African American family are fully developed as they reflect on the past and prepare for their future together.

True North: A Novel of the Underground Railroad [488]

Written by Kathryn Lasky

Hardcover: Blue Sky, Scholastic
Published 1996

A runaway slave, Afrika, and a white blue blood, Lucy, are girls of the same age but from extremely different worlds. The two meet when Lucy finds herself in the position to help Afrika continue her Underground Railroad journey from slavery. Afrika has made it as far as Boston, but now needs Lucy's help to trek the final distance to freedom in Canada. This expertly told story is a fictionalized account of the Underground Railroad and those who tried to infiltrate it to recapture runaway slaves.

Undying Glory: The Story of the Massachusetts 54th Regiment [489]

Written by Clinton Cox

Softcover: Scholastic
Published 1991

Black men's participation in the Civil War began with the 54th Regiment of Massachusetts, which joined the war effort between 1863 and 1865, after heated political debate about their inclusion. The regiment was undertrained, underrated, underpaid, and not supported by the army. But the men proved their bravery as they fought hundreds of battles, including the historic, skillfully fought battle at Fort Wagner, South Carolina. This historical novel captures the spirit of the times and the personalities of the soldiers. Young readers will learn that blacks were heavily involved in the fight for the liberation of their people.

> "*The pathway that they blazed would soon be followed by others, while the nation looked on in approval. Within six months, there were 60 black regiments in the army. None but the most biased now questioned the ability of black men to fight or the wisdom of using them to save the Union.*"

The Watsons Go to Birmingham—1963 [490]

Written by Christopher Paul Curtis

Hardcover and softcover: Bantam Doubleday Dell
Published 1995

Coretta Scott King Honor: Author
Newbery Honor

Ten-year-old Byron and his family leave their Flint, Michigan, home for Birmingham, Alabama, in an Ultra-Glide car to visit Grandma. Mr. and Mrs. Watson believe that exposure to the slower-paced lifestyle of the South will be good for their urban-raised children. Unfortunately, their trip comes in the midst of the turbulent summer of 1963. The Watsons experience the unfamiliar oppression of segregation and the supercharged racial hatred of the Deep South. This deeply felt novel will take young readers on a convincing journey into this dark period of recent American history.

The Well [491]

Written by Mildred D. Taylor

Hardcover and softcover: Penguin USA
Published 1995

The Logans, a back family in rural Mississippi in the early 1900s, have the only potable well in the area. They share generously with all of their neighbors, black and white. Despite their kindness, tensions grow between the young Logan boys and their white neighbors, which results in a tense, potentially explosive situation. Oppressive attitudes about blacks, reflective of the South in that era, are strongly stated in this book. Other novels about the Logan family include *Roll of Thunder, Hear My Cry* [469]; *The Road to Memphis*; *Song of the Trees* [479]; and *Let the Circle Be Unbroken*. **Nonstandard English. Use of N Word.**

Where Do I Go from Here? [492]

Written by Valerie Wilson Wesley

Softcover: Scholastic
Published 1993

Nia leaves the familiarity of her home to go to an exclusive Connecticut boarding school where she is uncomfortably different from the other students. On a full scholarship, Nia is one of only a few black students and not rich like most of the kids. She begins to adjust with the support of a new friend, Marcus. However, when he suddenly leaves the school without explanation, Nia is left to cope on her own. This is a provocative story that reveals the self-awareness and emotions of a complex teen girl.

Which Way Freedom? [493]

Written by Joyce Hansen   Coretta Scott King Honor: Author

Softcover: Avon, Hearst
Published 1986

Sixteen-year-old Obi, a runaway slave, joins a colored division of the Union Army to help fight for the freedom of his people. Obi is a highly principled young man who has been deeply affected by the pain of being sold away from his mother. He bravely runs away from his master and fights to help earn freedom and security for himself and his adopted slave family. This fictionalized story, based on actual events, establishes the significant role that runaway slaves played in the Civil War and their personal quest for freedom.

Who Is Carrie? [494]

Written by James Lincoln and Christopher Collier

Softcover: Yearling, Bantam Doubleday Dell
Published 1984

In this well-written historical novel, Carrie is a kitchen slave in a New York City tavern. She is totally unaware of the details of her past and does not even know her own last name. When she becomes the victim of an attempted kidnapping, she is determined to understand why she was targeted. She stumbles upon some profound facts about her own family and life when she attempts to help a friend who is trying to buy his own mother out of slavery. This suspenseful novel is accurately staged in the early years of George Washington's presidency. The story of Carrie's family continues in two other books: *War Comes to Willie Freeman* and *Jump Ship to Freedom*.

Wolf by the Ears [495]

Written by Ann Rinaldi

Hardcover and softcover: Scholastic
Published 1991

Fair-skinned Harriet is one of several children born to a slave woman, Sally Hemmings, and her master, Thomas Jefferson, the author of the Declaration of Independence. As young Harriet grows to womanhood, she is confused by the choices that she faces. She has the opportunity, promised since birth, to be freed and to leave her past behind by assuming a new life as a white woman. Plans are in place to educate her and prepare her to make the complete cultural transition into the white world. In this tantalizing work of historical fiction, written as Harriet's own journal, she is unsure that she can turn away from her slave family and the only life that she has known.

Won't Know Till I Get There [496]

Written by Walter Dean Myers

Hardcover: Viking, Penguin USA
Softcover: Puffin, Penguin USA
Published 1982

Fourteen-year-old Steve decides to show off for his newly adopted brother, Earl, in this fast-moving urban story. Transit police catch Steve and his brother spray-painting the side of a subway car. Because of Earl's past criminal record, the judge sentences them to a tough penalty—two months of social service work in a senior citizens' home with a feisty group of senior residents. This well-developed story, written as Steve's daily journal entries, contrasts the feelings and problems of the young and the old.

Yellow Bird and Me [497]

Written by Joyce Hansen

Softcover: Clarion, Houghton Mifflin
Published 1986

Doris, a young Bronx resident, makes a new friend, Yellow Bird. Yellow Bird is a troubled young man and a very poor student. Doris discovers, while trying to help him with his studies, that he is dyslexic. Once Yellow Bird's learning difference is discovered and addressed, he begins to succeed in school and to gain important self-esteem and motivation. This is a rich story of friendship, commitment, and self-discovery.

Yolanda's Genius [498]

Written by Carol Fenner   Newbery Honor

Hardcover and softcover: Margaret K. McElderry, Simon & Schuster
Published 1995

Yolanda is a streetwise, overweight fifth-grader who moves with her mother
and brother from Chicago to a smaller Midwestern town. She is fiercely protective of her younger brother, Andrew, who has severe learning and developmental problems. Andrew displays some genius, however, with his
harmonica. He is able to play it expertly and expresses himself through the
instrument. Yolanda executes a brilliant plan to bring attention to her
brother's masterful talent and special need in this moving book.

The Young Landlords [499]

Written by Walter Dean Myers   Coretta Scott King Award: Author

Softcover: Puffin, Penguin USA
Published 1979

Sixteen-year-old Paul Williams and his friends get more than they bargained
for in this entertaining novel. When the kids go to a local slumlord to com-
plain about the condition of Stratford Arms, a rundown apartment building
in their Harlem neighborhood, the crafty owner manages to trick them into
ownership of the dilapidated building. The teens name themselves the Action
Group and set out to become better landlords. But they had not anticipated
the cast of eccentric tenants or the challenges associated with managing a
building riddled with repair problems. Their experience teaches them that it
can be much more difficult to do something than to talk about it and that
there are not always easy answers to complex problems.

Zeely [500]

Written by Virginia Hamilton ☆ 80

Hardcover and softcover: Simon & Schuster
Published 1968

A creative young girl, Elizabeth, and her brother visit their uncle's farm for the
summer. There she meets Zeely, an older local girl who is the daughter of a
hog herder. When she finds a picture of a Watusi queen, Elizabeth becomes
convinced that it is really a picture of Zeely. Has her imagination run away
with her, or is Zeely really African royalty? Elizabeth sorts out the mystery
in this imaginative story.

Books for Parents and Families

As a natural extension of our work with African American children's books, we often find books that, although not specifically for children, are wonderful resources for African American parents and families. We would like to share a few of them with you.

Beloved Baby: A Baby Scrapbook and Journal by Michaela Angela Davis (Pocket Books, Simon & Schuster, 1995). This hardbound book will help devoted parents create a well-organized keepsake of their new baby. Sixty Afrocentrically illustrated pages are designed for pictures, developmental records, and special entries about your growing child.

Black Pearls for Parents: Meditations, Affirmations and Inspirations for African-American Parents by Eric V. Coppage (Quill, William Morrow, 1995). Three hundred sixty-five poignant thoughts, one for every day of the year, are organized in this palm-sized book to uplift and prepare parents for the important task of child rearing.

Different and Wonderful: Raising Black Children in a Race-Conscious Society by Dr. Darlene Powell Hopson and Dr. Derek S. Hopson (Simon & Schuster, 1992). This book details the difficult challenges faced by African American families raising their children in this race-conscious society and identifies tools for parents to help overcome those influences without losing sight of African American family values or ethnic pride.

Family Reunion Planner by Donna Beasley (Macmillan, Simon & Schuster, 1997). A comprehensive guide, designed specifically for African American families, helps one organize and execute a successful family reunion. This book offers practical advice and checklists on everything from budgeting and record keeping to registration and banquets.

Grandmother's Gift of Memories: An African American Family Keepsake by Danita Rountree Green; illustrated by James Ransome (Broadway, Bantam Doubleday Dell, 1997). This beautifully designed and illustrated book is ready to be filled with any of grandmother's fondest thoughts, recollections, photographs, recipes, mementos, and words of wisdom to be passed down, as a treasured keepsake, to her family.

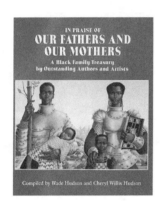

In Praise of Our Fathers and Our Mothers: A Black Family Treasury by Outstanding Authors and Artists compiled by Wade and Cheryl Willis Hudson (Just Us, 1997). This breathtaking anthology of writings and illustrations about African American mothers and fathers features the captivating works of forty-one renowned authors and illustrators, including Ashley Bryan, Gwendolyn Brooks, Walter Dean Myers, Tom Feelings, and Brian Pinkney.

The Joy and Challenge of Raising African American Children by Emma M. Talbott (Black Belt, 1997). A practical guide to help parents understand the special considerations and strategies necessary to raise African American children in our society, this book includes thoughts on topics from education and healthy lifestyle choices to child empowerment and role-modeling.

Juba This & Juba That: 100 African American Games for Children by Dr. Darlene Powell Hopson and Dr. Derek S. Hopson (Simon & Schuster, 1996). Culturally enriching games, songs, dances, and arts-and-crafts projects have been adapted from those of the African continent for our children.

Raising Black Children by James P. Comer, M.D., and Alvin F. Poussaint, M.D. (Plume, Penguin USA, 1992). Expressly written for African American parents raising their children amidst the pervasive messages of racism, this book offers expert advice and answers to almost a thousand common child-rearing questions, with emphasis on those uniquely about black children.

APPENDIX B

BOOK AWARDS

The Coretta Scott King Award was first conceived in 1969 at an American Library Association Conference. School librarians Mabel McKissick and Glyndon Greer and publisher John Carroll were lamenting the fact that in the more than sixty years of the Newbery and Caldecott Medals so few minority authors or illustrators had been recognized. The three award founders developed their idea and drew on other librarians to support their plan. Their next step was to determine a name for the award program. They decided to commemorate the life and work of Martin Luther King Jr. and to honor his wife, Coretta Scott King, for her "courage and determination in continuing the work for peace and brotherhood."

The first award presentation was made in 1970, although the award program was not officially adopted by the American Library Association until 1982. The Coretta Scott King Award is now a highly recognized and coveted professional honor. The criteria for selection include that "recipients are African American authors and illustrators whose distinguished books promote an understanding and appreciation of the culture and contributions of all people to the realization of the 'American dream.'"

THE
CORETTA
SCOTT KING
AWARDS

Coretta Scott King Author Awards

1998 AWARD: *Forged by Fire*, Sharon M. Draper [441]
    HONOR: *I Thought My Soul Would Rise and Fly: The Diary of Patsy, a Freed Girl*, Joyce Hansen
       Bayard Rustin: Behind the Scenes of the Civil Rights Movement, James Haskins

1997 AWARD: *Slam!*, Walter Dean Myers [476]
    HONOR: *Rebels Against Slavery: American Slave Revolts*, Patricia C. and Fredrick McKissack [467].

1996 AWARD: *Her Stories: African American Folktales, Fairy Tales and True Tales,* Virginia Hamilton [359]

HONOR: *The Watsons Go to Birmingham—1963,* Christopher Paul Curtis [490]
Like Sisters on the Homefront, Rita Williams-Garcia
From the Notebooks of Melanin Sun, Jacqueline Woodson

1995 AWARD: *Christmas in the Big House, Christmas in the Quarters,* Patricia and Fredrick L. McKissack [328]

HONOR: *I Hadn't Meant to Tell You This,* Jacqueline Woodson [448]
The Captive, Joyce Hansen [326]
Black Diamond: The Story of the Negro Baseball League, Patricia C. and Fredrick L. McKissack Jr. [426]

1994 AWARD: *Toning the Sweep,* Angela Johnson [487]

HONOR: *Brown Honey in Broomwheat Tea,* Joyce Carol Thomas [137]
Malcolm X: By Any Means Necessary, Walter Dean Myers

1993 AWARD: *The Dark-Thirty: Southern Tales of the Supernatural,* Patricia C. McKissack [434]

HONOR: *Mississippi Challenge,* Mildred Pitts Walter [458]
Sojourner Truth: Ain't I a Woman? Patricia C. and Fredrick L. McKissack [477]
Somewhere in the Darkness, Walter Dean Myers [478]

1992 AWARD: *Now is Your Time! The African American Struggle for Freedom,* Walter Dean Myers

HONOR: *Night on Neighborhood Street,* Eloise Greenfield [242]

1991 AWARD: *The Road to Memphis,* Mildred D. Taylor

HONOR: *Black Dance in America: A History Through Its People,* James Haskins
When I Am Old With You, Angela Johnson [113]

1990 AWARD: *A Long Hard Journey: The Story of the Pullman Porter,* Patricia C. and Fredrick L. McKissack

HONOR: *Nathaniel Talking,* Eloise Greenfield [238]
The Bells of Christmas, Virginia Hamilton
Martin Luther King, Jr., and the Freedom Movement, Lillie Patterson

1989 AWARD: *Fallen Angels,* Walter Dean Myers

HONOR: *A Thief in the Village and Other Stories,* James Berry
Anthony Burns: The Defeat and Triumph of a Fugitive Slave, Virginia Hamilton

1988 AWARD: *The Friendship*, Mildred D. Taylor
    HONOR: *An Enchanted Hair Tale*, Alexis DeVeaux [165]
        The Tales of Uncle Remus: The Adventures of Brer Rabbit, Julius
          Lester

1987 AWARD: *Justin and the Best Biscuits in the World*, Mildred Pitts Walter [370]
    HONOR: *Lion and the Ostrich Chicks and Other African Folk Tales*,
          Ashley Bryan
        Which Way Freedom?, Joyce Hansen [493]

1986 AWARD: *The People Could Fly: American Black Folktales*, Virginia Hamilton
          [393]
    HONOR: *Junius Over Far*, Virginia Hamilton
        Trouble's Child, Mildred Pitts Walter

1985 AWARD: *Motown and Didi: A Love Story*, Walter Dean Myers [460]
    HONOR: *Circle of Gold*, Candy Dawson Boyd [329]
        A Little Love, Virginia Hamilton

1984 AWARD: *Everett Anderson's Goodbye*, Lucille Clifton [167]
  CITATION: *The Words of Martin Luther King, Jr.*, Coretta Scott King
    HONOR: *The Magical Adventures of Pretty Pearl*, Virginia Hamilton
        Lena Horne, James Haskins
        Bright Shadow, Joyce Carol Thomas
        Because We Are, Mildred Pitts Walter

1983 AWARD: *Sweet Whispers, Brother Rush*, Virginia Hamilton [483]
    HONOR: *This Strange New Feeling*, Julius Lester [484]

1982 AWARD: *Let the Circle Be Unbroken*, Mildred D. Taylor
    HONOR: *Rainbow Jordan*, Alice Childress
        Lou in the Limelight, Kristin Hunter
        Mary: An Autobiography, Mary E. Mebane

1981 AWARD: *This Life*, Sidney Poitier
    HONOR: *Don't Explain: A Song of Billie Holiday*, Alexis DeVeaux

1980 AWARD: *The Young Landlords*, Walter Dean Myers [499]
    HONOR: *Movin' Up: Pop Gordy Tells His Story*, Berry Gordy Sr.
        Childtimes: A Three-Generation Memoir, Eloise Greenfield
          and Lessie Jones Little
        Andrew Young: Young Man with a Mission, James Haskins
        James Van Der Zee: The Picture Takin' Man, James Haskins
        Let the Lion Eat Straw, Ellease Southerland

1979 AWARD: *Escape to Freedom: A Play about Young Frederick Douglass,* Ossie Davis [340]

   HONOR: *Skates of Uncle Richard,* Carol Fenner

   Justice and Her Brothers, Virginia Hamilton

   Benjamin Banneker: Genius of Early America, Lillie Patterson

   I Have a Sister: My Sister Is Deaf, Jeanne Whitehouse Peterson

1978 AWARD: *Africa Dream,* Eloise Greenfield

   HONOR: *The Days When the Animals Talked: Black Folk Tales and How They Came to Be,* William J. Faulkner

   Marvin and Tige, Frankcina Glass

   Mary McLeod Bethune, Eloise Greenfield

   Barbara Jordan, James Haskins

   Coretta Scott King, Lillie Patterson

   Portia: The Life of Portia Washington Pittman, the Daughter of Booker T. Washington, Ruth Ann Stewart

1977 AWARD: *The Story of Stevie Wonder,* James Haskins

   HONOR: *Everett Anderson's Friend,* Lucille Clifton

   Roll of Thunder, Hear My Cry, Mildred D. Taylor [469]

   Quiz Book on Black America, Clarence N. Blake and Donald F. Martin

1976 AWARD: *Duey's Tale,* Pearl Bailey

   HONOR: *Julius K. Nyerere: Teacher of Africa,* Shirley Graham

   Paul Robeson, Eloise Greenfield

   Fast Sam, Cool Clyde, and Stuff, Walter Dean Myers [439]

   Song of the Trees, Mildred D. Taylor [479]

1975 AWARD: *The Legend of Africania,* Dorothy Robinson

1974 AWARD: *Ray Charles,* Sharon Bell Mathis

   HONOR: *A Hero Ain't Nothin' but a Sandwich,* Alice Childress

   Don't You Remember?, Lucille Clifton

   Ms. Africa: Profiles of Modern African Women, Louise Crane

   Guests in the Promised Land, Kristin Hunter

   Mukasa, John Nagenda

1973 AWARD: *I Never Had It Made: The Autobiography of Jackie Robinson,* Alfred Duckett

1972 AWARD: *17 Black Artists,* Elton Fax

1971 AWARD: *Black Troubadour: Langston Hughes,* Charlemae Rollins

   HONOR: *I Know Why the Caged Bird Sings,* Maya Angelou

   Unbought and Unbossed, Shirley Chisholm

I Am a Black Woman, Mari Evans
Every Man Heart Lay Down, Lorenz Graham
The Voice of the Children, June, Jordan, and Terri Bush
Black Means . . . , Gladys Groom and Barney Grossman
Ebony Book of Black Achievement, Margaret Peters
Mary Jo's Grandmother, Janice May Udry

1970 AWARD: *Dr. Martin Luther King, Jr., Man of Peace*, Lillie Patterson

Coretta Scott King Illustrator Awards

1998 AWARD: *In Daddy's Arms I Am Tall: African Americans Celebrating Fathers*,
Javaka Steptoe
HONOR: *Ashley Bryan's ABC of African American Poetry*, Ashley Bryan [7]
The Hunterman and the Crocodile: A West African Folktale,
Baba Wagué Diakité
Harlem, Christopher Myers [357]

1997 AWARD: *Minty: A Story of Young Harriet Tubman*, Jerry Pinkney [230]
HONOR: *The Palm of My Heart: Poetry by African American Children*,
Gregory Christie [392]
Running the Road to ABC, Reynolds Ruffins [271]
Neeny Coming, Neeny Going, Synthia Saint James [240]

1996 AWARD: *The Middle Passage: White Ships, Black Cargo*, Tom Feelings [457]
HONOR: *Her Stories: African America Folktales, Fairy Tales and True Tales*,
Leo and Diane Dillon [359]
The Faithful Friend, Brian Pinkney [169]

1995 AWARD: *The Creation*, James Ransome [152]
HONOR: *The Singing Man: Adapted from a West African Folktale*,
Terea Shaffer [277]
Meet Danitra Brown, Floyd Cooper [383]

1994 AWARD: *Soul Looks Back in Wonder*, Tom Feelings [403]
HONOR: *Brown Honey in Broomwheat Tea*, Floyd Cooper [137]
Uncle Jed's Barber Shop, James Ransome [294]

1993 AWARD: *The Origin of Life on Earth: An African Creation Myth*,
Kathleen Atkins Wilson
HONOR: *Little Eight John*, Wil Clay
Sukey and the Mermaid, Brian Pinkney [282]
Working Cotton, Carole Byard [312]

1992 AWARD: *Tar Beach*, Faith Ringgold [287]
    HONOR: *All Night, All Day: A Child's First Book of African-American Spirituals*, Ashley Bryan [118]
      Night on Neighborhood Street, Jan Spivey Gilchrist [242]

1991 AWARD: *Aïda: A Picture Book for All Ages*, Leo and Diane Dillon [318]

1990 AWARD: *Nathaniel Talking*, Jan Spivey Gilchrist [238]
    HONOR: *The Talking Eggs*, Jerry Pinkney [286]

1989 AWARD: *Mirandy and Brother Wind*, Jerry Pinkney [231]
    HONOR: *Under the Sunday Tree*, Mr. Amos Ferguson
      Storm in the Night, Pat Cummings [279]

1988 AWARD: *Mufaro's Beautiful Daughters: An African Tale*, John Steptoe [233]
    HONOR: *What a Morning! The Christmas Story in Black Spirituals*, Ashley Bryan

1987 AWARD: *Half a Moon and One Whole Star*, Jerry Pinkney [44]
    HONOR: *Lion and the Ostrich Chicks and Other African Folk Tales*, Ashley Bryan
      C.L.O.U.D.S., Pat Cummings

1986 AWARD: *The Patchwork Quilt*, Jerry Pinkney [256]
    HONOR: *The People Could Fly: American Black Folktales*, Leo and Diane Dillon [393]

1985 AWARD: None

1984 AWARD: *My Mama Needs Me*, Pat Cummings

1983 AWARD: *Black Child*, Peter Magubane
    HONOR: *All the Colors of the Race*, John Steptoe [319]
      I'm Going to Sing: Black American Spirituals, Ashley Bryan
      Just Us Women, Pat Cummings [214]

1982 AWARD: *Mother Crocodile: An Uncle Amadon Tale from Senegal*, John Steptoe
    HONOR: *Daydreamers*, Tom Feelings [334]

1981 AWARD: *Beat the Story Drum, Pum-Pum*, Ashley Bryan
    HONOR: *Grandmama's Joy*, Carole Byard [42]
      Count on Your Fingers African Style, Jerry Pinkney

1980 AWARD: *Cornrows*, Carole Byard [151]

1979 AWARD: *Something on My Mind*, Tom Feelings

1978 AWARD: *Africa Dream*, Carole Byard

1974 AWARD: *Ray Charles*, George Ford

1970 AWARD: None

The Newbery Medal is one of the highest and best known literary awards in the United States. The first Newbery Medal, named after distinguished English book-seller John Newbery, was awarded in 1922. Every year since then, the American Library Association selects the author of the most outstanding children's book published in the United States during the preceding year to receive the coveted medal. The ALA also selects other authors whose notable works are distinguished as Newbery Honor Books.

Since the inception of these awards, only five African American or African-themed children's books have won the prestigious medal and only twelve have been named as honor books.

Newbery Award Books with African American or African Themes

Medal Winners

1977	*Roll of Thunder, Hear My Cry*, Mildred D. Taylor	[469]
1975	*M.C. Higgins the Great*, Virginia Hamilton	
1974	*The Slave Dancer*, Paula Fox	
1970	*Sounder*, William H. Armstrong	
1951	*Amos Fortune: Free Man*, Elizabeth Yates	[320]

Honor Books

1997	*A Girl Named Disaster*, Nancy Farmer	
1996	*Yolanda's Genius*, Carol Fenner	[498]
	The Watsons Go to Birmingham—1963, Christopher Paul Curtis	[490]
1993	*The Dark-Thirty: Tales of the Supernatural*, Patricia C. McKissack	[434]
	Somewhere in the Darkness, Walter Dean Myers	[478]
1989	*Scorpions*, Walter Dean Myers	
1983	*Sweet Whispers, Brother Rush*, Virginia Hamilton	[483]
1976	*The Hundred Penny Box*, Sharon Bell Mathis	[361]
1975	*Phillip Hall Likes Me, I Reckon Maybe*, Bette Greene	[464]
1972	*The Planet of Junior Brown*, Virginia Hamilton	
1969	*To Be a Slave*, Julius Lester	[486]
1949	*Story of the Negro*, Arna Bontemps	

THE CALDECOTT AWARDS

Since its creation in 1937, the Caldecott Medal has been awarded annually by the American Library Association to the artist of the most distinguished American picture book for children. This prestigious medal, named after the nineteenth-century English illustrator Randolph J. Caldecott, was originated as an equivalent to the Newbery Medal, to honor the works of illustrating artists. While only one artist each year receives the Caldecott Medal, other outstanding artists receive the Caldecott Honor distinction for their excellent works.

Only three African American or African-themed children's books have been recognized as Caldecott Medal winners and fifteen have been named as Caldecott Honor books since the inception of the program.

Caldecott Award Books with African American or African Themes

Medal Winners

1977   *Ashanti to Zulu: African Traditions,* Leo and Diane Dillon [6]

1976   *Why Mosquitoes Buzz in People's Ears,* Leo and Diane Dillon

1963   *The Snowy Day,* Ezra Jack Keats [98]

Honor Books

1998   *Harlem,* Christopher Myers [357]

1997   *The Paperboy,* Dav Pilkey [254]

1996   *The Faithful Friend,* Brian Pinkney [169]

1995   *John Henry,* Jerry Pinkney [209]

1993   *Working Cotton,* Carole Byard [312]

1992   *Tar Beach,* Faith Ringgold [287]

1990   *The Talking Eggs,* Jerry Pinkney [286]

1989   *Mirandy and Brother Wind,* Jerry Pinkney [231]

1988   *Mufaro's Beautiful Daughters: An African Tale,* John Steptoe [233]

1987   *The Village of Round and Square Houses,* Ann Grifalconi [295]

1984   *Ten, Nine, Eight,* Molly Bang [103]

1980   *Ben's Trumpet,* Rachel Isadora

1975   *Jambo Means Hello: Swahili Alphabet Book,* Tom Feelings

1973   *Anansi the Spider,* Gerald McDermott

1972   *Moja Means One: Swahili Counting Book,* Tom Feelings [73]

1970   *Goggles,* Ezra Jack Keats

The *Reading Rainbow* public television program was created in 1983 with the primary goal of encouraging children to read for pleasure. The program selects books for children five to eight years old based on their literary merit, visual impact, artistic achievement, adaptability to the television format, and ability to interest children.

Reading Rainbow programs are theme-oriented and highlight a Feature Book that is the focal point for each episode. Additional Review Books are selected to support the program theme. Each program is carefully produced, employing the talents of well-cast celebrity narrators to help give voice to the stories.

Reading Rainbow selections include a significant number of outstanding African American and African-themed children's books. In the list below, Feature Books appear in **bold** type.

READING RAINBOW SELECTIONS

Reading Rainbow Selections with African American or African Themes

All the Colors of the Race, Arnold Adoff [319]

Alvin Ailey, Andrea Davis Pinkney [120]

Always My Dad, Sharon Dennis Wyeth

Amazing Grace, Mary Hoffman [121]

Ben's Trumpet, Rachel Isadora

Boundless Grace, Mary Hoffman

Bringing the Rain to Kapiti Plain, Verna Aardema

The Car Washing Street, Denise Lewis Patrick

Charlie Parker Played Be Bop, Chris Raschka

Daddy Is a Monster Sometimes, John Steptoe

Dancing with the Indians, Angela Shelf Medearis [154]

Daydreamers, Eloise Greenfield [334]

An Enchanted Hair Tale, Alexis DeVeaux [165]

Everett Anderson's Goodbye, Lucille Clifton [167]

Follow the Drinking Gourd, Jeanette Winter [176]

Galimoto, Karen Lynn Williams [182]

Grandmama's Joy, Eloise Greefield [42]

Great Women in the Struggle, Toyomi Igus

Half a Moon and One Whole Star, Crescent Dragonwagon [44]

Honey, I Love: And Other Love Poems, Eloise Greenfield [360]

How Many Stars in the Sky?, Lenny Hort

Jafta Series, Hugh Lewin

Jamaica's Find, Juanita Havill [58]

Jambo Means Hello: Swahili Alphabet Book, Muriel Feelings

Just Us Women, Jeannette Caines [214]

Kwanzaa, Deborah Newton Chocolate

Max Found Two Sticks, Brian Pinkney [228]

Mufaro's Beautiful Daughters: An African Tale, John Steptoe [233]

My Little Island, Frané Lessac [235]

Night on Neighborhood Street, Eloise Greenfield [242]

The Patchwork Quilt, Valerie Flournoy [256]

Pet Show!, Ezra Jack Keats

Peter's Chair, Ezra Jack Keats

A Picture Book of Harriet Tubman, David A. Adler

Shake It to the One That You Love Best, Cheryl Warren Mattox

The Snowy Day, Ezra Jack Keats [98]

Sweet Clara and the Freedom Quilt, Deborah Hopkinson [284]

The Talking Eggs, Robert D. San Souci [286]

Tar Beach, Faith Ringgold [287]

This Is the Key to the Kingdom, Diane Worfolk [104]

The Train to Lulu's, Elizabeth Fitzgerald Howard [291]

Uncle Jed's Barber Shop, Margaret King Mitchell [294]

Wagon Wheels, Barbara Brenner [298]

Why Mosquitoes Buzz in People's Ears, Verna Aardema

Zora Hurston and the Chinaberry Tree, William Miller [315]

INDEX OF TITLES

Italic type indicates a book that is mentioned only within the main entry or entries listed.
Bold type indicates the name of a series, not the title of an individual book.

INDEX OF AUTHORS

INDEX OF ILLUSTRATORS

INDEX OF TOPICS

Bold type indicates the name of a series, not the title of an individual book.

Africa/African themes
(continued)

Kofi and His Magic [216]
Lion's Whiskers: An Ethiopian
  Folktale [220]
Mandela: From the Life of the South
  African Statesman [226]
Masai and I [227]
The Middle of Somewhere: A Story of
  South Africa [384]
Moja Means One: Swahili Counting
  Book [73]
Mufaro's Beautiful Daughters: An
  African Tale [233]
Nanta's Lion: Search and Find
  Adventure [79]
The New King: A Madagascan Legend
  [241]
No Turning Back: A Novel of South
  Africa [462]
Ogbo: Sharing Life in an African
  Village [247]
Oh, No, Toto! [84]
The Old, Old Man and the Very Little
  Boy [248]
Only a Pigeon [249]
The Orphan Boy [250]
Over the Green Hills [252]
A Place in the Sun [394]
Sebgugugu the Glutton: A Bantu Tale
  from Rwanda, Africa [274]
The Singing Man: Adapted from a
  West African Folktale [277]
Stolen Kisses [481]
The Talking Cloth [285]
Themba [412]
Tower to Heaven [290]
Trouble [292]
The Village of Round and Square
  Houses [295]
Where Are You Going, Manyoni?
  [303]

alphabet. *See* preschool
skills: alphabet

art

The Block: Poems [325]
The Middle Passage: White Ships,
  Black Cargo [457]

Sing to the Sun [276]
Toussaint L'Ouverture: The Fight for
  Haiti's Freedom [415]

athletes/athletics. *See* sports

baby (new)

On the Day I Was Born [85]
She Come Bringing Me That Little
  Baby Girl [96]
Something Special [99]
Sweet Baby Coming [101]
Will There Be a Lap for Me? [115]

baby's day

Animal Sounds for Baby [5]
The Baby [9]
Baby Says [10]
Baby's Bedtime [11]
Billy's Boots: A First Lift-the-Flap
  Book [15]
Busy Baby [17]
Daddy and I [24]
Eat Up, Gemma [28]
Good Morning Baby [40]
Joshua by the Sea [61]
Look at You, Baby Face! [68]
Peekaboo, Baby [89]
Pretty Brown Face [90]

baseball. *See* sports: baseball

basketball. *See* sports: basketball

bedtime

Half a Moon and One Whole Star [44]
One Fall Day [86]
The Quilt [91]
Tell Me a Story, Mama [102]
Ten, Nine, Eight [103]

Bible stories. *See* religion: Bible
stories

biography

**African American Answer Book
  Series [421]**
Alvin Ailey [120]
Amos Fortune: Free Man [320]

Anthony Burns: The Defeat and
  Triumph of a Fugitive Slave [424]
Bill Pickett: Rodeo-Ridin'
  Cowboy [131]
**Black Americans of Achievement
  Series [425]**
Black Eagles: African Americans in
  Aviation [427]
Black Profiles in Courage: A Legacy
  of African American Achievement
  [428]
Black Stars in Orbit: NASA's African
  American Astronauts [324]
Buffalo Soldiers: The Story of
  Emanuel Stance [138]
Coming Home: From the Life of
  Langston Hughes [150]
Dare to Dream: Coretta Scott King
  and the Civil Rights Movement
  [332]
Dear Benjamin Banneker [159]
Dinner at Aunt Connie's House [160]
Escape to Freedom: A Play about
  Young Frederick Douglass [340]
Frederick Douglass: The Last Days of
  Slavery [344]
From Slave to Civil War Hero: The
  Life and Times of Robert Smalls
  [348]
Great African Americans in Civil
  Rights [354]
Great African Americans Series [187]
Great Black Heroes Series [188]
Grolier All-Pro Biography Series [190]
Hang a Thousand Trees with Ribbons:
  The Story of Phillis Wheatley [446]
Happy Birthday, Dr. King! [192]
Happy Birthday, Martin Luther
  King [191]
Jazz: My Music, My People [363]
**Junior Black Americans of
  Achievement Series [366]**
Mandela: From the Life of the South
  African Statesman [226]
Martin Luther King [380]
Minty: A Story of Young Harriet
  Tubman [230]
More Than Anything Else [232]
My Dream of Martin Luther King [234]
My Name Is York [236]
A Picture Book of Sojourner
  Truth [257]

family life/situations *(continued)*

Carousel [142]
Charlie Pippin [431]
Chevrolet Saturdays [327]
Chita's Christmas Tree [145]
Circle of Gold [329]
Cousins [331]
Dark Day, Light Night [155]
Dawn and the Round To-It [157]
Donovan's Word Jar [336]
Eat Up, Gemma [28]
Evan's Corner [166]
Families: Poems Celebrating the
    African American Experience [170]
Father and Son [30]
First Pink Light [174]
Flowers for Mommy [33]
Forged by Fire [441]
Gingerbread Days [184]
Grandmama's Joy [42]
Grandpa's Face [185]
Grandpa's Visit [186]
Happy Birthday, Daddy [46]
Hold Fast to Dreams [447]
The Hundred Penny Box [361]
I Love My Family [52]
In for Winter, Out for Spring [202]
Jamal's Busy Day [59]
Jonathan and His Mommy [60]
Just an Overnight Guest [367]
Just Family [452]
Just Us Women [214]
Justin and the Best Biscuits in the
    World [370]
Kelly in the Mirror [215]
The Leaving Morning [218]
Little Lil and the Swing-Singing Sax
    [221]
A Lullaby for Daddy [69]
Ma Dear's Apron [222]
Mama, I Want to Sing [456]
Mariah Loves Rock [379]
Me and My Family Tree [71]
Me, Mop, and the Moondance Kid
    [381]
Mississippi Chariot [459]
Neeny Coming, Neeny Going [240]
Not Yet, Yvette [83]
Off to School [246]

On the Day I Was Born [85]
Over the Green Hills [252]
Papa's Stories [253]
A Place Called Freedom [258]
Poppa's New Pants [259]
Roll of Thunder, Hear My Cry [469]
The Rolling Store [268]
Sister [473]
Something to Count On [402]
Somewhere in the Darkness [478]
Song of the Trees [479]
Stealing Home [405]
Striped Ice Cream [407]
The Stories Huey Tells [406]
Sunday [100]
The Sunday Outing [283]
Sweet Whispers, Brother Rush [483]
Talk about a Family [410]
Tell Me a Story, Mama [102]
Themba [412]
Toning the Sweep [487]
Uh-oh! It's Mama's Birthday! [107]
Uncle Jed's Barber Shop [294]
Wagon Wheels [298]
The Watsons Go to Birmingham—
    1963 [490]
What Mary Jo Shared [301]
What Will Mommy Do When I'm at
    School? [111]
Willie's Not the Hugging Kind
    [309]
Working Cotton [312]
Yolanda's Genius [498]
You're My Nikki [314]
Your Dad Was Just Like You [313]

fantasy

Carousel [142]
Cherries and Cherry Pits [21]
Dave and the Tooth Fairy [25]
Giant Hiccups [37]
Kim's Magic Tree [64]
Tar Beach [287]
This Is the Key to the Kingdom [104]

fears

Darkfright [156]
Halloween Monster [45]
Jenny Reen and the Jack Muh Lantern
    [207]

folktales, fairy tales, and legends

African

Chinye: A West African Folk Tale
    [144]
Fire Children: A West African
    Creation Tale [32]
Fire on the Mountain [172]
The Fortune-Tellers [178]
The Hunter Who Was King: And
    Other African Tales [48]
Imani in the Belly [200]
Kings, Gods, & Spirits from African
    Mythology [453]
Lion's Whiskers: An Ethiopian
    Folktale [220]
Mufaro's Beautiful Daughters: An
    African Tale [233]
The New King: A Madagascan
    Legend [241]
The Orphan Boy [250]
Sebgugugu the Glutton: A Bantu Tale
    from Rwanda, Africa [274]
The Singing Man: Adapted from a
    West African Folktale [277]
Tower to Heaven [290]
The Village of Round and Square
    Houses [295]

American

The Confetti Company Series [23]
Freedom's Fruit [180]
Her Stories: African American
    Folktales, Fairy Tales, and True
    Tales [359]
Jenny Reen and the Jack Muh Lantern
    [207]
John Henry [209]
Sukey and the Mermaid [282]
The Talking Eggs [286]
Traditional Fairy Tales Series [105]

Caribbean

The Faithful Friend [169]
The House in the Sky: A Bahamian
    Folktale [196]
Tukama Tootles the Flute: A Tale from
    the Antilles [106]
A Wave in Her Pocket: Stories from
    Trinidad [418]

religion

Bible stories

All Night, All Day: A Child's First Book of African-American Spirituals [118]
Climbing Jacob's Ladder: Heroes of the Bible in African American Spirituals [147]
The Creation [152]
Noah [82]
Who Built the Ark? [305]

church

Big Meeting [129]
Come Sunday [149]

religious concepts

Baby Jesus, Like My Brother [125]
Designed by God, So I Must Be Special (African American Version) [26]

responsibility

Get Lost, Laura! [35]
It Takes a Village [55]
The Paperboy [254]

role model

Do Like Kyla [27]
Jamal's Busy Day [59]
Justin and the Best Biscuits in the World [370]
Mighty Menfolk [72]

romance

Motown and Didi: A Love Story [460]
Phillip Hall Likes Me, I Reckon Maybe [464]
Stolen Kisses [481]
This Strange New Feeling [484]

school

Amazing Grace [121]
Be Patient, Abdul [127]
The Best Bug to Be [128]
Chevrolet Saturdays [327]
Darnell Rock Reporting [333]
Definitely Cool [435]

Fast Talk on a Slow Track [440]
The Girl on the Outside [444]
Joshua's Masai Mask [211]
Off to School [246]
Once Upon a Time in Junior High [391]
Rachel Parker, Kindergarten Show-Off [262]
Running the Road to ABC [271]
Sky Man: 18 Pine Street [475]
Something Special [99]
The Story of Ruby Bridges [280]
What Mary Jo Shared [301]
What Will Mommy Do When I'm at School? [111]
Where Are You Going, Manyoni? [303]
Yellow Bird and Me [497]

seasons and weather

Big Wind Coming! [130]
Can't Sit Still [141]
Knoxville, Tennessee [65]
One Hot Summer Day [87]
Rain Talk [92]
Snow on Snow on Snow [97]
The Snowy Day [98]

self-confidence/self-esteem/self-image

All the Colors of the Race [319]
Amazing Grace [121]
Annie's Gifts [122]
The Best Bug to Be [128]
The Black Snowman [133]
Bright Eyes, Brown Skin [16]
Brown Honey in Broomwheat Tea [137]
Can You Dance, Dalila? [140]
Cornrows [151]
Darnell Rock Reporting [333]
Designed by God, So I Must Be Special (African American Version) [26]
An Enchanted Hair Tale [165]
Fall Secrets [438]
For the Love of the Game: Michael Jordan and Me [177]
I Like Me! [51]
Indigo and Moonlight Gold [203]

JoJo's Flying Side Kick [210]
Joshua's Masai Mask [211]
Kelly in the Mirror [215]
May'naise Sandwiches & Sunshine Tea [229]
My Hair Is Beautiful . . . Because It's Mine! [77]
My Skin Is Brown [78]
Nina Bonita [80]
Nappy Hair [237]
Our People [251]
The Palm of My Heart: Poetry by African American Children [392]
Poor Girl, Rich Girl [466]
Somebody's New Pajamas [278]
What I Want to Be [110]
White Socks Only [304]
Wild Wild Sunflower Child Anna [307]

sexual abuse

Forged by Fire [441]
I Hadn't Meant to Tell You This [448]

shapes. *See* preschool skills: shapes

siblings

Baby Jesus, Like My Brother [125]
Baby Says [10]
Do Like Kyla [27]
Finding the Green Stone [171]
Get Lost, Laura! [35]
Girl Wonder and the Terrific Twins [351]
Moriah's Pond [385]
Oh, Brother [389]
The Train to Lulu's [291]
The Twins Strike Back [417]
Yolanda's Genius [498]

slavery

emancipation

The Amistad Slave Revolt and American Abolition [423]
Dancing with the Indians [154]
Freedom's Gifts: A Juneteenth Story [181]
If You Please, President Lincoln [449]
Juneteenth Jamboree [213]

Meet Addy: An American Girl [382]
Now Let Me Fly: The Story of a Slave
Family [244]
The People Could Fly: American
Black Folktales [393]
Rebels Against Slavery: American
Slave Revolts [467]
Seminole Diary: Remembrances of a
Slave Family [398]

slave life

The Captive [326]
Christmas in the Big House,
Christmas in the Quarters [328]
Irene Jennie and the Christmas
Masquerade: The
Johnkankus [204]
Jumping the Broom [212]
Long Journey Home: Stories from
Black History [455]
Many Thousand Gone: African
Americans from Slavery to
Freedom [378]
The Middle Passage: White Ships,
Black Cargo [457]
Nightjohn [461]
A Picture of Freedom: The Diary of
Clotee, A Slave Girl, Belmont
Plantation, Virginia 1859 [465]
Second Daughter: The Story of a Slave
Girl [471]
This Strange New Feeling [484]
To Be a Slave [486]
The Wagon [296]
Who Is Carrie? [494]
Wolf by the Ears [495]

Underground Railroad

Aunt Harriet's Underground Railroad
in the Sky [124]
Barefoot: Escape on the Underground
Railroad [126]
Follow the Drinking Gourd [176]
Freedom Crossing [345]

Get on Board: The Story of the
Underground Railroad [349]
Harriet and the Promised Land [194]
. . . If You Traveled on the
Underground Railroad [199]
Next Stop Freedom: The Story of a
Slave Girl [388]
North Star to Freedom: The Story of
the Underground Railroad [463]
Sweet Clara and the Freedom
Quilt [284]
True North: A Novel of the
Underground Railroad [488]

sports

baseball

Baseball Legends Series [323]
Black Diamond: The Story of the
Negro Baseball League [426]
Stealing Home [405]
Teammates [288]
What Kind of Baby-Sitter Is This? [300]

basketball

Allie's Basketball Dream [119]
For the Love of the Game: Michael
Jordan and Me [177]
NBA by the Numbers [239]
Slam! [476]
Those Who Love the Game: Glenn
"Doc" Rivers on Life in the NBA
and Elsewhere [485]

football

Red Dog, Blue Fly: Football
Poems [397]

other

**Grolier All-Pro Biography Series
[190]**
I Am a Jesse White Tumbler [362]
JoJo's Flying Side Kick [210]
Run for Your Life [470]

Sports Reports Series [404]
Wilma Unlimited: How Wilma
Rudolph Became the World's
Fastest Woman [310]

toddler skills and development

Getting Dressed [36]
I Don't Eat Toothpaste Anymore!
[50]
Kia Tanisha Drives Her Car [63]
No Diapers for Baby! [81]
See What I Can Do! [93]

toys

The Chalk Doll [20]
Golden Bear [39]
Galimoto [182]

Underground Railroad. *See*
slavery: Underground Railroad

virtue

Bimmi Finds a Cat [132]
Chinye: A West African Folk
Tale [144]
Finding the Green Stone [171]
The House in the Sky: A Bahamian
Folktale [196]
Jamaica's Find [58]
Mufaro's Beautiful Daughters: An
African Tale [233]
The Old, Old Man and the Very Little
Boy [248]
Rachel Parker, Kindergarten Show-
Off [262]
Sebgugugu the Glutton: A Bantu Tale
from Rwanda, Africa [274]

weather. *See* seasons

Permissions and Credits

Every effort has been made to locate and credit the copyright holders of the material quoted in this book. Grateful acknowledgment is made for permission to reprint excerpts from the following books:

Allie's Basketball Dream by Barbara E. Barber, with the permission of the publishers, Lee & Low Books. Copyright © 1996 by Barbara E. Barber.

Baby Jesus, Like My Brother by Margery Wheeler Brown, with the permission of the publishers, Just Us Books, 365 Glenwood Ave., East Orange, NJ 07017. All rights reserved. Text copyright © 1995 by Margery Wheeler Brown.

The Black Snowman by Phil Mendez, with the permission of the publishers, Scholastic Inc. Copyright © 1989 by Phil Mendez.

Designed by God, So I Must Be Special (African American Version) by Bonnie Sose, with the permission of the publishers, Character Builders for Kids. Copyright © 1988 by Bonnie Sose.

Down Home at Miss Dessa's by Bettye Stroud, with the permission of the publishers, Lee & Low Books. Copyright © 1995 by Bettye Stroud.

Grandfather and I by Helen E. Buckley, with the permission of the publishers Lothrop, Lee & Shepard Books, a division of William Morrow & Company. Text copyright © 1994 by Helen E. Buckley.

Hold Christmas in Your Heart: African American Songs, Poems and Stories for the Holidays by Cheryl Willis Hudson, with the permission of the publishers, Scholastic Inc. Copyright © 1995 by Cheryl Willis Hudson.

Indigo and Moonlight Gold by Jan Spivey Gilchrist, with the permission of the author, Jan Spivey Gilchrist. Copyright © 1993 by Jan Spivey Gilchrist.

Jaha and Jamil Went Down the Hill: An African Mother Goose by Virginia Kroll, with the permission of the publishers, Charlesbridge Publishing, Watertown, Massachusetts 02172, e-mail: books@charlesbridge.com. Copyright © 1995 by Charlesbridge Publishing.

Juneteenth Jamboree by Carole Boston Weatherford, with the permission of the publishers, Lee & Low Books. Copyright © 1995 by Carole Boston Weatherford.

Kelly in the Mirror by Martha Vetreace, with the permission of the publishers, Albert Whitman & Company. Copyright © 1993 by Martha M. Vertreace.

Lion's Whiskers: An Ethiopian Folktale by Nancy Raines Day, with the permission of the publishers, Scholastic Inc. Copyright © 1995 by Nancy Raines Day.

More Than Anything Else by Marie Bradby, with the permission of the publishers, Orchard Books. Copyright © 1996 by Marie Bradby.

My Name Is York by Elizabeth Van Steenwyk, with the permission of the publishers, Rising Moon: Books for Young Readers, Northland Publishing. Copyright © 1997 by The Donald and Elizabeth Van Steenwyk Family Trust.

Off to School by Gwendolyn Battle-Lavert, with the permission of the publishers, Holiday House. Copyright © 1995 by Gwendolyn Battle Lavert.

Oh, No, Toto! by Katrin Hyman Tchana and Louise Tchana Pami, with the permission of the publishers, Scholastic Inc. Copyright © 1997 by K.H. Tchana and L.T. Pami.

The Paperboy by Dav Pilkey, with the permission of the publishers, Orchard Books. Copyright © 1996 by Dav Pilkey.

Puzzles by Dava Walker, with the permission of the publishers, Lollipop Power Books. Copyright © 1996.

Rum-A-Tum-Tum by Angela Shelf Medearis, with the permission of the publishers, Holiday House. Copyright © 1997 by Angela Shelf Medearis.

The Story of Ruby Bridges by Robert Coles, with the permission of the publishers, Scholastic Inc. Copyright © 1995 by Robert Coles.

Uh-oh! It's Mama's Birthday! by Naturi Thomas, with the permission of the publishers, Albert Whitman & Company. Text copyright © 1997 by Naturi Thomas.

What Mary Jo Shared by Janice May Udry, with the permission of the publishers, Albert Whitman & Company. Text copyright © 1966, 1994 by Janice May Udry.

When I Am Old with You by Angela Johnson, with the permission of the publishers, Orchard Books. Text copyright © 1990 by Angela Johnson.

When I Was Little by Toyomi Igus, with the permission of the publishers, Just Us Books. All rights reserved. Text copyright © 1992 by Toyomi Igus.

Working Cotton by Sherley Anne Williams, with the permission of the publishers, Harcourt Brace & Company. Text copyright © 1992 by Sherley Anne Williams.

The following illustrations are reprinted with permission:

Page 11: Cover illustration by Jan Spivey Gilchrist from *Aaron and Gayla's Alphabet Book* by Eloise Greenfield. Illustrations copyright © 1993 by Jan Spivey Gilchrist. Reprinted by permission of Jan Spivey Gilchrist. All rights reserved.

Page 12: Cover illustration by Culverson Blair from *Afro-Bets 123 Book* by Cheryl Willis Hudson. Illustrations copyright © 1987 by Culverson Blair. Reprinted by permission of Just Us Books. Cover illustration by George Ford from *Animal Sounds for Baby* by Cheryl Willis Hudson. Illustrations copyright © 1995 by George Ford. Published by Cartwheel Books by arrangement with Just Us Books, Inc. Reprinted by permission of Scholastic, Inc. Cartwheel Books is a registered trademark of Scholastic Inc.

Page 14: Cover illustration by John Steptoe from *Baby Says* by John Steptoe. Illustrations copyright © 1988 by John Steptoe. Reprinted by permission of the John Steptoe Literary Trust and William Morrow & Company. Cover illustration by Sylvia Walker from *Baby's Bedtime* by Nikki Grimes. Illustrations copyright © 1995 by Golden Books Publishing Company, Inc. Reprinted by permission of the publisher. Cover illustration by Keaf Holliday from *Baby's Colors* by Naomi McMillan. Illustrations copyright © 1995 by Golden Books Publishing Company, Inc. Reprinted by permission of the publisher.

Page 17: Cover illustration by George Ford from *Bright Eyes, Brown Skin* by Cheryl Willis Hudson and Bernette G. Ford. Illustrations copyright © 1990 by George Ford. Reprinted by permission of Just Us Books.

Page 19: Cover illustration by Cheryl Munro Taylor from *Coconut Mon* by Linda Milstein. Illustrations copyright © 1995 by Cheryl Munro Taylor. Reprinted by permission of Tambourine Books, a division of William Morrow & Company.

Page 20: Cover illustration by James E. Ransome from *Do Like Kyla* by Angela Johnson. Illustrations copyright © 1990 by Orchard Books. Reprinted by permission of the publisher.

Page 21: Cover illustration by Jan Ormerod from *Eat Up, Gemma* by Sarah Hayes. Illustrations copyright © 1988 by Jan Ormerod. Reprinted by permission of Mulberry Books, a division of William Morrow & Company.

Photo credits:

About the Authors

Donna Rand graduated from the University of California, Sacramento, in 1975. Immediately after graduation, she embarked on a professional sales and marketing career, serving fourteen years with Xerox Corporation in a variety of sales, marketing, and management positions, including an international marketing management assignment. She also spent two years with MCI Telecommunications before joining Black Books Galore! Ms. Rand lives in Stamford, Connecticut, with her husband and two school-aged children.

Toni Trent Parker is a graduate of Oberlin College and did graduate work in Black Studies at the University of California, Berkeley. Ms. Parker's professional credentials include service as a Program Officer for the Phelps-Stokes Fund. An original member of the Black Family Cultural Exchange, Ms. Parker lives with her husband and three daughters in Stamford, Connecticut, where she is active in a variety of civic organizations.

Sheila Foster holds a B.A. degree from the University of California, San Diego, and a M.S.W. from the University of Southern California. She is an original member of the Black Family Cultural Exchange and is involved in several community-based projects and fund-raising activities. Ms. Foster lives in Greenwich, Connecticut, with her husband and two daughters.